Affective and Cognitive Factors and Foreign Language Achievement

A Study of Chinese Undergraduate EFL Learners

T0381052

Meihua Liu and Wenxia Zhang

Department of Foreign Languages
Tsinghua University, Beijing

Note: This project was funded by Research in Humanity and Social Science, the Chinese Ministry of Education (the Youth Fund — 06JC&400010) in 2006.

Order this book online at www.trafford.com
or email orders@trafford.com

Most Trafford titles are also available at major online book retailers.

Printed in Victoria, BC, Canada.

ISBN: 978-1-4251-8538-1 (Soft)

Our mission is to efficiently provide the world's finest, most comprehensive book publishing service, enabling every author to experience success. To find out how to publish your book, your way, and have it available worldwide, visit us online at www.trafford.com

Trafford rev. 01/08/2010

 www.trafford.com

North America & international
toll-free: 1 888 232 4444 (USA & Canada)
phone: 250 383 6864 ♦ fax: 812 355 4082

Also by Meihua Liu:

Reticence and anxiety in oral English lessons. Berne: Peter Lang, 2009.

Also by Wenxia Zhang:

The rhetorical patterns found in Chinese EFL student writers' examination essays in English and the influence of these patterns on rater response. Beijing: Tsinghua University Press, 2004.

Preface

Widely agreed is that numerous factors may interact together to affect the learning outcomes of a second/foreign language. Given the importance of English and the huge number of EFL (English as a foreign language) learners in China, research on the interacting effect of various factors in English learning has been far from sufficient. Situated in EFL classroom learning within three formal learning institutions in Beijing, this study, via questionnaires and reflective journals, aims to examine various aspects of Chinese EFL learners' anxiety, motivation, English-learning and test-taking strategy use, and the interactive effect of these variables on their achievements in English: manifestations, general patterns, differences in terms of gender, proficiency level and learning contexts, coping strategies and so on. Complicated statistical analyses, coupled with content thematic analyses, reveal a series of insightful findings. For example, mixed findings were found concerning gender differences in the measured variables; the measured variables generally significantly correlated with one another and the students' performance in English; and the SEM results of the four samples were generally similar, however, some striking differences existed due to certain reasons. Because of the nature of the sample and the methods used to collect data, most of the findings are sure to be generalizable in other Chinese EFL contexts, or even similar contexts outside China.

Acknowledgments

We feel greatly indebted to the teachers and students at Tsinghua University, Chinese University of Petroleum, and Beijing Forestry University for their great support and help during the data collection process. Special thanks go to Miss Qing CHANG, Mr. Hui DING, Miss Shan ZHAO, and Miss Xiuling GU and their students for their full support and participation, which rendered this research study a reality.

Our special thanks also go to the Department of Foreign Languages (esp. professor Lisheng LUO) at Tsinghua University for sponsoring the publication of this book.

Finally we would like to express our earnest thanks to Junhua LIU, Ph.D student at the School of Economics and Management at Tsinghua University, for providing technical support, and to Qiong XIE and Xiaofang Li, two MA students at the Department of Foreign Languages of the University, for proofreading the manuscript.

List of Abbreviations

TU = Tsinghua University
BFU = Beijing Forestry University
CUP = China University of Petroleum
CAS = the Classroom Anxiety Scale
WS = the whole sample
ELMS = the English Learning Motivation Scale
ELM = English learning motivation
InsM = Instrumental motivation
IntM = Integrative motivation
ELSI = the English Learning Strategy Inventory
MS = Memory strategies
CogS = Cognitive strategies
ComS = Compensation strategies
MetaS = metacognitive strategies
AS = Affective strategies
SS = Social strategies
ETSI = the English Test-taking Strategy Inventory
TMS = Test-taking memory strategies
TCogS = Test-taking cognitive strategies
TComS = Test-taking compensation strategies
TMetaS = Test-taking metacognitive strategies
TAS = Test-taking affective strategies
TSS = Test-taking social strategies
SEM = structural equation modeling

Table of Contents

ix

List of Tables

List of Diagrams

Chapter 1   Introduction

1.1 Research problem

Because of the increasing status of English as a world language, people in Mainland China are becoming more and more aware of the importance of English. This awareness was reflected in the new *College English Curriculum* (1999), which required that undergraduate non-English majors acquire a strong ability in English reading and a certain ability in English listening, speaking, writing and translating; and master good English learning strategies. Thereafter, learning English has gained much more weight than ever in Mainland China.

Despite this general awareness of the importance of English, college students in Mainland China, similar to learners in other foreign language contexts (Daly, Vangelisti & Weber, 1995; Horwitz, Horwitz & Cope, 1986; MacIntyre and Gardner, 1989, 1991a), have been observed to be anxious and/or reticent to varying degrees during English classes (Cortazzi & Jin, 1996; Liu, 2006a, 2006b). They also often complain English is too difficult to learn and are (strongly) dissatisfied with the quality of the learning outcome. Consequently, both students and teachers become frustrated. This makes it urgent to examine students' anxiety, motivation, English learning and test-taking strategies to enhance the learning and teaching of English there.

1.2 Rationale for the research

Because of the complex nature of language learning, various variables such as learning and test-taking strategies, foreign language anxiety, motivation, self-perceived proficiency in the target language, and access to the target language exert differing effects on the learning of a foreign language (Clément et al., 1994; Gardner, 1985; Horwitz et al., 1986; Oxford, 1990; Horwizt & Young, 1991). Thus, the effect of these variables on students' proficiency in a foreign/second language has been consistently researched to better the teaching and learning of the target language (Horwitz et al., 1986; Liu, 2006a, 2006b; Oxford, 1990).

Second/Foreign language researchers and theorists have long realized that anxiety is often associated with language learning and is a major obstacle to the learning of a foreign language (Bailey, Daley &

Onwuegbuzie, 1999; Horwitz et al., 1986; MacIntyre & Gardner, 1989; Sellers 2000). High-anxious people are less willing to participate in second/foreign language classroom activities and tend to achieve less in second/foreign language learning (Hilleson, 1996; Tsui, 1996; Ely, 1986).

In addition, anxiety is found to be interwoven with many variables such as attitudes and motivation (Clément et al., 1994; Ehrman & Oxford, 1989) and learning strategies (Bailey et al., 1999; Ehrman & Oxford, 1995; Oxford, 1999) to affect the learning of a foreign language.

Likewise, motivation has also long been researched and found to be a great contributor to the learning of a second/foreign language (Gardner et al. 1987; Gardner et al., 1989; Gardner & MacIntyre, 1991; Tremblay & Gardner, 1995). Learners high in integrative motivation will learn better than those low in integrative motivation. Meanwhile, motivation interacts with such variables as language aptitude, proficiency, second language learning situation, and language anxiety to have an impact on second language learning.

Since 1970s, much work has been done to establish a relationship between learning strategies and successful language learning (Abraham & Vann, 1987; O'Malley & Chamot, 1990). It is revealed that the types of language learning strategies used by different learners vary according to various variables such as motivation, cultural background, task type, age, L2 proficiency, learning style, intelligence, language aptitude, personalities of learners, and gender (Grainger, 1997; Oxford, 1989; Skehan, 1989; Yang, 1999).

Though issues of anxiety, motivation and learning strategies have captured more and more attention in Mainland China (Gao et al., 2004; Liu, 2006a, 2006b; Wen, 1996, 2001), still more research in these areas is needed given the large number of SL/FL learners there. Meanwhile, even fewer studies have combined the research on these issues in the same learning situation. In addition, though the potential effect of test-taking strategies on the learning of a foreign/second language has been acknowledged, it has been scarcely researched. Considering the fact that many Chinese EFL learners study English in order to pass various exams, we reckon that test-taking strategies will probably affect their achievement in English. Thus, English test-taking strategies and their effects on students' achievement in English merit more research in different situations in the country, which is also a strong motivation for the present study. Additionally, the relationships between strategy use and performance were mainly examined by means of frequency counts, correlations, ANOVA or t-tests; few used more sophisticated statistical procedures. In this sense, structural equation modeling (SEM) allowed for the possibility of investigating the interrelationships between observed and latent variables and of specifying models (Purpura, 1998).

Mainly adopting a quantitative approach, the present research sought to investigate foreign language anxiety, motivation, English learning and test-taking strategies and their effects on students' achievement in English at the tertiary level in Mainland China, hoping to contribute to our understanding of these issues in foreign language learning situations.

1.3 Research questions

To investigate the issues illustrated above, the present study was situated in three universities in Beijing and the following questions were formulated.

1.3.1 Foreign language anxiety

(1) To what extent do Mainland Chinese university students suffer anxiety in English classrooms?

(2) What is the difference in foreign language anxiety between male and female students?

(3) What is the difference in foreign language anxiety between/among students at different English proficiency levels and among those from different universities?

1.3.2 English learning motivation

(4) To what extent are Mainland Chinese university students motivated to learn English?

(5) What is the difference in English learning motivation between male and female students?

(6) What is the difference in English learning motivation between/among students at different English proficiency levels and among those from different universities?

1.3.3 English learning strategy use

(7) What is the broad profile of English learning strategy use by Mainland Chinese university students?

(8) What is the difference in English learning strategy use between male and female students?

(9) What is the difference in English learning strategy use between/among students at different English proficiency levels and among those from different universities?

1.3.4 English test-taking strategy use

(10) What is the broad profile of English test-taking strategy use by Mainland Chinese university students?

(11) What is the difference in English test-taking strategy use between male and female students?

(12) What is the difference in English test-taking strategy use between/among students at different English proficiency levels and among those from different universities?

1.3.5 Relationships among the measured variables

(13) How do the measured variables relate to one another?

(14) How do the measured variables relate to students' performance in English?

(15) Does the use of certain English learning/ test-taking strategies relate to students' performance in English?

1.4 Significance

The large-scale survey administered in the present research revealed whether and to what extent Mainland Chinese university EFL learners experienced anxiety in English class and were motivated to learn English, and how often they used various strategies when learning English and taking English exams. Reflective journals made it possible to better understand students' feelings and perceptions of these issues. More complicated statistical analyses helped to explore the directions of causality among the measured variables and students' achievements in English. Based on the findings, certain implications for Mainland Chinese EFL teachers and learners could be provided. In this way, the present research hoped to draw more attention to anxiety, motivation and English learning and test-taking strategies in Mainland China and contribute to the overall literature of research on these issues in second/foreign language learning.

1.5 Organization of the book

The present book consists of eight chapters. Chapter 2 reviews existing theories and studies on foreign language anxiety, motivation, English learning and test-taking strategies. Chapter 3 describes the methodology used in the present research. The middle four chapters are mainly concerned with the presentation of findings: chapter 4 presents the findings of the whole participant sample, and chapters 5 to 7 report the results of each of the three university samples respectively. Chapter 8 provides a detailed discussion of the findings, draws conclusions, and discusses limitations of the present study and suggestions for future research.

Chapter 2   Review of Related Studies

As English is gaining increasing importance in our daily life, much research has been done on various aspects of the teaching and learning of the target language in both ESL and EFL situations. However, second/foreign language learners have not progressed as much as might have been anticipated. And learning outcomes vary greatly even in the same learning situation. A possible explanation is that various variables (e.g., affective variables, personality and individual characteristics, etc.) play an important role in determining the level of achievement in learning the target language (Ely, 1986; Gardner, 1985; MacIntyre, Baker, Clément & Conrod, 2001; Onwuegbuzie, Bailey & Daley, 2000).

Situated in Chinese university English language classrooms, the present study seeks to investigate such variables influencing Chinese EFL learners' performance in English as foreign language anxiety, English learning motivation, English learning and test-taking strategies.

2.1 Foreign language anxiety

Interest in affective variables of second/foreign language teaching and learning, which had been emergent since the 1970s (Brown, 1973; Lozanov, 1978), was brought to the fore by Krashen's (1982) hypothesis that stressful classroom environments contributed to a "filter" blocking easy acquisition of the target language. Krashen (1982) hypothesized that anxiety contributed negatively to an "affective filter", which made an individual less responsive to language input.

Anxiety experienced in the course of learning a foreign language is specific and unique (Horwitz et al., 1986; MacIntyre & Gardner, 1989). It is best described as a form of situation-specific anxiety (Bailey et al., 1999; Horwitz et al., 1986; MacIntyre & Gardner, 1989, 1991a). Foreign language anxiety is a complex, multidimensional phenomenon (Young, 1991b). It was defined as "the feeling of tension and apprehension specifically associated with second language contexts, including speaking, listening, and learning" (MacIntyre & Gardner, 1994b: 284). Williams defined anxiety in the foreign language classroom as "a response to a condition in which the external element is or is perceived as presenting a demand that threatens to exceed the student's capabilities and resources for

6

meeting it" (1991: 25). The acceptance of the situation as threatening then manifested itself as a psychological emotion and/or a physiological response which distracted the student's focus, attention and effort away from mastery of the assigned task, which otherwise could be used to master the task presented (Williams, 1991). "The essence of second/foreign language learning is the communication of personally meaningful and conversationally appropriate messages through unfamiliar syntactic, semantic, and phonological systems" (Horwitz, 1995: 573). Thus, many second/foreign language learners find the basic requirements of second/foreign language learning inherently stressful (Horwitz, 1995).

To investigate foreign language anxiety, Horwitz and his colleagues developed a general theory about foreign language classroom anxiety (Horwitz et al., 1986). They described foreign language classroom anxiety as "a distinct complex of self perceptions, beliefs, feelings, and behaviors related to classroom language learning arising from the uniqueness of the language learning process" (1986: 128). They claimed that there were three components of foreign language anxiety: communication apprehension, test anxiety, and fear of negative evaluation. Because complex and non-spontaneous mental operations were required in order to communicate, "any performance in the L2 is likely to challenge an individual's self-concept as a competent communicator and lead to reticence, self-consciousness, fear, or even panic" (1986: 128). In order to identify anxious university students and measure their anxiety, the researchers developed the Foreign Language Classroom Anxiety Scale (FLCAS), which has gained widespread popularity in subsequent research studies (Cheng, Horwitz & Schallert, 1999; Kitano, 2001; Onwuegbuzie et al., 2000; Phillips, 1992; Saito et al., 1999; Sellers, 2000; Yan & Wang, 2001). These studies reveal that a considerable number of students experience anxiety in the foreign language classroom and foreign language classroom anxiety mainly inhibits students' learning of the target language.

Similarly, Gardner and his associates have also long noticed the important role of anxiety in second/foreign language acquisition. He (1985) believed that individual differences in achievement would be influenced by intelligence, aptitude, motivation, and/or anxiety. Situational anxiety affected not only formal language training but informal language experiences. During the course of developing the socio-educational model, Gardner has worked with other researchers, especially MacIntyre, to explore the issue of language anxiety and has developed more measure scales such as the Classroom Anxiety Scale and the French Use Anxiety Scale from the French Class Anxiety Scale (MacIntyre & Gardner, 1989, 1991a, 1991b, 1994a, 1994b). Language anxiety, according to MacIntyre and Gardner, was the apprehension experienced when a situation requires the use of a second language with which the individual is not fully proficient. It is, therefore, seen as a stable personality trait referring to the propensity for an individual to react in a nervous manner when speaking, listening, reading, or writing in the second language (1994a: 5). They postulated that language anxiety was characterized by derogatory self-related cognitions, feelings of apprehension, and physiological responses such as increased heart rate. In the case of second/foreign language learning, fear of negative evaluation was likely to be manifested in a student's over-concern with academic and personal evaluations of his/her performance and competence in the target language (MacIntyre & Gardner, 1991a). Although language learning could not occur without errors, errors could be the source of anxiety in some individuals because they drew attention to the difficulty of making positive social impressions when speaking a new language (MacIntyre & Gardner, 1989). This idea has been supported by a host of research studies (Clément et al., 1994; Gardner & MacIntyre, 1992; MacIntyre & Gardner, 1991a, 1991b; MacIntyre & Thivierge, 1995; Saito & Samimy, 1996).

To study anxiety and its effect of production, MacIntyre and Gardner (1989) administered nine anxiety scales to 94 first-year college students in Canada: Classroom Anxieties, French Use Anxieties, Trait Anxieties, Computer Anxieties, Test Anxieties, Audience Sensitivity, State Anxieties, Paired Associates and Vocabulary Test. They determined communicative apprehension and social-evaluative anxiety had a negative effect on production. The students with high communicative anxiety tended to have lower scores on free recall on the paired-associates learning task and oral and written vocabulary tests. Thus, the researchers concluded that "the results presented tend to indicate that anxiety leads to deficits in learning and performance" (1989: 271). The study revealed that communication apprehension and social evaluation were part of the elements of foreign-language classroom anxiety.

For the study of the relationship among language anxiety, perceived competence and actual competence, MacIntyre, Noels & Clément, (1997) included 37 Anglophones in English-language sections of a mandatory first-year class at a bilingual university in Canada. All these participants had considerable exposure to French, their L2. The participants completed a questionnaire followed by a series of French proficiency tests during the testing session. The questionnaire included a language anxiety measure adapted from Gardner's French Use Anxiety and French Class Anxiety scales and a scale of self-rated L2 proficiency in terms of can-do items. Corresponding to each of the areas of the can-do, tasks covering a wide range of difficulty were administered to the students to test their proficiency in L2 speaking, reading, writing, and comprehension. The results showed that actual competence, perceived competence, and language anxiety were all significantly interrelated. Students who produced more output tended to produce better output and those who were more proficient tended to perceive themselves as more proficient. In addition, all the correlations involving language anxiety were negative. As language anxiety scores increased, the ratings of ideas expressed, output quality, and self-rated competence declined. Moreover, these relations were consistent across speaking, reading, writing and comprehension tasks, indicating a strong relationship between language anxiety and measures of language achievement. Further analysis supported the hypothesis that anxious students tended to underestimate their ability and the more relaxed students tended to overestimate their ability. Highly anxious students did not perceive their competence to be as high as a more objective analysis revealed it to be. The arousal of anxiety probably made some students more reluctant to speak.

Saito and Samimy (1996) examined the role of language learner anxiety and other affective variables (gender, year in college, length of time in Japan, strength of motivation, etc.) of university students of Japanese in relation to their language performance at three different instructional levels. The participants were 257 students enrolled in beginning, intermediate, and advanced levels of Japanese courses at the University of Texas at Austin. The instruments were Language Class Anxiety, Language Class Risk-taking, Language Class Sociability, Strength of Motivation, Attitude toward the Japanese Class, and Concern for the Grade adapted from Ely (1986) and Gardner (1985). The results indicate that the predictive variable of the participants' performance was different from the beginning level to the intermediate- and the advanced-level students. For beginning students, the Year in College was identified as the best predicting factor, while Language Class Anxiety was the best predictor for both intermediate and advanced-level students. The results also implied that foreign language anxiety had a negative impact on Japanese learners' performance. The influence of foreign language anxiety became more important as Japanese learners' instructional levels increased.

In summary, language anxiety mainly inhibits language learning and is related to the familiarity of audience and context (MacIntyre & Gardner, 1991a, 1991b; MacIntyre & Thivierge, 1995). The less anxious learners tended to be more confident (MacIntyre & Gardner, 1991b).

2.2 English learning motivation

Initiated by Gardner and Lambert (1972), the study of motivation in second language acquisition became a distinguished research topic after they published a comprehensive summary of the results of a long-term research program (Dörnyei, 1990; Spolsky, 2000). In their book *Attitudes and Motivation in Second Language Learning* (Gardner & Lambert, 1972), a socio-psychological model on motivation research was advanced and motivation was defined as influenced by attitudes towards and orientations to learn a second language (L2). Advanced in this model, integrative and instrumental motivations became the fundamental concepts in motivation research, which characterizes all the later research in this field (Dörnyei, 2001). According to Gardner and Lambert (1972), motivation to learn a second language is grounded in positive attitudes toward the second language community and in a desire to communicate with valued members of that community and become similar to them. This latter desire is integrative orientation, which is a better support for language learning, while an instrumental orientation is associated with a desire to learn L2 for pragmatic gains such as getting a better job or a higher salary (Dörnyei, 2001; Gardner & Lambert, 1972). The role of orientation is to help arouse motivation and direct it towards a set of goals, either with a strong interpersonal quality (integrative orientation) or a strong practical quality (instrumental orientation) (Dörnyei, 2001).

To measure learners' motivation for a second language, Gardner (1985) developed the Attitude/Motivation Test Battery (AMTB)—a multi-component motivation test made up of over 130 items involving variables such as attitudes towards French Canadians, European French people and learning French, interest in foreign languages, orientation to learn French, French class anxiety, parental encouragement, motivation intensity, desire to learn French, and motivation index.

10

Though the AMTB was designed for learners in SL learning contexts, its adaptations have been used in several data-based studies of L2 motivation all over the world (Clément, Dörnyei & Noels, 1994; Crookes & Schmidt, 1989; Gardner, Lalonde & Moorcroft, 1985; Gardner, Lalonde & Pierson, 1983; Gardner, Lalonde, Moorcroft, & Evers, 1987; Gardner, Moorcroft, & Metford, 1989; Gardner & MacIntyre, 1991; Gardner, Day, & MacIntyre, 1992; Tremblay & Gardner, 1995). The results evidence that attitude and motivation are positively related to second/foreign language learning achievement and support Gardner's (1983) prediction that individuals who were integratively motivated and/or held the more positive attitudes would be more active in language learning context, work harder and learn faster. As empirical studies on second language learning motivation blossom, it has been found integrative and instrumental orientations are not opposite ends of a continuum (Belmechri & Hummel, 1998; Dörnyei, 1994; Huang & Wen, 2005; Qin & Wen, 2002). Instead, they are positively related and both are affectively loaded goals that can sustain learning. They both may be in return enhanced by better proficiency and higher achievement in the target language (Oxford & Shearin, 1994; Belmechri & Hummel, 1998; Dörnyei, 1994, 2001). Ely (1985) found that motivation and attitudes were positively correlated with risk-taking, persistence and competence while negatively correlated with test anxiety. Moreover, MacIntyre and his associates (1998, 2001) revealed that attitudes and motivation were closely related to communicating in a second language.

2.3 English learning strategy use

Since 1970s, much work has been done to identify what might be good language learning strategies and to establish a relationship between these and successful language learning (Rubin, 1975; Stern, 1975). Qualitative studies (Abraham & Vann, 1987; Nam & Oxford, 1998; O'Malley & Chamot, 1990; Takeuchi, 2003) have uncovered that successful L2 learners are aware of the strategies they use and why they use them. Such learners are able to choose appropriate strategies to specific tasks and combine different strategies together to solve problems. Less successful learners are also able to identify their own strategies; however, they do not know how to choose the appropriate strategies or how to link them together into a useful strategy chain (Block, 1986; Vann & Abraham, 1990). Meanwhile, quantitative studies reveal that different patterns of language learning strategy use can occur in different ESL/EFL situations (Ehrman & Oxford, 1989; Green & Oxford, 1995; Huang & Van Naerssen, 1985; Oxford & Cohen, 1992; Oxford & Nyikos, 1989). In general, it is widely agreed that the types of language learning strategies used by different learners may vary according to various variables such as motivation, cultural background, task type, age, L2 proficiency, learning style, intelligence, language aptitude, personalities of learners, and gender (Grainger, 1997; Ko, 2002; Liao, 2000; Oxford, 1989; Peng, 2001; Skehan, 1989; Yang, 1996).

Then, what is language learning strategy? How is language learning strategy identified and classified? What is the relationship between language learning strategy use and learning outcomes? ... All these will be the focus of this chapter which briefly reviews the research in this area. Section 2.2 discusses the definition of language learning strategy and gives a brief description of models on language learning strategy; section 2.3 reviews the classification and research on language learning strategy; section 2.4 is a brief summary; and section 2.5 proposes research questions for the present study.

2.3.1 Definition and models of language learning strategy

Because of the complex nature of language learning strategies, considerable debate exists about how to define language learning strategies (Ellis, 1999). Rubin defined learning strategies as "strategies which contribute to the development of the language system which the language learner constructs and affect learning directly" (1987: 23). Apparently, this definition only reveals an incomplete view of the function of learning strategies. Cognitive psychologists Weinstein and Mayer defined learning strategies as "the behaviors and thoughts that a learner engages in during learning that are intended to influence the learner's encoding process" (1986: 315). Though acknowledging the cognitive functions of learning strategies, this definition fails to identify that some strategies may be metacognitive in nature.

According to Chamot (1987: 71), learning strategies "are techniques, approaches or deliberate actions that students take in order to facilitate the learning and recall of both linguistic and content area information". Wenden referred to learner strategies as "language learning behaviors learners actually engage in to learn and regulate the learning of a second language ... what they know about the strategies they use ... what they know about aspects pf their language learning other than the strategies they use" (1987: 6). The common feature of these two definitions is that both emphasize the behavioral nature of learning strategies though they both are more extensive than previous definitions.

Even though criticized to be essentially behavioral (Ellis, 1999), Oxford's definition remained the most frequently applied one in empirical studies which states "learning strategies are specific actions taken by the learner to make learning easier, faster, more enjoyable, more self-directed, and more transferable to new situations" (1990: 8). This definition was then extended, saying language learning strategies "are specific actions or techniques that students use, often intentionally, to improve their progress in developing L2 skills" (Green & Oxford, 1995). "A language-learning strategy is a technique or a specific action used consciously by a learner to assist some aspect or aspects of language learning" (Grainger, 1997: 378). Cohen (1998b: 5) believed that "second language learner strategies encompass both second language learning and second language use strategies. Taken together they constitute the steps or actions consciously selected by learners either for the learning of a second language, the use of it, or both".

In conclusion, most researchers emphasize that language learning strategy use, by definition, must involve some degree of consciousness, awareness, and internationality (Lan & Oxford, 2003).

Many recent models of second language acquisition and learning have included language learning strategies (Hsiao & Oxford, 2002; McDonough, 1999; McLaughlin, 1987; Skehan, 1989). Skehan (1989) regarded language learning strategies as one of the most important individual difference factors in L2 acquisition, as evidenced by his detailed review of learning strategy research in the context of various models of acquisition. When discussing declarative and procedural knowledge, Ellis (1985) classified the three processes for developing L2 knowledge as learning strategies, production strategies, and communication strategies. And McLaughlin (1987) adopted this three-part distinction in his own integrated model of L2 teaching and learning. Nevertheless, other researchers argued that it was impossible to separate these three kinds of strategies and that often times all three result in learning (Oxford, 1990).

Social psychologists have also added to the theory of language learning the use of language learning strategies (Gardner & MacIntyre, 1993; MacIntyre, 1994). Gardner and MacIntyre (1993) found that language learners' individual characteristics, situational variables, and types of learning strategies interacted in a complicated way to influence proficiency in a second language. According to Green and Oxford (1995), a very insightful strategy-related model of language learning was the one proposed by MacIntyre (1994), who highlights the importance of affective factors and links the use of a given language learning strategy with task demands, proficiency, aptitude, situation, attitude, motivation, previous success, anxiety, self-confidence, actions against strategy use, goals, and criteria for success. In this model, students must be aware of the strategy, must have a reason to use it, and must have a reason not to use it.

2.3.2 Research on and classification of language learning strategies

Since language learning strategy use captured researchers' and educators' attention, much work has been done in this area. Based on the findings, various language learning strategies have been identified and classified (Naiman et al., 1978; O'Malley, Chamot, Stewner-Manzanares & Russo, 1985a; Oxford, 1990) and the classification is becoming more and more systematic.

"Attempts to define and classify language-learning strategies have been followed by attempts to identify strategies that appear effective in promoting different aspects of language learning" (Bruen, 2001: 217). One set of qualitative studies examines the strategies that good language learners report using (Naiman, 1978; O'Malley et al., 1985a; Rubin, 1975, 1981; Takeuchi, 2003), while another uses statistical techniques to explore the relationships between reported strategy use and language-learning outcomes for larger groups of language learners (Ku, 1995; Ehrman & Oxford, 1995; Oxford & Ehrman, 1995; Oxford & Nyikos, 1989).

2.3.2.1 Qualitative studies on language learning strategy use

Early language learning strategy studies mainly centered around good language learners based on data gathered through interviews, diaries, recordings, and observations. Studies of good language learners generally reveal that good language learners use more and better learning strategies than do poor language learners (Matsumoto, 1994; Naiman et al., 1978; Nam & Oxford, 1998; O'Malley et al., 1985a; Rubin, 1975, 1981; Takeuchi, h2003). According to Rubin (1975), the good language learner was a willing and accurate guesser; had a strong, persevering drive to communicate; focused on form by looking for patterns; took advantage of

14

all practice opportunities; monitored his/her own speech as well as that of others; and paid attention to meaning.

In order to study how children increased in communicative competence in English, Wong-Fillmore (1976, 1979) investigated five Mexican school children in California with an age range of 5.7 to 7.3 years. Each child was paired with a native American child, and their interactions were recorded for an hour each week when they were in a school playroom. The analyses showed that extremely wide differences in English proficiency occurred over the nine-month study. When accounting for the differences, the researcher believed the cognitive and social strategies employed by the children played a major a role and identified three social and five cognitive strategies, as presented in Table 2.1.

Table 2.1: Children's Use of Language Learning Strategies

Social strategies	Cognitive strategies
1. Join a group and act as if you understand what's going on, even if you don't. 2. Give the impression that you speak the language. 3. Count on your friends for help.	1. Assume what people are saying is relevant to the situation at hand. 2. Get some expressions you understand, and start talking. 3. Look for recurring parts in the formulas you know. 4. Make the most of what you've got. 5. Work on the big things first: save the details for later.

Based on 34 interviews with successful language learners, Naiman et al. (1978) identified five major strategies. Each major strategy is associated with a number of minor and more specific substrategies. (1) Active task approach: good language learners actively involve themselves in the language learning task by (a) responding positively to the given learning opportunities, or by identifying and seeking preferred learning environments and exploiting them, (b) adding related language learning activities to the regular program, and/or intensifying their efforts, (c) engaging in a number of practice activities and (d) changing the purpose of an activity in order to focus on L2 learning. (2) Realization of language as a system: good language learners develop or exploit an awareness of language as a system. In dealing with language as a system, good language learners (GLLs) (a) refer back to their native language judiciously (translate into L1) and make effective cross-lingual comparisons at different stages of language learning, and (b) analyze the target language and make inferences about it. (3) Realization of language as a means of communication and interaction: GLLs develop and exploit an awareness of language as a means of communication (i.e. conveying and receiving messages) and interaction (i.e. behaving in a culturally appropriate manner). In the earlier stages of language learning GLLs may emphasize fluency over accuracy. They seek out situations in which they can communicate with members of the target language and/or increase their communicative skills in the language, and display critical sensitivity to language use, for example, by attempting to find out socio-cultural meanings. (4) Management of affective demands: GLLs realize initially or with time that they must cope with affective demands made upon them by language learning and succeed in doing so. (5) Monitoring of L2 performance: GLLs constantly revise their L2 systems. They monitor the language they are acquiring by testing their inferences (guesses): by looking for needed adjustments as they learn new material or by asking native informants when they think corrections are needed.

Aside from these strategies, Naiman et al. (1978) discovered quite a few more specific techniques, among which the most commonly used were:

- repeating aloud after the teacher and/or native speaker
- following the rules as given by the grammar books or textbooks
- making up vocabulary charts and memorizing them
- listening to radio, TV, records, etc.
- having contact with native speakers
- reading anything: magazines, newspapers, professional articles, comics.

Naiman et al.'s (1978) study demonstrates the richness that can be gained from qualitative study. But their findings have to be interpreted with caution because the strategies used by good language learners might also be used by poor language learners.

By way of directed self-report with a focus on particular types of cognitive processes, Rubin (1981) proposed a list of strategies: (1) clarification/verification (e.g., asking for examples of how to use a word/expression; putting word in sentence to check understanding; looking up word in the dictionary; and paraphrasing a sentence to check understanding); (2) monitoring (e.g., correcting error in own/other's pronunciation, vocabulary, spelling, grammar, style; and noting sources of own errors, such as own language interference and other language interference); (3) memorization (e.g., taking notes of new items with or without examples, contexts, or definitions; and finding some association); (4) guessing/inductive inferencing (e.g., using clues from the following to guess the meaning—other items in the sentence or phrase, syntactic structure, context of discourse; and ignoring difficult word order); (5) deductive reasoning—looking for and using general rules (e.g., comparing native/other language to target language to identify similarities and differences; inferring grammatical rules by analogy; noting exceptions to rules; and finding meaning by breaking down word into parts); and (6) practice (e.g., experimenting with new sounds in isolation and in context, uses mirror for practice; talking to self in target language; and drilling self on words in different forms.

Later on, Rubin (1981, 1987) identified these strategies contributed to language learning success as either direct (e.g., inductive inferencing, practice, and memorization) or indirect (e.g., creating practice opportunities, and using production tricks) strategies.

According to Skehan (1989), these strategies all have a cognitive orientation and suggest considerable scope for self-awareness in the process of learning.

A major study in the 1980s was that conducted by O'Malley et al. (1985a) in the United States. Based on interviews with secondary-school ESL learners, interviews with their teachers and observations, the researchers uncovered 26 strategies, as listed below.

Table 2.2: O'Malley et al.'s Classification of Strategies

Learning strategies	Description
A. Metacognitive strategies	
Advance organizers	Making a preview of the organizing concept or principles in a learning activity
Directed orientation	Deciding in advance what to attend to in a learning task
Selective attention	Deciding in advance to attend to specific aspects of the language input or situational details in a task
Self-management	Understanding and arranging for the conditions that help one learn
Advance preparation	Planning for and rehearsing linguistic components necessary for a language task
Self-monitoring	Correcting one's speech for accuracy or for appropriateness to context
Delayed production	Consciously deciding to postpone speaking in favor of initial listening

Self-evaluation	Checking learning outcomes against internal standards
Self-reinforcement	Arranging rewards for successfully completing a language learning activity
B: Cognitive strategies	
Repetition	Imitating a language model, including overt practice and silent rehearsal
Resourcing	Using target language reference materials
Directed physical response	Relating new information to physical action as with directives
Translation	Using the first language to understand and produce the second language
Grouping	Reordering or reclassifying material to be learned
Note-taking	Writing down main ideas, important points, outlines, or summaries of information.
Deduction	Conscious application of rules
Recombination	Constructing language by combining known elements in a new way
Imagery	Relating new information to visual concepts in memory
Auditory representation	Retention of the sound or similar sound for a word, phrase, etc.
Keyword	Remembering a new word in the second language by mnemonic or associational techniques, e.g. keywords.
Contextualization	Placing a word or phrase in a meaningful language sequence
Elaboration	Relating new information to existing concepts
Transfer	Using previously acquired knowledge to facilitate new learning
Inferencing	Using available information to guess meanings of new items, predict outcomes, etc.
Questions for clarification	Asking a teacher, etc. for repetition, paraphrasing, explanation, and/or examples.
C: Social Mediation	
Cooperation	Working with one or more peers to obtain feedback, pool information, etc.

It is striking that many of the strategies reported by Naiman et al. (1978) are not included here. There is little emphasis on the Strategy of Realization of Language as a Means of Communication, Management of Affective Demands. Equally striking is the greater focus on metacognitive strategies, of which there are nine. These partly correspond to the

Monitoring Strategies identified by Naiman et al. (1978), but for O'Malley et al. (1985b) monitoring is only one among a number of metacognitive strategies. According to them, "metacognitive strategies involve thinking about the learning process, planning for learning, monitoring of comprehension or production while it is taking place, and self-evaluation of learning after the language activity is completed. Cognitive strategies are more directly related to individual learning tasks and entail direct manipulation or transformation of the learning materials ..." (O'Malley et al., 1985b: 560-561).

In addition, O'Malley et al. (1985b) found that intermediate-level students tended to use a greater proportion of metacognitive strategies, while the beginning level learners emphasized more the actual handling of data and direct learning processes. The study revealed that the most frequently used strategies were concerned with rote learning, not transformation or engagement with the learning material. Greater strategy use tended to be linked with activities which were less conceptually complex. The most strategy generating activities were vocabulary learning, pronunciation and oral drills. Fewer strategies were used in more complex activities like analysis, inferencing and making oral presentations.

Chamot, Kupper and Impink-Hernandez (1988) examined strategy use and second language performance with beginning, intermediate and advanced students of Spanish and Russian over a period of four semesters. They first asked teachers to group learners as 'effective' or 'ineffective' and then analyzed the learners' strategy use over time. They found effective students used a larger range of strategies and made more appropriate strategy choices for particular tasks than did their ineffective peers. They also noted that the effective learners demonstrated a greater degree of 'comprehension monitoring' than 'production monitoring' or attention to discrete linguistic features. Meanwhile, the study revealed that effective learners made better use of their knowledge schemata and their second language linguistic knowledge than did the ineffective ones. Apparently, these findings attest to a strong relationship between strategy use and the ability to perform well in a language learning environment.

Five French, three Spanish and six Japanese immersion programs in Washington and fourteen immersion teachers participated in Chamot and El-Dinary's (1999) study. Data collected by way of think-aloud protocols revealed that no significant differences emerged between high- and low-rated students in overall measures of strategy use or metacognitive awareness statements for either reading or writing. It also showed that high-rated students might have used a greater proportion of metacognitive strategies than low-rated students, while the latter might have used more cognitive strategies than the former. Low students used a greater proportion of phonetic decoding than did high students, whereas the latter used a greater proportion of background-knowledge strategies than the former. Less effective learners were also found to focus too much on the details, while more effective learners focused on the task as a whole.

2.3.2.2 Quantitative studies on language learning strategy use

In addition to qualitative studies, there is another set of studies seeking to examine the patterns of behaviors and the relationship between strategy use and second/foreign language performance/proficiency by means of statistical analyses (Bacon, 1992; Bialystok, 1981, 1983; Chamot & Küpper, 1989; Grainger, 2003; Magogwe & Oliver, 2007; Mangubhai, 1991; Politzer & McGroarty, 1985; Vandergrift, 1996, 1997, 2003, 2005). This set of quantitative studies came to flourish, especially after Oxford (1990) publicized her classification of language learning strategies and the Strategy Inventory for Language Learning.

Synthesizing previous research results, Oxford's (1990) classification system distinguishes direct and indirect strategies, which are then divided into six groups: memory strategies, cognitive strategies, compensation strategies, metacognitive strategies, affective strategies and social strategies. Memory strategies relate to the storing and retrieval of information (e.g., 'I use new English words in a sentence so I can remember them'). Cognitive strategies are "unified by a common function: manipulation or transformation of the target language by the learner" (e.g., 'I use the English words I know in different ways') (Oxford, 1990: 43). Compensation strategies "enable learners to use the new language for either compensation or production despite limitations in knowledge" (e.g., 'To understand unfamiliar English words I make guesses) (Oxford, 1990: 47). Metacognitive strategies "allow learners to control their own cognition" (e.g., 'I look for people to talk to in English') (Oxford, 1990: 135). Affective strategies are concerned with the regulation of feelings and attitudes (e.g., 'I try to relax whenever I feel afraid of using English'), and social strategies are those which take account of the fact that language is a form of social behavior, involving communication with other people (e.g., "I practice English with other students'). This fairly exhaustive list of strategies is described by Ellis as "perhaps the most comprehensive classification of learning strategies to date" (1999: 539). Based on this classification, Oxford (1990) developed the Strategy Inventory for Language Learning (SILL) to explore EFL/ESL learners' use of language strategies. Designed on a 5-point Likert scale, the SILL has been widely used in various learning contexts and achieved high reliability and validity (Akbari & Hosseini, 2008; Ehrman & Oxford, 1989; Griffiths, 2003; Hong-Nam & Alexandra, 2006; Oxford & Burry-Stock, 1995; Oxford & Cohen, 1992; Oxford & Nyikos 1989; Wang, 2002; Wu, 2000).

Based on data collected via the SILL and self-ratings, Oxford and Nyikos (1989) found that students' self-rated proficiency in speaking, listening, or reading was positively related to their frequency of strategy use and that greater strategy use was accompanied by self-perceptions of higher proficiency. The study also revealed that females reported using strategies far more often than did males in formal rule-related practice, general study strategies, and conversational input elicitation strategies. Ehrman and Oxford (1995) also discovered significant gender differences in the SILL, but the differences lied in general study strategies, strategies for authentic language use, strategies for searching for and communicating meaning, and metacognitive or self-management strategies.

In order to describe the patterns of variation in overall strategy use, strategy use by SILL categories, and strategy use at the individual level by male and female students at three different proficiency levels, Green and Oxford (1995) administered the SILL, along with some proficiency tests, to 374 prebasic-, basic-, and intermediate- English level students at the University of Puerto Rico. The statistical analyses showed that (1) significant differences only occurred between the prebasic-level and the other two level students, (2) females used more strategies than males, (3) proficiency level had a significant effect on the cognitive, compensation, metacognitive, and social strategies, and (4) significant differences existed at individual strategy item level. More proficient and successful learners reported greater strategy use.

Bremner (1999) distributed the SILL to 149 participants to investigate the strategy use of Hong Kong university students and the relationship between strategy use and language proficiency, The results indicated that (1) the learners used compensation strategies the most frequently, followed by metacognitive, cognitive, social, memory and affective strategies, (2) significantly positive relationships existed between proficiency and cognitive and compensation strategies while proficiency was significantly negatively correlated with affective strategies, and (3) some individual strategy items were significantly correlated with proficiency.

Wakamoto's (2000) study attempted to explore the relationship between language learning strategies and personality variables. Administering the SILL and MBTI to 254 junior college students majoring in English, the researcher found that extroversion significantly correlated with functional practice strategies and social-affective strategies. The extroverts employed some of the specific strategy items more significantly such as encouraging oneself to speak English, asking questions in English and asking help form English speakers.

Ko (2002) investigated how 161 junior high students' EFL learning strategies were affected by their perceptual learning style preferences. Data collected through the SILL and the Perceptual Learning Style Preference Questionnaire indicated that students with a multiple style and students with a visual/nonverbal style had higher English achievements than those with other style preferences. No significant differences occurred in overall strategy use among groups with different perceptual style preferences. Kinesthetic/tactile-style learners used significantly more memory, compensation, and social strategies than did other style groups. The visual/nonverbal and the multiple style learners deployed significantly more affective strategies than other style groups. Nevertheless, the strategies were generally not used with a high frequency.

Administering the children's SILL to 379 six-grade Taiwan students, Lan and Oxford (2003) discovered that the students used all the six categories of strategies moderately. The most frequently used strategies were compensation, affective and social strategies, whereas the least frequently used was memory strategy. Significant difference was found to exist between gender, proficiency level and liking English in relation to overall strategy use and some categories of strategies, while no interactions among the independent variables were significant.

Based on the data collected through survey and in-depth interviews, Huang and Van Naerssen (1985) examined the strategy use of the top and bottom thirds of a group of 65 students. Statistical analyses showed that no significant differences existed between the high and low performers with regard to formal practice and monitoring, but significant differences did emerge between the groups on functional practice strategies. This lent some support to a relationship between strategy use and second language performance.

Based on Chinese EFL learning contexts, Wen (1996, 2001) advanced a relatively new classification system of language learning strategies. According to her, language learning strategy is a system composed of two subsystems: one is of beliefs and the other is of strategies. Then these two subsystems can be further divided into two parts: management and language learning. Therefore, four subcategories emerge in Wen's classification: management beliefs, language learning beliefs, management strategies, and language learning strategies. In order to measure students' language strategy use, Wen (1993) developed the Language Learner Factors Questionnaire (LLFQ) involving statements about beliefs and learning strategies. Although Wen's classification might better reflect the Chinese EFL learning context, questions also arise in that beliefs much probably do not turn into strategies used by the learners. Maybe due to this reason, not much application of her system could be reviewed.

2.3.3 Summary

Studies on strategy use have provided many valuable insights concerning L2 learning. Studies on good language learners discovered that more proficient language learners used more learning strategies and more types of strategies and were more able to choose strategies appropriate to the task. These studies also reveal that good language learners often seek ways to practice the L2 and maintain a conversation (Naiman et al., 1978; O'Malley et al., 1985a; Rubin, 1987); to have a positive attitude towards speakers of the target language (Oxford, 1990); to organize and plan learning around preferred ways of learning (Ellis & Sinclair, 1989; Oxford, 1990); to monitor their speech and that of others (Ellis & Sinclair, 1989; Naiman et al., 1978; Oxford, 1990); to seek verification and clarification, attend to both form and meaning, look for patterns, use deduction, and make inferences (Ellis & Sinclair, 1989; O'Malley et al., 1985a; Oxford, 1990; Rubin, 1987); and to be active participants in the learning process (Wenden, 1985). It is also generally agreed that successful learners demonstrate a greater use of learning strategies or more appropriate application of strategies to the learning task, whereas less successful or unsuccessful students use a limited or inappropriately applied repertoire of language learning strategies. In addition, it is revealed that females usually demonstrate a greater use of language learning strategies (Cohen, 1998b;

Oxford & Nyikos, 1989; Ehrman & Oxford, 1989, 1995) although Tran (1988) and Wharton (2000) reported different findings. The former study revealed that Vietnamese women used fewer learning strategies than men and the latter found no absence of gender difference on the overall SILL but only at specific item level (Li, 2005).

Meanwhile, a number of quantitative studies have shown that L2 strategy use is associated with proficiency (Akbari & Hosseini, 2008; Huang & Van Naerssen, 1985; Lan & Oxford, 2003; Purpura, 1997), learning style (Ehrman & Oxford, 1995; Oxford & Cohen, 2004; Reid, 1987), gender (Ehrman & Oxford, 1989; Grainger, 2003; Oxford & Nyikos, 1989; Phakiti, 2003; Young & Oxford, 1997), motivation (Oxford & Nyikos, 1989), and academic major or career choice (Ehrman & Oxford, 1989; Oxford & Nyikos, 1989). However, the correlational studies were only partially successful in establishing a substantive link between strategy use and SL acquisition or performance (Bialystok, 1983; Huang & Van Naerssen, 1985; Mangubhai, 1991).

2.4 English test-taking strategy use
According to Cohen (2000), language test-taking strategies consisted of both language use strategies and test-wiseness strategies.

Concerning the use of strategies during language tests, much research can be found in quasi-testing conditions (Anderson, 1991; Black, 1993; Cohen, 1998a). Administering a response strategy checklist and a multiple-choice reading comprehension test to 42 tenth Hebrew graders of French, Nevo (1989) found that it was possible to obtain feedback from respondents on their strategy use after each test item if the checklist was provided for quick labeling of the processing strategies utilized. In order to investigate strategy use in cloze tests and its relationship with cloze test performance, Black (1993) recruited six female university students and asked them to think aloud when doing a cloze test. She found that (1) overall totals of strategy use failed to explain the cause of a participant's success or failure, (2) less successful learners used as broad a variety of strategies as their successful peers, (3) all participants used more monitoring/evaluating strategies than any other type, (4) different strategies suited different learners, (5) the quality of the thought processes engaged in by the learners when encountering problem-solving situations considerably affected the outcome of their efforts, and (6) successful item solution did not always involve the use of strategies.

Focusing on the relationships between test takers' reported cognitive and metacognitive strategy use and patterns of performance on language tests, Purpura (1997) examined the putative effects of strategy use on second language test performance in a construct validation study. Administering an 80-item cognitive and metacognitive strategy questionnaire and a 70-item standardized language test to 1,382 students in Spain, Turkey and the Czech Republic, and using structural equation modeling as a primary analytical tool, he found that metacognitvie strategy use had a significantly positive and direct effect on cognitive strategy use but had no significantly direct impact on SL test performance. The researcher also discovered that cognitive strategy use had no significant and direct effect on reading ability, but influenced reading indirectly through lexico-grammatical ability. To be specific, the comprehending processes had no significant, direct impact on reading or lexico-grammatical ability, and the retrieval processes yielded a small, but significant positive effect on lexico-grammatical ability; while the memory processes had a significantly direct negative effect on lexico-grammatical ability. Alternatively, the more test takers invoked memory strategies in a speeded test situation, the worse they performed on the test, while the less they utilized them, the better they performed. These findings further confirm the implication that relationships between strategy use and second language proficiency are extremely complex, and at times very subtle, given the multidimensional nature of the constructs involved and the number of possible interactions that could occur between and among various variables (Chamot, et al., 1988; Wesche, 1987).

As such, few studies have been done to explore strategies used in standardized language tests, probably due to the fact that test-takers usually disperse soon after finishing the tests, which makes it rather difficult to elicit introspective ideas closely related to the tests. However, by looking at the test-taking strategies used by L2 learners, as Cohen (2000) claimed, we can improve both the assessment instruments themselves and the success that learners have in responding to these instruments. Moreover, when test takers sit in a test, many factors such as anxiety, motivation and self-confidence may have varying effects on them and their strategy use, thus making their strategy use different from that in non-testing conditions. There, investigating test-taking strategy use is also of interest or value.

2.5 Summary

As reviewed above, most studies mainly focused on the use of general language learning strategies, few targeted language test-taking strategies. Fewer studies have employed complicated statistical procedures to explore the use of language learning or test-taking strategies (Purpura, 1997). Moreover, not much research has examined the interaction of strategy use with other individual characteristics of the learners in the same learning situation (Ehrman & Oxford, 1989, 1995; Oxford & Cohen, 2004; Oxford & Nyikos, 1989). Deploying statistical procedures to analyze data, the present study attempted to investigate the use of English learning and test-taking strategies and its interactive effect on students' test performance with such affective variables as anxiety and motivation in a Chinese EFL context.

Chapter 3　Research Method

The present research utilized a mixed method to investigate foreign language classroom anxiety, English learning motivation, English learning strategy use, and test-taking strategy use in EFL learning contexts in Mainland China and their impact on students' performance in English at the tertiary level. Section 4.1 describes the context of the research; section 4.2 provides a detailed discussion of the study of the research: participants, instrument, procedure, and ways of analyzing the data.

3.1 Context of the study

Targeting first-year undergraduate non-English majors, the present research was situated in three EFL teaching and learning contexts in Beijing: Tsinghua University, Beijing Forestry University, and China University of Petroleum. The first two lies in the center of the city while the last is located in the suburb. Though all being top universities in China, the mode of English teaching and learning in these universities is quite different, as detailed below. Another difference is that undergraduate non-English majors at Tsinghua University are exempt from the College English Test (CET) band 4 (a nation-wide English proficiency test which is a must for undergraduate non-English majors to be granted the degree certificate), whereas those at the other two universities must take the test in order to be granted the B.A/B.S degree on time. To help students to pass CET band 4 is also the aim of their teachers. Moreover, non-English majors at these three universities have to take the same Beijing English placement test upon entering the university. The test, consisting of listening comprehension, reading comprehension and cloze (writing and oral test are excluded maybe due to their complex nature), aims to measure students' English proficiency and place them into different band groups. Nevertheless, only students at Tsinghua University and China University of Petroleum are actually divided into different band groups according to their scores in the test.

3.1.1 Tsinghua University

As one of the top two universities in Mainland China, only the best students from each province across the country who are good at every content subject and those who are talented in certain areas such as music and sports can be admitted to Tsinghua University (TU). Coupled with the advanced facilities and highly qualified faculties provided by the University, it is generally believed that students at Tsinghua University soon become far better in knowledge and skills than most of those in other universities.

As a comprehensive university, Tsinghua contains several Schools and has a variety of study programs such as Chinese, English, Law and Civil Engineering. The majority of the students, however, major in science and engineering, and all students except English majors are required to take English courses for at least one term. To pass the Tsinghua English Proficiency Test I (TEPTI) is a precondition for their graduation. The Department of Foreign Languages is responsible for offering various English courses, organizing, and grading English tests.

To improve the teaching of English, first-year non-English majors are placed in different band groups to study English at Tsinghua University. Generally speaking, there are three band groups, the band 1 group representing the lowest English proficiency level and the band 3 group representing the highest level. Upon entering the University and before starting their formal studies at the University, all freshmen are given the Beijing English placement test. Those who score below 70 are put in the band 1 group, those with scores from 70 to 79 are placed in the band 2 group, and those who score above 80 are in the band 3 group. Usually, a large body of the population is placed in the band 2 group, with a small number in band 1 and 3 groups respectively. After having been assigned to different band groups, the students are randomly placed into different classes, which often contain the maximum number of 35 students. Therefore, the case is often that students of the same class are from several different Departments instead of the same Department.

English teaching and learning usually lasts for 16 weeks each term, two weeks before the term ends. During these 16 weeks, students and their English course teachers meet once a week, each time lasting 90 minutes. The final-term exam for students from all band groups is often held on Saturday morning of the 16th week. Because freshmen always start their formal English learning 2 weeks later than sophomores, juniors and seniors, they actually have only 14 weeks of formal learning of English during the first term.

The teaching of English at all band levels is mainly based on a set of textbooks designed and compiled by the staff at the Department of

Foreign Languages, Tsinghua University. This set of textbooks, called *New English Course*, consisting of Reading, Writing & Translation and Listening & Speaking, has been revised every four or five years since its first publication in 1987. Both textbooks have four books (Book I, II, III, & IV), each for one term of teaching and learning. Generally, book I is for band 1 students, book II for band 2 students and so on. For first-term freshmen, Reading, Writing & Translation is compulsory and taught by Chinese teachers of English; Listening & Speaking which is offered by native speakers is optional. As the names indicate, Reading, Writing & Translation mainly serves to improve students' abilities in English reading, writing and translation between English and Chinese, with a focus on reading; whereas Listening & Speaking seeks to enhance students' abilities in English listening and speaking. What is worth pointing out is that the teaching and learning of English at Tsinghua University is not exam-orientated but for the sake of improving students' real competence in English. After the first term's teaching and learning of English, all English courses become elective thereafter.

In addition to formal classroom teaching, other learning facilities have also been established by the Department of Foreign Languages to create more opportunities for students to learn English on their own. FM Radio, Tsinghua University was set up in 2001 to offer students a variety of air programs at noon and in the evening. A Language Lab was also opened to students for skill learning and communication with English teachers. Furthermore, English lectures given by English native speakers are regularly held during the teaching period. To provide more access to native English, a 3-week English summer camp has been held for three consecutive years for freshmen since 2004, which offers students enormous opportunities for intensive training and learning of English.

Before starting the lessons, the teachers are often offered such information from the Department of Foreign Languages about their students as ID numbers, Departments and scores in the placement test. Thus, they often do not take a further step to obtain more information about their students after the commencement of the lessons.

When the study was carried out, most of the first-year undergraduate non-English majors took Listening & Speaking during the first term in addition to Reading, Writing & Translation. For each course, they met the instructor once a week, with each meeting lasting 90 minutes.

3.1.2 Beijing Forestry University

Though not so outstanding as Tsinghua University, Beijing Forestry University (BFU) is also a key comprehensive university in China and the most famous university in its field. In addition to programs related to forestry, the University offers a variety of other study programs such as accounting, business and management, English, and computer engineering. The majority of the students major in science and all students except English majors are required to take English courses for two years. The Department of Foreign languages is responsible for offering various English courses, organizing, and grading English tests.

Though the students are required to take the Beijing English placement test upon entering the University, they are not placed into different band groups. Students are generally placed into different classes according to their majors, with each class having about 45 students with mixed English abilities.

English teaching and learning usually lasts for 16 weeks each term. The teaching and learning of English is mainly based on a set of textbooks issued by Shanghai Higher Education Press. This set of textbooks, called *College English*, has Intensive Reading, Extensive Reading, Listening & Speaking, and Fast Reading and has been updated several times since its first publication in 1985. Each has four books (Book I, II, III, & IV), with one book for one term of teaching and learning. Generally, book I is for band 1 students, book II for band 2 students and so on. Intensive Reading, covering careful reading, translation and writing with focus on careful reading, is always compulsory for students.

In addition to compulsory courses, students can also take optional English courses, especially after they have passed CET band 4. Furthermore, there are some other English learning facilities established by the Department of Foreign Languages to create more opportunities for students to learn English on their own, such as English corners and English competitions.

Like those at Tsinghua University, English teachers at Beijing Forestry University can get such information from their Department about their students as ID numbers, Departments and scores in the placement test before starting the lessons. Consequently, they often do not take further trouble to obtain more information about their students thereafter.

When the study was conducted, all freshmen took Intensive Reading which was offered twice a week, each meeting lasting 90 minutes.

They were also required to take Listening & Speaking which was offered once a week; the meeting lasted 90 minutes as well. Each Intensive Reading class often had 30 students, whereas each Listening & Speaking class consisted of around 60 students. The final exams for both courses were administered to all students at the same time in the 19th week.

3.1.3 China University of Petroleum

Though not so good as the previous two universities, China University of Petroleum (CUP) is also a key comprehensive university in China and the most famous in its field. Thus, it also offers a variety of study programs such as oil engineering, chemistry, English, business, and communication. The majority of the students, like those at the other two universities, major in science, and all students except English majors are required to take English courses for two years. The Department of Foreign Languages is responsible for offering various English courses, organizing, and grading English tests.

To improve the teaching of English, non-English majors at China University of Petroleum are as well placed in different band groups to study English according to their scores in the Beijing English placement test upon entering the University. Generally speaking, there are three band levels: band 1 represents the lowest English proficiency level and band 3 represents the highest level. Those who score below 60 are put in the band 1 group, those with scores from 60 to 75 are placed in the band 2 group, and those who score above 76 are in the band 3 group. Usually, a large body of the population is placed in the band 2 group, with a small number in band 1 and 3 groups respectively. After having been assigned to different band groups, the students are placed into different classes mainly according to their majors. Each class often consists of 45 students with various majors.

English teaching and learning usually lasts for 18 weeks each term. The teaching of English at all band levels is as well based on the set of textbooks called *College English* issued by Shanghai Higher Education Press. For first-term freshmen, the compulsory course is Intensive Reading, which is offered three times a week, each meeting lasting for two hours each time. The final-term exam for students from all band groups is often held on Saturday morning of the 18th week. In addition to compulsory courses, students can also take selective English courses, especially after they have passed CET band 4. Furthermore, there are some other English learning facilities established by the Department of Foreign Languages to create more opportunities for students to learn English on their own, such as English corners and English competitions.

Like those at the other two universities, English teachers at China University of Petroleum are offered such information from their Department about their students as ID numbers, Departments and scores in the placement test before starting the lessons. Consequently, they often do not take further trouble to obtain more information about their students thereafter.

When the study was conducted, there were only around 90 band 1 students, the majority fell in band 2 and 3 groups. Therefore, the band 1 students were excluded from the study. Further, the compulsory textbook for the teaching and learning of English for freshmen at the time was Intensive Reading which focused on reading and translation, with 10% of the teaching time for listening and speaking.

3.2 The study

3.2.1 Participants

The data for the study were collected at two phases. In phase 1, one intact class from each band group at each university were required to write two reflective journals. In phrase 2, a large-scale survey was conducted at three universities. Thus, the participants in these two phases were different.

3.2.1.1 Journal respondents

Altogether, six intact classes at three universities, with one class from each band group participated in journal writing: 3 TU classes, 1 BFU class and 2 CUP classes. Among 95 TU journal participants, 34 (28 male and 6 female) were band 1 students, 33 (28 male and 5 female) band 2 and 28 (24 male and 4 female) band 3 learners. Of 37 BFU journal participants, 18 were male and 19 were female. Of 83 CUP journal correspondents, 41 (35 female and 6 male) were band 2 learners and 42 (32 female and 10 female) band 3 students. It should be noted that since the BFU did not adopt any bench system in English teaching, only one class was randomly selected for journal writing. It was also worth noting that these students, in addition to writing reflective journals, also answered the battery of questionnaires. However, since not all them completed the survey or finished the two journals, the numbers of journal and survey participants and the actual numbers of these classes might be different. As such, Table

3.1 only records the real number of journal writers from each band group at each university.

Table 3.1: Participants in the Case Study (Source: journals)

	Band 1		Band 2		Band 3		Total
	Male	Female	Male	Female	Male	Female	
TU	28	6	28	5	24	4	95
BFU	18 male and 19 female						37
CUP	0	0	35	6	32	10	83
Total	165 male and 50 female						215

With an average age of 18.3, these journal participants, though from different universities, majored in various areas, ranging from Chinese Literature, to Chemistry, to Civil Engineering, to Business Management, to International Politics, and to Medicine.

3.2.1.2 Survey respondents

In the second phase, a battery of questionnaires was distributed to approximately 1500 first-year students at different English proficiency levels at three universities from various Departments such as Computer Science, Architecture, Management and Chinese. Of 1431 collected questionnaires, 1203 were found valid (the others were discarded because of incompleteness) with general information presented in Table 3.2.

Table 3.2: General Information about Survey Respondents

TU (451)		BFU (327)		CUP (425)		Whole sample (1203)		Average age
Male	Female	Male	Female	Male	Female	Male	Female	18.7
336	115	116	211	312	113	764	439	

	Band 1	Band 2	Band 3	Total
TU	113 (93 M/20 F)	205 (150M/55F)	133 (93M/40F)	451
BFU	/	/	/	327
CUP	0	289 (216M/73F)	136 (96M/40F)	425

Among 1203 respondents, 764 (63.5%) were male and 439 (36.5%) were female. 451 (336 male and 115 female) respondents came from Tsinghua University, among whom 113 (93 male and 20 female) were band 1 students, 205 band 2 students (150 male and 55 female) and 133 band 3 students (93 male and 40 female). 327 participants were from Beijing Forestry University, among whom 116 (35.5%) were male and 211 (64.5%) female. 425 respondents came from China University of

Petroleum, among whom 289 (216 male and 73 female) were band 2 students and 136 (96 male and 40 female) band 3 students. More students from the band 2 group at both Tsinghua University and China University of Petroleum were selected for the study because they represented the first-year students at both universities in terms of number, population diversity, English proficiency, major diversity, and gender difference. With an age range from 16 to 25 and an average age of 18.7, the majority of these students started to learn English formally from the junior high school.

3.2.2 Instrument

In this study, data were collected by way of reflective journals and survey, as detailed below.

Reflective journal. Though questionnaires can be administered to a large number of respondents in a short period of time (Nunan, 1992; Richards, 2001; Wallace, 1998), the measurement is usually inferential and indirect (Bailey, 1983; Nunan, 1992; Richards, 2001; Wallace, 1998). They are often problematic because the respondents "tend to give answers that are associated with their perceptions of the predispositions of the researcher" (Oller, 1979: 17, cited in Bailey, 1983). To solve this dilemma, diaries and journals were used to add an element of triangulation by providing additional data about personal and affective variables in language learning (Allwright, 1983; Bailey, 1983). By reflecting the processes that go on inside the learners' minds, diaries open up fields that are "normally not accessible to researchers, and are thus able to provide an important complement to other research tools" (Halbach, 2000: 85). Thus, diaries, logs and journals are employed in many research studies to ask students to introspect about learning, and comment on a class, and therefore constitute a useful source of information about the students' use of strategies and their skills in language learning (Bailey, 1983; Peck, 1996; Wenden, 1986).

Therefore, one intact class representing each band level from three universities were asked to write two journal entries to reflect and comment on their English learning experiences (see Appendix I). For each journal entry, focus of writing was provided beforehand, which covered these aspects: (1) English learning motivation, (2) anxiety, (3) English learning strategies and (4) test-taking strategies. In addition to the topics suggested, the learner could also write about other aspects related to his/her language learning experiences. In case the students might have difficulty

34

understanding the guide in English, it was translated into Chinese before being implemented.

Survey. Based on the results of the pilot study and review of related work, a 309-item survey was developed, which comprised a modified 8-item Classroom Anxiety Scale (CAS) (Gardner, 1985, cited in Young, 1999), a modified 26-item English Learning Motivation Scale (ELMS) (Noels, Clément & Pelletier, 2000; Vandergrift, 2005), a self-developed 184-item English Learning Strategy Inventory (ELSI), and a self developed 91-item English Test-taking Strategy Inventory (ETSI). In addition, respondents were asked to rate their English proficiency, English learning motivation and access to English on a scale of 1-5.

Classroom Anxiety Scale (CAS). This 8-item Classroom Anxiety Scale developed by Gardner (1985, cited in Young, 1999) was to measure to what degree students would feel anxious, especially when speaking, in English class. To suit the foreign language learning situation in Mainland China, some modifications were made. The words "language" and "foreign language" used in the original CAS were consistently replaced with "English" (see 1-8, Appendix II). For example, the original CAS item "I don't usually get anxious when I have to respond to a question in foreign language class" was modified to be "I don't usually get anxious when I have to respond to a question in English class".

English Learning Motivation Scale (ELMS). This 26-item English Learning Motivation Scale was developed with reference to Vandergrift's (2005) and Noel et al.'s (2000) foreign language learning motivation survey. To suit the present research, items about interest in and attitude toward the target language and so on were deleted, whereas items about instrumental and integrated motivation were either maintained or modified. At the same time, items peculiar to Chinese EFL learning were added such as learning English for certificates and high marks in exams. Finally this ELMS scale included 26 items and intended to measure whether (items 9-10) learners were motivated to learn English and for what reasons (instrumental or integrated) (items 11-34) they were motivated to do so (see 9-34, Appendix II).

English Learning Strategy Inventory (ELSI). To explore Chinese university students' English learning strategy use, Oxford's (1990) Strategy Inventory for Language Learning (SILL) was adopted. But to better suit the present research, more items were added to the SILL with reference to Li's (2005) self-developed English learning strategy survey.

35

For example, item 53 "I often memorize English words according to a vocabulary book or a dictionary" was added because Chinese EFL learners often depended on vocabulary books or even dictionaries to learn more English words. These books could also be easily bought in bookstores or markets. Item 56 "I say or write new English words several times" was added in that Chinese EFL learners reinforced their memory of English words by repeated saying or writing due to limited exposure to English. Finally, a 184-item English Learning Strategy Inventory (ELSI) was developed. Adopting Oxford's (1990) classification system as the base model, the present ELSI also covers six aspects of English language learning strategy use: (a) 20-item memory strategy, (b) 44-item cognitive strategy, (c) 21-item compensation strategy, (d) 75-item metacognitive strategy, (e) 13-item affective strategy, and (f) 11-item social strategy (see 35-218, Appendix II).

English Test-taking Strategy Inventory (ETSI). In order to examine what strategies were used when taking English tests, a 91-item English Test-taking Strategy Inventory was developed with reference to Zhang and Liu's (2008) Test-taking Strategy Inventory. Like the ELSI, the ETSI involved six aspects of English test-taking strategy use: (a) 6-item memory strategy, (b) 17-item cognitive strategy, (c) 12-item compensation strategy, (d) 48-item metacognitive strategy, (e) 4-item affective strategy and (f) 4-item social strategy.

Open-ended question. In addition to the survey, an open-ended question was designed to allow the respondents to write down any other ideas about the learning or test-taking strategies they have adopted.

Performance in English. Students' final course grades were obtained at the end of the term as a global measure of performance in English (Aida, 1994; Saito, Horwitz & Garza, 1999; Saito & Samimy, 1996).

All the survey items except the background questionnaire were designed on a 5-point Likert scale, ranging from 'Strongly Disagree' to 'Strongly Agree' with values 1-5 assigned to them respectively. The reliability scores of these scale and their subscales are presented in Table 3.3.

Table 3.3: Characteristics of Instruments

Name of the instruments	No. of items	R of the whole sample	Mean item-total correlation of the whole sample ($P = .01$)	R of TU	R of BFU	R of CUP
Classroom Anxiety Scale (CAS)	8	.753	.605	.797	.738	.713
English Learning Motivation Scale (ELMS)	26	.786	.40	.760	.810	.777
Memory Strategy (MS)	20	.777	.439	.79	.761	.774
Cognitive Strategy (CogS)	44	.825	.346	.846	.810	.818

Compensation Strategy (ComS)	21	.779	.447	.804	.784	.742
Metacognitive Strategy (MetaS)	75	.932	.410	.941	.924	.928
Affective Strategy (AS)	13	.730	.486	.771	.667	.722
Social Strategy (SS)	11	.726	.517	.774	.652	.72
English Learning Strategy Inventory (ELSI)	184	.959	.436	.965	.953	.956
Test-taking Memory Strategy (TMS)	6	.705	.599	.711	.694	.639
Test-taking Cognitive Strategy (TCogS)	17	.783	.466	.814	.794	.787
Test-taking Compensation Strategy (TComS)	12	.705	.503	.744	.707	.654
Test-taking Metacognitive Strategy (TMetaS)	48	.899	.430	.915	.887	.890
Test-taking Affective Strategy (TAS)	4	.409	.604	.460	.435	.326
Test-taking Social Strategy (TSS)	4	.558	.658	.564	.571	.531
English Test-taking Strategy Inventory (ETSI)	91	.942	.437	.951	.938	.935

Notes: R = reliability; N of whole participant sample = 1203
N of TU = 451; N of BFU = 327; N of CUP = 425

3.2.3 Procedure

Prior to the design of the study, six second-year students from Tsinghua University were invited for an informal interview to talk about their English learning motivation, anxiety, and learning and test-taking strategies. Based on this pool and review of related work, the focus for reflective journals and the survey items were developed. The instrument was first sampled to ten band 2 freshmen at Tsinghua University to test whether anything was missing, superfluous or inappropriate. The results led to a devised instrument to be used in the study.

The study was conducted during the first term of the academic year of 2005-2006 which lasted from 14 to 18 weeks for freshmen depending on which university they were from. One intact class from each band group at Tsinghua University and China University of Petroleum, and one intact class from Beijing Forestry University were randomly selected for writing journals. Considering the fact that the majority of the freshmen needed time to become accustomed to the new teaching and learning mode at university and university life, their ideas and attitudes about English learning might change as well. They were thus asked to write the journals during the tenth and eleventh weeks. Each time, the course teachers would describe the requirements of journal writing and distribute to the students the topics for each entry in both Chinese and English a week beforehand. By the end of the twelfth week, all the journal entries had been collected. After that, all the journal entries were read and commented on by the researchers. Then, they were photocopied and returned to the students in early December.

Because of the large number of survey items, the battery of questionnaires was distributed to 13, 8 and 8 intact classes (altogether about 1500 students) at Tsinghua University, Beijing Forestry University and China University of Petroleum respectively in the twelfth week, including the classes required to write reflective journals. Students were asked to complete the survey after class and give it back to their course teachers during the following class meeting. Finally, 1431 questionnaires were gathered by the researchers, of which 1203 were valid for statistical analysis.

3.2.4 Data analysis

The survey and its components were first analyzed to measure their reliability and validity. Then for each scale, statistical analyses and analysis of ANOVA were conducted.

To have a broad profile of students' level of anxiety and learning motivation, the scales were computed in terms of mean, standard deviation, median, mode, maximum and minimum. Likewise, Oxford's (1990) key to understanding mean scores on SILL-based instruments whose scale range is 1 to 5 was adopted to obtain an overall picture of students' use of English learning and test-taking strategies. To complement these analyses, the responses to each Classroom Anxiety Scale and English Learning Motivation Scale items were counted in terms of frequency and percentage; the most and least frequently used English learning and test-taking strategies were identified and analyzed. In order to test the differences among students from different universities and at different proficiency levels, analysis of various ANOVA (Duncan's) was conducted in terms of these variables.

Then, correlation analyses were run to explore the relationships between these measured variables and students' performance in English. Finally, structural equation modeling (SEM) was conducted for each sample to further understand these relationships.

Responses to the open-ended questions and the reflective journals were subjected to a thematic content analysis (Krippendorff, 1980), which was then integrated into the discussion of survey results.

According to Krippendorff (1980), content analysis can be used to analyze narratives, descriptions, folklores and political materials, and so on when source materials are voluminous and complicated, when they contain all sorts of different kinds of subject matters, and/or when the source material is used to complement some other kind of data during an inquiry. Before analyzing the content of communications, it is important to classify the content into units, which can be word, phrase, sentence, syntax, reference, time, size, proposition, and/or theme (Neuendorf, 2002). Since the reflective journals and open-ended questions in the present research were conducted according to a set of purposes or key questions, they could be best analyzed according to thematic units. The primary purpose in this study was to identify whether the students felt anxious in English class and motivated to learn the target language, what provoked anxiety in them and their coping strategies, what motivated them to learn the language, and what strategies they often used when learning English and taking English exams. Based on the analyses, some calculations were carried out, for example, about how many students felt anxious in English class.

Chapter 4   Results of the Whole Participant Sample

This chapter reports the results of the whole participant sample. For each measured variable, descriptive analysis and analysis of ANOVA (Duncan's) were conducted. Subsequently, correlation coefficients were computed to determine the associations among the measured variables and performance in English. Finally, SEM was run to further explore these relationships.

4.1 English language classroom anxiety of the whole sample

4.1.1 General picture of English language classroom anxiety of the whole sample

With a reliability score of .753 in the present research, the Classroom Anxiety Scale (CAS) measured the extent to which students felt anxious in English language classrooms.

4.1.1.1 Item analysis of the CAS of the whole sample

Table 4.1 summarizes students' responses (the first number means the real number and the second percentage) to the CAS (Classroom Anxiety Scale) items. All percentages refer to the number of students who (strongly) disagreed, neither disagreed nor agreed, or (strongly) agreed with the statements (percentages were rounded to the nearest whole number).

Table 4.1: CAS Items with Numbers and Percentages of Students Selecting Each Alternative (N = 1203)

	SD/D	N	A/SA
1. I don't usually get anxious when I have to respond to a question ….	404/34.4	130/10.8	659/54.8
2. I am always afraid that other students would laugh at me if I speak ….	851/70.7	152/12.6	200/16.7
3. I always feel that other students are more at ease than I am in … .	586/48.7	290/24.1	317/27.2
4. I am never embarrassed to volunteer answers in English class.	510/42.4	289/24.1	404/33.6
5. I am generally tense whenever participating in English class.	928/77.1	150/12.5	125/10.4

6. I never understand why other students are so nervous in English class.
    511/42.5   378/31.4   304/26.1
7. I usually feel relaxed and confident when active participation takes ….
    392/32.6   300/24.9   511/42.5
8. Whenever I have to answer a question, … I get nervous and ….
    767/63.8   180/14.9   256/21.3

Notes: SD → Strongly disagree;   D → Disagree
N → Neither disagree nor agree; A → Agree;   SA → Strongly agree

As shown in Table 4.1, consistent with the mean scores of the CAS items presented in Appendix II, most students (strongly) disagreed with statements reflective of speech anxiety such as "whenever I have to answer a question, out loud, I get nervous and confused in English class" (item 8) (63.8%); "I am always afraid that other students would laugh at me if I speak up in English class" (item 2) (70.7%); "I am generally tense whenever participating in English class" (item 5) (77.1%). This suggests many students did not feel anxious or even feel confident and relaxed in English class. Nevertheless, they rejected the CAS items indicative of confidence when speaking in English class such as "I usually feel relaxed and confident when active participation takes place in English class" (item 7) (32.6%); "I don't usually get anxious when I have to respond to a question in English class" (item 1) (34.4%); "I am never embarrassed to volunteer answers in English class" (item 4) (42.4%); and "I never understand why other students are so nervous in English class" (item 6) (42.5%). This indicates that significant anxiety was experienced by at least a third of the students in English language classrooms, like that reported in previous studies (Gardner & MacIntyre, 1992; Horwitz et al., 1986; Horwitz, 2001; Liu, 2006a, 2006b, 2007b; Liu & Jackson, 2008). Anxious students reported that they were afraid to speak and felt deeply self-conscious when speaking English in the presence of other people.

    This finding is generally supported by the result of the journal data. Of 215 journal participants, 166 reported that they were (very/a little/sometimes) anxious in English classrooms, especially when speaking/using the language publicly in class. The principal reasons were: low English proficiency, lack of practice, lack of vocabulary, lack of confidence, lack of preparation, personality, and so on, as detailed in Table 4.6.

4.1.1.2 General tendency of the CAS of the whole sample

In order to know the general tendency of students' anxiety in English class, the total score, mean, standard deviation, median, mode, maximum and minimum of the CAS were computed. When computing these scores, the researchers adjusted the values assigned to different alternatives from 'Strongly Disagree' (1) to 'Strongly Agree' (5) of some items. Namely, for items 1, 4, 6 and 7 which expressed confidence in speaking English, the response 'Strongly Disagree' got a value of 5 instead of 1, the response 'Strongly Agree' got a value of 1 instead of 5, and so on. Thus, the total score of the CAS revealed respondent's anxiety in English classrooms. The higher the score, the more anxious the respondents felt.

Since there are 8 items on the CAS, a total score of more than 32 on the scale implies that the respondent is very anxious in English classrooms. A total score of 24 to 32 signifies moderate anxiety and a total score of less than 24 indicates no/little anxiety in English class. The results are shown in Table 4.2.

Table 4.2: Statistical Analyses of the CAS of the Whole Sample

	Mean	Standard Deviation	Median	Mode	Range
Male (764)	21.33	5.30	21.00	20.00	8.00-37.00
Female (439)	21.21	4.79	21.00	22.00	8.00-34.00
Total (1203)	21.29	5.12	21.00	20.00	8.00-37.00

As reflected by Table 4.2, though some students (with a score of 37.00) felt extremely nervous, a mean of 21.29, a median of 21.00 and a mode of 20.00 on the CAS, all below the average score of 24.00, indicates that the majority felt relaxed and that only around a third experienced anxiety in English class. These findings are consistent with the results of item analysis of the CAS and the mean scores of CAS items shown in Appendix II.

In addition, according to Table 4.2, female students with a mean of 21.21 reported to be slightly less anxious than males with a mean of 21.33 in English class, unlike that in Aida's (1994) study but similar to Wang's (2003) and Wang and Ding's (2001). Yet, the difference was not significant, as proved by the Independent-samples t Test result: $t = .397$, $p = .69$.

4.1.2 Differences in English language classroom anxiety among students from different universities

In order to know the differences in English language classroom anxiety among students from different universities, the total scores, means, standard deviations, medians, modes, maximums and minimums of the CAS were computed, as done in section 4.2.1.2. Thus, the total score of the CAS represented respondents' anxiety in English class, the higher the score, the more anxious/nervous the respondent felt. The results and further analyses are presented in the following Tables.

Table 4.3: Statistical Analyses of the CAS across Universities

	Mean	Standard Deviation	Median	Mode	Range
TU (451)	21.57	5.40	22.00	20.00	8.00-37.00
BFU (327)	21.50	4.91	22.00	22.00	9.00-36.00
CUP (425)	20.82	4.93	21.00	20.00	8.00-36.00

Notes: TU → Tsinghua University; BFU → Beijing Forestry University
CUP → China University of Petroleum

Table 4.4: ANOVA Results of the CAS of the Whole Sample

Measure	F	P	F*	University (Mean) TU = 451; BFU = 327; CUP = 425			Location of sig. difference
				TU	BFU	CUP	
CAS	2.75	.064	2.77	21.57	21.50	20.82	/

Note: F* → Critical F value for Duncan's test at .05 level (Black, 1999).

As seen from Table 4.3, although some students (with a mean of 36.00 or 37.00) felt extremely anxious and nervous in English class, the mean score, median and mode, all below 24.00, of each university show the majority from each university did not feel nervous in English classrooms. Nevertheless, these scores also reveal at least a third of the students from each university experienced anxiety in English class, in accordance with the finding of the whole participant sample, as found in previous studies (Chen, 2002; Kitano, 2001; Saito, Horwitz & Garza, 1999; Liu, 2006a, 2006b; Wang & Ding, 2001).

According to Table 4.3, Tsinghua (TU) students scored the highest while those from China University of Petroleum (CUP) scored the lowest on the CAS. The TU students not only had the highest mean score (21.57) but also the highest median (22.00) and the maximum (37.00); the CUP students had the lowest scores (mean = 20.82; median = 21.00; maximum = 36.00); and their BFU counterparts had the mean (21.50) in middle but the highest mode (22.00) and minimum (9.00). It appears that the TU students felt the most nervous while the CUP learners felt the least in English class. Alternatively, the students from the best university or at the highest English proficiency level experienced the most anxiety; whereas, those from the lowest top university or at the lowest English proficiency level suffered anxiety the least in English class. This is still out of our expectation though the difference was statistically insignificant, as indicated by the ANOVA results reported in Table 4.4.

This finding is again proved by that of the journal data, as reported in Table 4.5.

Table 4.5: Student Anxiety Reported in Journals (whole sample)

	Total No.	(Very) N N/%	A little N N/%	Sometimes N/%	Not N N/%	Not mentioned N%
TU	95	52/54.7%	22/23.2%	3/3.2%	18/18.9%	0
BFU	37	31/83.8%	0	0	5/16.1%	1/2.7%
CUP	83	30/36.1%	15/18.1%	13/15.7%	20/24.1%	5/6%
Total	215	113/52.6%	37/17.2%	16/7.4%	43/20%	6/2.8%

Note: N = nervous

Table 4.5 shows that over half of the journal participants (52.6%) reported feeling (very/a little/sometimes) nervous in English class due to various reasons. A closer comparison of the three groups reveals that more BFU students (83.8%) self-reported to be anxious than their TU (54.7%) and CUP (36.1%) peers, whereas the fewest CUP learners were anxious in English class. This finding partially confirmed the statistical result that the CUP students were the least anxious in English classrooms.

4.1.3 Causes for and consequences of language classroom anxiety of the whole sample

As previously discussed, around half of the participants from the three universities reported feeling anxious in English class. But the reasons might vary, as listed in Table 4.6.

Table 4.6: Causes for Language Classroom Anxiety (WS)
(Source: journals)

	TU (Total N = 95) N/%	BFU (Total N = 37) N/%	CUP (Total N = 83) N/%
Low English proficiency	19/20%	16/51.6%	14/16.9%
Lack of /limited vocabulary	13/13.7%	10/32.2%	21/25.3%
Lack of practice	3/3.2%	13/41.9%	11/13.3%
Personality	19/20%	4/12.9%	16/19.3%
Lack of confidence	9/9.5%	5/16%	10/12%
Not understanding what the teacher is saying	2/2.1%	9/29%	1/1.2%
Poor oral English	10/10.5%	4/12.9%	5/6%
Other students' wonderful performance	14/14.7%	0	3/3.6%

Lack of preparation	2/2.1%	0	10/12%
Poor/Bad pronunciation	2/2.1%	3/10%	0
Poor listening	1/1.1%	4/12.9%	0
Being unable to find appropriate words to express myself	4/4.2%	0	3/3.6%
Fear of being the center of attention	4/4.2%	0	1/1.2%
English being a foreign language	3/3.2%	0	2/2.4%
Fear of making mistakes	0	0	7/5.4%
Being afraid of being laughed at	0	5/16%	0
Not knowing how to express oneself in English	0	0	5/6%
English lessons being difficult	0	0	3/3.6%
Being unable to catch classmates	0	0	3/3.6%
Coming from the countryside where English teaching is poor	1/1.1%	1/3.2%	0
Fear of being unable to understand the teacher	1/1.1%	0	2/2.4%
Lack of familiarity with classmates	1/1.1%	0	1/1.2%
Inadequate grammatical knowledge	3/3.2%	0	0
Having never spoken English before so many people	3/3.2%	0	
Teachers always speaking English in the whole class	0	1/3.2%	0
Being afraid of being asked	0	1/3.2%	0
Having not finished homework	0	1/3.2%	0
English being difficult	0	0	2/2.4%
Different teaching method	2/2.1%	0	0
Teaching and learning tradition	2/2.1%	0	0
Not liking speaking English	2/2.1%	0	0
Hating English	0	0	1/1.2%
The pressure given by the teacher	0	0	1/1.2%
Fear of speaking	1/1.1%	0	0
Slow progress	1/1.1%	0	0
Taking speaking seriously	1/1.1%	0	0
Hating being required to write down a word that I can't spell	1/1.1%	0	0
Inability to organize speech when speaking	1/1.1%	0	0
Not knowing the keys to questions	1/1.1%		0

Notes: WS = the whole sample

As shown in Table 4.6, the three main factors contributing to the whole sample's anxiety in English class were low English proficiency (20%, 51.6% and 16.9% for TU, BFU and CUP samples respectively), lack of vocabulary (13.7%, 32.2% and 25.3% for TU, BFU and CUP samples respectively), and lack of practice (3.2%, 41.9% and 13.3% for TU, BFU and CUP samples respectively).

Low English proficiency, to many of these participants, especially the BFU correspondents, provoked anxiety the most, as found in Liu's (2006a, 2007b) studies. Due to poor English, they became "afraid of speaking English, and worry about being asked to answer questions. When I have to speak English, I become very nervous (Li, male, BFU)". Similarly, lack of vocabulary could produce anxiety in many of the participants in that it made them unable to express themselves. Some students felt anxious when speaking/using English because they had had little practice with the language.

The next three important reasons were personality (mainly introversion and shyness based on their own description) (20%, 12.9%, and 19.3% respectively), lack of confidence (9.5%, 16%, and 12% respectively), and not understanding what the teacher was saying (2.1%, 29%, and 1.2% respectively). Personality was also identified as a great contributor to their anxiety in English class by around 20% of each university sample. Because of shyness or introversion, some students would easily become nervous when using/speaking English, especially when it happened in front of others. It was the same with lack of confidence and incomprehensible input.

The other factors ranged from fear of being the focus of attentions, to inadequate grammatical knowledge, to the difficulty of English and English lessons, etc., with varying weights assigned to them by different band students.

In addition to identifying anxiety-provoking factors in English class, these participants also commented on the impact of anxiety on their learning of English. Of 215 journal participants, 154 (71.6%) thought that anxiety negatively affected their learning of English, 13 (6%) believed anxiety to be beneficial, 8 (3.7%) regarded anxiety as something both good and bad, 16 (7.4%) maintained that anxiety could produce no effect, and 21 (9.8%) didn't give any comment. The results are presented in Table 4.7.

Table 4.7: Impact of Anxiety on Students' Learning of English
(the whole sample) (Source: journal)

	Bad	Good	Good and bad	No effect	No comment
TU (95)	64/67.4%	7/7.4%	6/6.3%	10/10.5%	8/8.4%
BFU (37)	32/86.5%	2/5.4%	0	2/5.4%	1/2.7%
CUP (83)	58/69.9%	4/4.8%	2/2.4%	6/7.2%	13/15.7%
Total (215)	154/71.6%	13/6%	8/3.7%	16/7.4%	21/9.8%

Table 4.7 reveals that more than 60% of each university sample believed that anxiety exerted a negative effect on their learning of English. These students reflected that due to anxiety, they could not perform as well as they should have, made slow progress, and studied inefficiently. Around 5% of each sample regarded anxiety as something conducive to their learning of the language in that it served as a motivation and urged them to study harder. Meanwhile, 6.3% of the TU and 2.4% of the CUP participants respectively maintained that anxiety affected their learning of English both negatively and positively: anxiety motivated them to work harder but at the same time prevented them from performing better.

Comparison of the three samples shows that more BFU participants (86.5%) believed anxiety to be a debilitator than did their TU (67.4%) and CUP (69.9%) peers, while more TU learners (7.4%) regarded it as something conducive than their BFU (5.4%) and CUP (4.8%) counterparts.

Although the majority of each sample held that anxiety negatively affected their learning of English, only a few had purposefully taken some measures to cope with it, such as breathing deeply, telling oneself to be brave and/or encouraging oneself by saying that "you are the best". The majority seemed to be helpless while hoping more contact with the target language could gradually reduce their anxiety, as found in Liu's (2006a) study. Nevertheless, they offered some suggestions for language learners and teachers to help reduce/overcome learners' foreign language anxiety, as demonstrated in Table 4.8.

Table 4.8: Students' Suggestions to Cope with Anxiety for Language Learners and Teachers (the whole sample) (Source: journal)

Suggestions for teachers	Com. to all the Ss	Create a relaxing and comfortable classroom environment.
		Encourage students to speak more.
		Give students more chances to express themselves.
		Be friendly and helpful.
	Com. to TU & CUP Ss	Often praise students.
		Choose interesting topics.
		Give students some time to prepare the answers.
		Treat students equally.
		Let students talk in pairs.
	Com. to TU & BFU Ss	Ask students to answer questions.
		Slow down speech.
		Smile more.
		Help students feel confident.

		Play games in class.
		Let students talk in pairs.
	Com. to BFU & CUP Ss	Be humorous.
	Particular to TU Ss	Arrange consistent meetings for students to gather and practice oral English.
		Teach according to students' English proficiency and personality, etc.
		Help students discover the beauty of English.
		Develop students' interest in English.
		Explain difficult words.
		Help students with examples.
		Give more chances to nervous students.
		Organize some interesting activities.
	Particular to BFU Ss	Help students to pronounce correctly
		Ask students to read more, write more and speak more
		Organize more activities in class.
		Teach useful things.
		Communicate with/ pay more attention to shy students.
		Have patience and love for students.
		Make simple conversations in class.
		Cancel exams.
		Use Chinese sometimes.
		Solve the problem together with students.
		Correct students' mistakes.
		Introduce new ways of study
	Particular to CUP Ss	Ask students in turn.
		Help students overcome some difficulties.
		Let students speak loud in the classroom.
		Have a talk with students.
		Make students feel free.
		Set proper assignments.
		Give more advice on how to study English.
		Ask certain students to answer questions.
	Com. to all the Ss	More practice.
		Be more self-confident.
		Be brave.
		Improve English.
		Don't be afraid of making mistakes.
		Study harder.
		Enlarge vocabulary.

		Be well prepared.
Suggestions for students	Com. to TU & BFU Ss	Believe in yourself.
		Don't give up.
		Don't laugh at others.
	Com. to TU & CUP Ss	Love English.
		Make a study plan.
		Communicate with other students.
	Particular to TU Ss	Change personality.
		Care little about marks.
		Improve grammatical knowledge.
		Focus on the teachers' lessons.
		Fix several groups.
		Read English as often as possible.
		Don't fear being laughed at.
		Speak to themselves.
		Don't lose heart.
		Telling yourself "it's a good chance to show yourself".
		Be optimistic.
		Develop positive attitudes toward English learning.
	Particular to BFU Ss	Communicate with the teachers
		Read English novels
		Take part in psychological lessons
		Read more and loudly
		Have passion
		Spend more time on it
		Recite useful sentences and paragraphs
	Particular to CUP Ss	Learn English songs.

Notes: Ss → students; Com. = common

According to Table 4.8, all the correspondents suggested that they would become less nervous when using/speaking English in class if the teachers could create a relaxing classroom environment, encourage them more, give them more chances for practicing the target language, and be friendly and helpful in class. The TU and BFU students also hoped English teachers to ask students to answer questions (frequently), slow down speech, smile often, help them to feel confident and play some games in class. The TU and CUP participants advised English teachers to choose interesting topics, praise students often, ask them to talk in pairs, treat them equally and give them some thinking time before answering questions, as found in Liu's (2006a) and Tsui's (1996) studies. Meanwhile, both the BFU and CUP learners believed that a humorous teacher could help them feel more at ease. As to the specific suggestions proposed by each university sample, they will be discussed in more detail in Chapters 5-7 respectively. On the whole, the CUP students advised English teachers to create more opportunities for their students to practice the language orally; the BFU learners also suggested English teachers ask their students to practice more, and at the same time to help them with their pronunciation and grammar; the TU participants hoped English teachers to facilitate their study by giving examples and explanation, developing their interest in the language and helping them discover the beauty of the language. As such, the TU respondents seemed to be much more demanding compared with their BFU and CUP peers.

As far as language learners were concerned, all the participants, as suggested by previous researchers (Donley, 1998; Jackson, 2002; Tsui, 1996), commented that they should have more practice, be more confident, be brave and well-prepared, study hard, enlarge vocabulary, improve English and not fear making mistakes in order to become more confident when using/speaking English in class.

Apart from the common suggestions, the students from different universities suggested other ways to overcome anxiety in English class. In spite of differences in wording, the essence lay in improving English, having more contact with and practice of English, and supporting each other in the classroom. Some BFU learners even suggested anxious students take psychological lessons to help reduce/overcome anxiety. This was surprising yet brilliant in that psychological consult has been rare in China.

4.2 English learning motivation of the whole sample

4.2.1 General picture of English learning motivation of the whole sample

Achieving a reliability score of .786, the English Learning Motivation Scale (ELMS) in the present research examined whether and why the students were motivated to learn English.

4.2.1.1 Item analysis of the ELMS of the whole sample

Table 4.9 presents the students' responses (the first number means the real number and the second percentage) to ELMS (English Learning

Motivation Scale) items, in the same way as the presentation of their responses to CAS items.

Table 4.9: ELMS Items with Numbers and Percentages of Students Selecting Each Alternative (the whole sample) (N = 1203)

SD/D	N	A/SA
9. Honestly, I don't know whether I am motivated to learn English.		
769/63.9	169/14.1	265/22.0
10. I have the impression that I am wasting my time in studying English.		
994/72.6	97/8.1	102/9.3
11. I study English in order to get a good job later on.		
428/35.6	190/15.8	586/48.7
12. I study English in order to earn more money later on.		
486/40.4	250/20.8	467/38.8
13. I study English for higher education later on.		
192/15.9	188/15.6	823/68.4
14. I study English in order to go abroad later on.		
268/22.2	228/19.0	707/58.8
15. I study English because I think it is important for my future work.		
173/14.4	164/13.7	866/72.0
16. I study English because I want to get high marks in English exams.		
496/41.2	214/17.7	493/41.0
17. I study English because it is required with credits at my university.		
565/47.0	190/15.8	448/37.3
18. I study English because I want to … competence in the language ….		
663/55.1	251/20.9	289/24.0
19. … I have to pass English exams; otherwise, I would not learn it.		
938/78.0	136/11.3	129/10.7
20. … I am good at English listening, … thus interested in it.		
508/42.3	297/24.7	398/23.1
21. I study English because I want to improve my English abilities ….		
200/16.6	155/12.9	848/70.5
22. … I think it is important for my personal development.		
86/7.2	81/6.8	1036/86.1
23. I study English because I would feel guilty if I didn't know English.		
621/51.6	264/21.9	318/26.4
24. I study English because I would feel ashamed if I couldn't ….		

519/43.2   262/21.8   422/35.1

25. … I choose to be … who can speak more than one language.
217/18.0   201/16.7   785/65.3

26. … I choose to be the kind of person who can speak English.
192/15.9   222/18.5   789/65.6

27. I study English for the satisfied feeling I get in finding out new things.
281/23.3   355/29.5   567/47.2

28. … I experience in knowing more … literature.
360/29.9   407/33.8   436/36.2

29. … I enjoy the feeling of learning… and their way of life.
416/34.6   336/27.9   451/37.5

30. I study English … understand a difficult idea in English.
509/42.3   396/33.0   298/24.8

31. … I feel when I am doing difficult exercises in English.
682/56.7   294/24.5   227/18.9

32. I study English for the good feeling … than I thought in English class.
361/30.0   337/28.0   505/42.0

33. I study English for the excitement that I get while speaking English.
569/47.3   308/25.6   326/27.1

34. I study English for the excitement … speaking a foreign language.
635/52.8   292/24.3   276/23.0

Notes: SD → Strongly disagree;   D → Disagree
N → Neither disagree nor agree;   A → Agree;   SA → Strongly agree

As shown in Table 4.9, the majority of the respondents rejected such ELMS items indicative of little English learning motivation as "Honestly, I don't know whether I am motivated to learn English (item 9)" (63.9%) and "I have the impression that I am wasting my time in studying English (item 10)" (72.6%). This strongly suggests that the students were motivated to learn English and considered it worthwhile to learn the language.

The frequencies and percentages of response to items 9 to 21 presented in Table 4.9 and ELMS item mean scores reported in Appendix II also reveal that the students were highly instrumentally motivated to learn English. They reported being motivated to learn the language for various instrumental reasons such as going abroad (item 14) (58.8%); higher education (item 13) (68.4%); improving English abilities in four basic skills (item 21) (70.5%); future career (item 15) (72.0%); and personal development (item 22) (86.1%), as found in Liu's (2009) study. Meanwhile, they disagreed with statements expressing learning English for certificates and passing exams, as demonstrated by their responses to items 18 (55.1%) and 19 (78.0%).

When it comes to integrative reasons, most students attributed their motivation to learn English to such reasons as the good feeling of doing better in class (item 32) (42%); the satisfaction of finding out new things (item 27) (47.2%); choosing to speak more than one language (item 25) (65.3%) and English (item 26) (65.6%). At the same time, they denied being motivated to learn English for such reasons as excitement of speaking English (item 33) (47.3%); feeling guilty (item 23) (51.6%); excitement of hearing someone speaking English (item 34) (52.8%); and satisfaction of doing difficult exercises in English (item 31) (56.7%). These clearly indicate that the students' integrative motivation was more concerned with their school performance than their liking for the language, as supported by the mean scores of ELMS items presented in Appendix II as well.

This finding was also supported by the students' self-reports in their journal journals. Of 215 journal participants, 192 reported to be motivated to learn English in university because of a variety of reasons, as listed in Table 4.10.

Table 4.10: Reasons for Students' Motivation to Learn English
(the whole sample) (Source: Journal)

		TU (95)	BFU (37)	CUP (83)
No Motivation	Number	10/10.5%	1/2.7%	3/3.6%
	Reason	Don't like English So many new words and hard texts No pressure Not use English outside the classroom	Don't like English	No interest in English
Motivation	Number	85/ 89.5%	36/97.3%	71/85.5%

	Reason			
		To do things for the Olympic Games 2008 To find a good/better job To improve English To go abroad To get more knowledge from English books Pass the TEPT 1 English being useful English being not so hard now To be a postgraduate Admire those who can speak well To talk with foreigners To change the present situation To feel very proud English being important Being interested in English English being a beautiful language To have more better opportunities To communicate with others easily To become a serious English speaker Passion and curiosity Learning English being fun	To find a better/good job To go abroad To pass CET band 4 Being interested in English To communicate with foreigners To become graduate students English being a requirement for computer majors To listen to English To speak good English To understand the difference between dreams and reality For a beautiful future American movies being funny Teachers being interesting and not stiff Realizing what has been learned is limited To enjoy the new learning environment To learn more for graduation To see English movies To play computer games To improve English To do something for the Olympic Games 2008 College English being more interesting Being envious of those who can speak English smoothly English being very important/useful English being funny	To find a better/good job Interest in English English being useful English being important Desire to speak English fluently To learn more things from English books To pass examinations To communicate with others better To go abroad To be happy in English class To improve English To do as teachers said To be better than friends To communicate with foreigners For further study

As noted from Table 4.10, the common reasons for the three university samples to be motivated to learn English were to find a good/better job, to go abroad, to pursue further study, to pass exams, to improve English, and to communicate with foreigners. English being useful and important and being interested in English tool were also shared motivations. The TU and CUP learners were motivated also because they wanted to learn more things from English books and to communicate with others (more) easily. Desire to speak English fluently motivated both the BFU and CUP participants to learn the language. The TU and BFU correspondents also shared a motivation which was to do something for the Olympic Games 2008.

In addition to these common motivations, each sample had some specific ones. For example, the TU participants were motivated to learn English because the language, to them, was beautiful and learning the language was fun. They also admired those who spoke the language well and thus thought they would feel proud if they could speak it fluently as well. By learning English well, they might be able to change the present situation and have more and better opportunities. The BFU students were motivated because, in their eyes, English and English movies were interesting. They also wanted to play computer games, to enjoy the new learning environment and to understand the differences between dreams and reality. The CUP learners were motivated to learn English because their teachers told them to study it hard. Meanwhile, they wanted to be happy in English class and be better than their friends.

Generally speaking, each sample was motivated to learn English both integratively and instrumentally. And the TU participants seemed to have more integrative motivations while their CUP peers appeared to be more instrumentally motivated.

4.2.1.2 Factor analysis of the ELMS of the whole sample

A factor analysis with varimax rotation was conducted on the English Learning Motivation Scale (ELMS) to investigate if the statements formed clusters matching different hypothesized views. The analysis yielded three factors—English learning motivation (ELM), instrumental motivation (InsM) and integrative motivation (IntM) (Table 4.6), as expected by the researchers. Two items (9-10) were included in interpreting the first ELMS component—ELM, which accounted for 36.29% of the total variance. Twelve items (11-22) were included in interpreting the second ELMS component—InsM, which had in common a sense of learning English for instrumental purposes and accounted for 45.4% of the total variance. The other twelve items (23-34) were included in interpreting the third ELMS component—IntM, which were reflective of learning English for integrative purposes and explained 18.32% of the total variance. The results are displayed in Table 4.11.

Table 4.11: Varimax Rotated Loadings for Factor Analysis of the ELMS (the whole sample) (N = 1203)

	1	2	3
9. Honestly, I don't know … to learn English.	.658		
10. I have the … time in studying English.	.676		
11. I study English in order to get a good job later on.		.775	
12. I study English in order to earn more money later on.		.745	
13. I study English for higher education later on.	.297	.489	
14. I study English in order to go abroad later on.	.353	.468	
15. I study English … it is important for my future work.	.369	.546	
16. I study English … to get high marks in English exams.	-.207	.652	

55

17. I study English ... with credits at my university.	-.341	.607	
18. I study English ... my competence in the language.	-.176	.555	.147
19. I study English ... otherwise, I would not learn it.	-.634	.143	-.107
20. I study English ... and thus interested in it.	.281		.417
21. I study English ..., reading and/or writing.	.516		.206
22. I study English ... for my personal development.	.600	.249	
23. I study English ... if I didn't know English.	-.182	.168	.417
24. I study English ... friends in English.		.160	.464
25. I study English ... speak more than one language.	.369	.143	.453
26. I study English ... who can speak English.	.426	.125	.467
27. I study English ... I get in finding out new things.	.353		.579
28. I study English ... more about English literature.	.282	-.115	.650
29. I study English ... people and their way of life.	.237		.621
30. I study English ... a difficult idea in English.			.724
31. I study English ... difficult exercises in English.			.662
32. I study English ... I thought in English class.		.156	.582
33. I study English ... I get while speaking English.	.141		.623
34. I study English ... speaking a foreign language.			.587

Notes: Loadings of less than .10 are excluded from the Table.

Factor 1 (ELM) = English learning motivation

Factor 2 (InsM) = Instrumental motivation

Factor 3 (IntM) = Integrative motivation

The loadings displayed in Table 4.11 reveal that the majority of the items within a subcomponent of the ELMS were highly correlated with that subcomponent: items 9 to 10 significantly positively correlated with the ELM with coefficients ranging from .658 to .676; items 11 to 22 highly related to the InsM with a coefficient range of .000 to .775, with 8 being higher than .40; items 23 to 34 highly positively correlated with the IntM with coefficients ranging from .417 to .724, with all being higher than .40. This suggests the English motivation, instrumental motivation and integrative motivation were important subcomponents of the ELMS. Meanwhile, these three subcomponents were significantly correlated with the ELMS (r = .323, .718 and .829 for the ELM, InsM and IntM respectively), which is reported in Table 4.12.

Table 4.12: Correlations between the ELMS and its Subscales (WS)

	InsM	IntM	ELMS
ELM	.035	.213**	.323**
InsM	1	.238**	.718**
IntM		1	.829**

Notes: WS = the whole sample; **. p < .01

Table 4.12 also demonstrates these three subcomponents were significantly related to one another, which implies students who were instrumentally motivated to learn English also tended to be integratively motivated.

4.2.1.3 General tendency of the ELMS of the whole sample

In order to know the general tendency of the students' English learning motivation, the total score, mean, and standard deviation of the ELMS were computed. When doing so, the researchers adjusted the values assigned to different alternatives in a similar way to the computation of the CAS. Items 9 and 10 which expressed no motivation had values assigned to their alternatives reversed. Thus, the total score of the ELMS revealed the respondent's motivation to learn English. The higher the score, the more motivated the students were to learn the language. Since the ELMS consists of 26 items, a total score of more than 104 on the scale implies the respondent is highly motivated to learn English; a total score of 78 to 104 signifies moderate motivation and a total score below 78 indicates no/little motivation.

It is worth noting that the ELMS consists of three components: English learning motivation (ELM), instrumental motivation (InsM) and integrative motivation (IntM). The mean, standard deviation, median, mode, maximum and minimum of each of these three subscales were also computed. Given the total number of items of each subscale, a total score of more than 8 on the ELM which has 2 items (with a score range of 2 to 10) indicates high motivation, a total score of 6 to 8 suggests moderate motivation and a score below 6 means no/little motivation. A total score of more than 48 on the InsM which has 12 items (with a score range of 12 to 60) implies that a respondent is strongly instrumentally motivated to learn English, a total score of 36 to 48 represents moderate instrumental motivation and a score of less than 36 signifies no/little instrumental motivation. A total score of more than 48 on the IntM which has 12 items (with a score range of 12 to 60) implies that a respondent is strongly integratively motivated to learn English, a total score of 36 to 48 represents moderate integrative motivation and a score below 36 signifies no/little integrative motivation. It holds true for all the three subscales that the higher the score the more motivated the respondent was to learn

English integratively or instrumentally. The results are shown in Table 4.13.

Table 4.13: Statistical Analyses of the ELMS and its Subscales
(WS) (N = 1203)

	Mean	Standard Deviation	Median	Mode	Range
ELMS	81.93	10.81	82.00	80.00	43.00-124.00
ELM	7.81	1.75	8.00	8.00	2.00-10.00
InsM	38.00	5.60	38.00	36.00	15.00-56.00
IntM	36.12	7.16	36.00	36.00	12.00-59.00

Note: WS = the whole sample

As presented in Table 4.13, though some students (with a score of 43.00) had little motivation to learn English, a mean of 81.93, a median of 82.00 and a mode of 80.00, all above the average score of 78.00, imply that the majority were moderately or highly motivated to learn the language, as found in numerous other studies (Hao et al., 2004; Hu, 2002; Liu, 2009; Zhou, 1998). In addition, a mean of 7.81, a median and a mode of 8.00 on the ELM reflect the majority had moderate or strong motivation to learn English. Likewise, a mean of 38.00, a median of 38.00 and a mode of 36.00 on the InsM, all above the average score of 36.00, suggest the students were moderately or strongly instrumentally motivated, as usually found in other studies (Dörnyei, 2001; Gardner & MacIntyre, 1993; Liu, 2009, 2007a). Similarly, the students reported being moderately integratively motivated as well, as indicated by their IntM mean (36.12), median (36.00) and mode (36.00) presented in Table 4.13, similar to Lamb's (2004) study but different from Liu's (2007).

Moreover, as implied by the InsM and IntM mean scores shown in Table 4.13, the students seemed to be more instrumentally than integratively motivated to learn English, as found in other studies in Chinese EFL situations (Gao, Zhao, Cheng & Zhou, 2004; Liu, 2007a). And the difference was statistically significant, as supported by the results of paired samples t Test: t = 7.9993, p = .000.

Further, the results of statistical analyses reported in Table 4.7 indicate that female students were generally more motivated to learn English both instrumentally and integratively than their male peers; and their motivation was stronger as well. The differences were all statistically significant, as proved by the results of Independent-samples t Tests presented in Table 4.14.

Table 4.14: Gender Differences in the ELMS and its Subscales (WS)

	Mean		Standard Deviation		t-test result	
	Male	Female	Male	Female	t	p
ELMS	80.81	83.88	10.72	10.70	-4.79	.000.
ELM	7.68	8.04	1.80	1.64	-3.505	.000
InsM	37.68	38.56	6.11	5.75	-2.458	.014
IntM	35.45	37.28	7.17	7.00	-4.293	.000

Notes: WS = the whole sample; Male = 764;   Female = 439

4.2.2 Differences in English learning motivation among students from different universities

In order to know the differences in English learning motivation among students from different universities, the total scores, means, standard deviations, medians, modes, maximums and minimums of the ELMS and its subscales were computed, as done in section 4.2.1.3. Thus, the total scores of the ELMS, ELM, InsM and IntM represented respondents' overall motivation, English learning motivation, instrumental and integrative motivation respectively. It holds true for all that the higher the score, the more motivated the students were. The results and further analyses are presented in the following Tables.

**Table 4.15: Statistical Analyses of
the ELMS and its Subscales across Universities**

Measures	University	Mean	Standard Deviation	Median	Mode	Range
ELMS	TU (451)	80.08	10.27	80.00	81.00	43.00-123.00
	BFU (327)	83.07	11.44	82.00	75.00	50.00-122.00
	CUP (425)	83.01	10.62	83.00	80.00	50.00-124.00
ELM	TU (451)	7.85	1.69	8.00	8.00	2.00-10.00
	BFU (327)	7.67	1.86	8.00	8.00	2.00-10.00
	CUP (425)	7.88	1.73	8.00	10.00	2.00-10.00
InsM	TU (451)	36.42	6.12	36.00	36.00	15.00-56.00
	BFU (327)	38.92	5.92	39.00	37.00	16.00-55.00
	CUP (425)	38.97	5.57	39.00	38.00	23.00-56.00
IntM	TU (451)	35.80	6.81	36.00	37.00	12.00-57.00
	BFU (327)	36.48	7.21	36.00	36.00	16.00-59.00
	CUP (425)	36.17	7.48	36.00	40.00	12.00-58.00

Table 4.16: ANOVA Results of the ELMS and its Subscales (WS)

Measures	F	P	F*	University (Mean) TU = 451; BFU = 327; CUP = 425			Location of sig. difference (a = .05)
				TU	BFU	CUP	
ELMS	10.73 *	.000	2.77	80.08	83.07	83.01	TU & BFU; TU & CUP
ELIM	1.47	.231	2.77	7.85	7.67	7.88	/
InsM	26.00 *	.000	2.77	36.42	38.92	38.97	TU & BFU; TU & CUP
IntM	.85	.426	2.77	35.80	36.48	36.17	/

Notes: WS = the whole sample

F* → Critical F value for Duncan's test at .05 level (Black, 1999).

As reported in Table 4.15, the mean scores, medians and modes of the universities on the ELMS and its subscales clearly show that the majority of each university students had moderate or even strong motivation to learn English. They were also moderately or even strongly instrumentally/ integratively motivated to learn the language. This finding generally conforms to that of the whole participant sample.

According to Table 4.15, Tsinghua (TU) students had the lowest mean scores on all the scales except the ELM; the BFU students had the highest mean scores on the ELMS and the IntM; CUP students achieved the highest mean scores on the ELM and the InsM; and their medians and modes were somewhat similar on all these scales. It appears that the TU respondents had the lowest overall motivation to learn English. They were also the least motivated to learn the language both instrumentally and integratively. The BFU students had the highest overall motivation and the most integratively motivated to learn English. The CUP learners were the most instrumentally motivated. Namely, students from the best university or at the highest English proficiency level were the least motivated to learn English both instrumentally and integratively, while students from the other not so good universities were more motivated either instrumentally or integratively. And some of the differences were statistically significant, as indicated by the ANOVA results reported in Table 4.16. The TU participants significantly differed from their BFU and CUP counterparts on the ELMS and the InsM; whereas no significant differences were found on other scales. This finding was surprising. Generally speaking, learners better at a foreign language are more motivated to learn that language (Belmechri & Hummel, 1998; Clément et al., 1994; Dörnyei, 1994; Oxford & Shearin, 1994), while the case was just the opposite in the present research. This might be attributed to the fact that the TU students were exempt from the national CET band 4 while both the BFU and CUP students had to pass the exam to obtain degree certificates on time. This might also explain why the TU students were the least instrumentally motivated to learn English. The facts that the TU learners generally had more and better exposure to English and that they had a brighter future after graduation could also partially account for the finding. Further, this findings may be attributed to the fact that the TU learners, quite proficient in English, had more difficulty making great(er) progress, which was (much) easier to their CUP and BFU peers. Nevertheless, these explanations need to be confirmed in future research.

4.3 English learning strategy use by the whole sample

4.3.1 Factor analysis of the ELSI of the whole sample

A factor analysis with varimax rotation was conducted on the English Learning Strategy Inventory (ELSI) to investigate if the statements formed clusters matching different hypothesized views. The analysis yielded six factors—(a) memory strategies (MS), (b) cognitive strategies (CogS), (c) compensation strategies (ComS), (d) metacognitive strategies (MetaS), (e) affective strategies (AS), and (f) social strategies (SS) (Table 4.17), which is consistent with the view held by the researchers based on Oxford's (1990) model.

Twenty items (35-54) were included in interpreting the first ELSI component—MS, which accounted for 42.35% of the total variance; forty-four items (55-98) were included in interpreting the second ELSI component—CongS, which explained 26.26% of the total variance. Twenty-one items (99-119) were included in interpreting the third ELSI component—ComS, which had in common a sense of making guesses and/or overcoming limitations in speaking and writing and accounted for 8.66% of the total variance; seventy-five items (120-194) were included in the forth ELSI component—MetaS, which explained 19.69% of the total variance. The fifth ELSI factor—AS included thirteen items (195-207), which accounted for 1.96% of the total variance; and the last ELSI factor—SS included eleven items (208-218), which explained 1.28% of the total variance. The results are reported in Table 4.17.

Table 4.17: Varimax Rotated Loadings for Factor Analysis of the ELSI (the whole sample) (N = 1203)

	1	2	3	4	5	6
35. I remember English ... synonyms.	.439					
36. I remember English ...letter clusters.	.242		.336		-.15	
37. I remember a new word	.366		.355			
38. I think of relationships ... English.	.426		.335		-.14	
39. When learning ... I already know.	.419		.347		-.111	
40. I remember ... with others.	.493		.135	.155		
41. I use new English ... them.	.464		.163	.182		
42. I use the English ... different ways.	.425		.197	.229		.115
43. I connect ... remember the word.	.367		.244			
44. I remember ... or on a street sign.	.212				.271	
45. I remember ... word might be used.	.442		.265	.128		
46. I remember ... semantic relations.	.332		.294			
47. I use rhymes to remember new	.360			.189	.232	
48. I remember ... its pronunciation.	.126	.108	.354			
49. I often review what	.334			.153		.298
50. I copy down ... them regularly.	.332			.148		.229
51. I ... act out new English words.	.335		-.131	.282	.286	
52. I use flashcards ... English words.	.283		-.143	.198	.251	
53. I often memorize ... or a dictionary.	.275			.127	.184	.117
54. I often recite English essays.	.353			.191	.108	.194
55. I often ...understand every word.	.102	.339		.141		.223
56. I say or write new English words	.199	.176				.270
57. I reread an English text to	.191	.306				.213
58. I practice the sounds of English.	.277	.285	.229	.177	-.133	.184
59. I practice pronunciation ...rules.	.423	.337		.163		
60. I try to imitate ... native speakers.	.258	.303	.199	.266	-.137	
61. I often do ... listening exercises.		.326		.271	.111	.141
62. I try to talk like native English	.183	.236	.139	.208		
63. I often practice reading English	.312	.250		.297	-.110	.181
64. ..., I ... deduce grammatical	-.162	.482		.151		.147
65. I often try to ... in English.		.328	.289		-.134	.128
66. I try to find patterns in English.		.386	.154			.147
67. I often try to put together ...d.		.453	.123	.139		.197
68. I watch ... or English movies.		.316	.258	.223	-.199	
69. I read for pleasure in English.	.206	.203	.274	.206	-.164	
70. I'm much concerned ... in English.					.218	.248
71. I keep on listening to English		.391				
72. ..., I ... pay attention to grammar.	-.143	.303	.323		.165	
73. I first skim ... read carefully.	.203		.332	.120	.104	
74. ..., I skip unimportant information.		.104	.388			
75. I often try to enlarge my	.290	.131	.170	.316	-.154	.158
76. ..., I ... but learn how to use it.		.366	.158	.123	-.129	
77. I ... looking up every new word.		.403				

78. I ... before listening to English.		.106	-.208		.364	
79. ..., I read the transcript.			-.180		.363	
80. ...or Chinese-English dictionary.			.207			.189
81. ..., I ...related to what I am reading.	-.224	.104			.296	-.133
82. I often remember English	.196	.364			-.166	
83. ..., I ...opinion and ... intention.	.226	.431				.148
84. ..., I analyze the structure ... text.	-.190	.378		.237		
85. I often learn English grammar	-.168	.363	-.168	.271	.103	.163
86. ..., I ... the sentence structures.	-.244	.432	-.244	.109	.105	
87. I find the meaning ... I understand.	.270		.176	.124		
88. I often analyze the structure	.457	-.188				.107
89. I often pay attention to the		.353	.203	.184		
90. I look for words in my own			.276	-.117	.195	.136
91. I often translate what I learn	.103	-.112			.355	.141
92. I try not to translate			.300		-.111	
93. I practice writing ... writing ability.	.227			.149		.196
94. I often transfer my knowledge	.205			.109	.288	.114
95. I take notes while reading English.	.227	-.108		.104	.160	.334
96. I take notes while listening to	.157			.221		.310
97. I make summaries ... in English.	.269			.284	.121	.213
98. I highlight certain phrases or	.143	.338				.267
99. ..., I make guesses	.190		.527			
100. ..., I make guesses			.665	.102		
101. I often use linguistic clues		-.102	.519		-.111	
102. ..., I often try to remember....	.193		.320	.174		
103. I try to guess what the other			.433	.236		
104. I use contextual clues to			.613			
105. I use background knowledge to....			.621			
106. I use background knowledge to....			.582			
107. I make guesses about the			.547	.131		
108. ..., I use visual aids to			.635			
109. I try to predict the content	.103		.497		.107	
110. I try to guess what the other			.517	.149		
111. I often switch to Chinese			.187	-.130	.410	
112. I often ask for other people's			.145		.158	.283
113. ..., I use body language.			.417	.119	.137	
114. I will give it up if I can't					.436	
115. I often try to avoid using English.			-.144	-.118	.505	
116. I often choose the topics which I....			.430	-.109	.215	
117. I often turn to use simple, ...			.518	-.218	.104	
118. I make up new words				.287	.393	
119. ... I use a word or phrase that			.574	-.185		.170
120. ..., I often try to link it with		.134	.548			.192
121. ..., I often try to link the topic	.160		.531			.202
122. I pay attention to the	.231	-.170	.351			.256
123. ..., I try to find out topic	.158	-.178	.350			.215
124. I won't look it up in a			.389			

125. I pay attention to the beginning....	.130		.417			.132
126. ..., I definitely don't use words	.115	-.104		.205		.146
127. I look up the words in			.426	-.155		.174
128. I look up in dictionary only			.354			.109
129. I look up in dictionary only			.281			.135
130. I pay attention when someone			.414			.237
131. I pay attention to new	.306	-.279		.258		.207
132. I try to use a variety of sentence	.187	-.218	.349	.112	-.231	.136
133. I try to use a variety of words	.169	-.269	.377	.140	-.228	.155
134. I try to make as few		-.240	.449		-.205	.169
135. I try to make it coherent when	.121	-.198	.518		-.169	.199
136. I keep to the main idea when		-.248	.478		-.114	.234
137. I pay attention to paragraphing		-.233	.445		-.106	.274
138. I am attentive		-.211	.367			.320
139. ..., I focus my attention on	-.124	.239	.375		.125	
140. I often focus on listening			.283		.172	.163
141. I try to find out how to be a			.351		-.103	.311
142. ..., ... own English learning plan.	.197		.119	.278	-.155	.344
143. I plan my schedule	.135			.219		.353
144. ..., I organize my ideas quite	.133	-.174	.341		-.128	.250
145. I often put forward a new	.192	-.136	.127	.369	.101	.133
146. I have clear goals for improving	.175		.148	.291		.402
147. I often set short-term and	.181			.327		.408
148. I often identify the purpose	.253	-.151		.320		.358
149. ..., I ... evolve around an idea.	.108	-.233	.300	.155		.126
150. ..., I often state the main idea		-.219	.351			.146
151. ..., I often make a summary		-.205	.431			.241
152. I select different learning	.138		.268			.364
153. I often outline before starting to	.128	-.204		.293		.168
154. ..., I often try to list the ideas	.109	-.225	.292	.122		.286
155. I select English learning			.398			.276
156. I often think out a title		-.126	.252	.131	.146	.263
157. I try to write notes and book	.163			.609		
158. I keep on listening to the		.132	.268	.274		.143
159. I write emails and/or letter in	.122			.629		
160. I try to write diaries and/or				.496		
161. I have a notebook ready for	.135			.521	.106	.116
162. I try to find as many ways	.228		.121	.474	-.140	.202
163. I murmur the answer to myself	.133			.237		.216
164. I try to voluntarily seek chances	.158			.571		
165. I often speak English to myself.		.229	.220	.372	-.163	.162
166. I look for opportunities to read	.154	.121	.158	.456		.254
167. I initiate to greet and converse				.681		
168. I initiate to make friends with			-.184	.688		
169. I initiate to talk to teachers in	.105		-.162	.705		
170. I often participate in various	.119		-.111	.656		
171. I actively take part in various	.155		-.138	.652		

	Col1	Col2	Col3	Col4	Col5	Col6
172. I pay attention to the	.157		.164	.396	-.201	.175
173. I pay attention to the English	.122	.153	.259	.262	-.230	.220
174. I pay attention to the English		.132	.345	.219	-.232	.270
175. I read English instructions of			.188	.455	-.115	.149
176. I often search for various	.117			.657		.148
177. I often download audio		.133		.421		.226
178. I often surf various English				.620		.114
179. I don't pursue grammaticality		.202	.402			.169
180. I repeatedly revise my English		-.201		.280		.371
181. I notice my English mistakes		-.161	.254		-.113	.456
182. ..., I note down the cases	.201	-.101		.319	.127	.375
183. ..., I think about how I could			.276	.139		.418
184. I pay attention to learning from	.145		.245			.502
185. I make adjustment	.188		.298			.451
186. I check my progress in English	.221		.211	.112		.495
187. I assess my English learning	.217		.239	.131		.457
188. I study my personality	.192		.282	.137		.392
189. I adjust my reading speed			.255			.145
190. I pay attention to the feedback	.132	-.161	.240	.134		.407
191. ..., I repeatedly read and revise it.	.197	-.183		.307		.332
192. ..., I check spelling and	.201	-.233	.127	.146		.360
193. I usually read English articles, ...	.200	.137	.275	.250		.245
194. I often test myself on English ...	.212			.436	.118	.275
195. I try to relax		.127	.295		.138	.290
196. I breathe deeply		.104	.183	.221	.230	.246
197. I often try to laugh				.390	.294	
198. I encourage myself not to lose			.451			.336
199. I encourage myself to use....	.187	.177	.344	.189		.349
200. I often purposefully take	.210	.191	.282	.399		.304
201. I often purposefully use certain	.160	.169	.371	.197		.270
202. I often purposefully make			.491			.194
203. I give myself a reward or treat			.185	.175	.248	.220
204. I notice if I am tense or nervous			.302		.124	.261
205. I often use a checklist to note	.151		-.136	.445	.369	.104
206. I write down my feelings in			-.109	.453	.268	.213
207. I talk to someone else				.260		.465
208. I ask for help from English	.102			.304		.394
209. ..., I... slow down or say it again.		.112	.361			.402
210. ..., I ask for clarification.	.111		.279			.335
211. I ask English speakers to....				.201		.440
212. I ask my English teachers to			.298			.409
213. I practice English ... outside class.	.132			.508		.262
214. I talk to my peers about how to	.100	.141		.252		.462
215. I talk to more proficient		.118	.126	.213		.522
216. I try to learn about the culture		.185	.285	.118	-.220	.316
217. ..., I just care for what I need		-.130	-.208	.282	.353	
218. ..., I use various ways to		.147	.342	.149		.297

Notes: Loadings of less than .10 are excluded from the Table.

Factor 1 (MS) = Memory strategies

Factor 2 (CogS) = Cognitive strategies

Factor 3 (ComS) = Compensation strategies

Factor 4 (MetaS) = metacognitive strategies

Factor 5 (AS) = Affective strategies; Factor 6 (SS) = Social strategies

The loadings presented in Table 4.17 indicate the majority of the items within a subcomponent of the ELSI was highly correlated with that subcomponent: items 35 to 54 highly positively related to MS with coefficients ranging from .126 to .493, with 15 being higher than .30; items 55 to 98 highly positively correlated with CogS with a coefficient range of -.244 to .482, with around a half being higher than .30; items 99 to 119 highly related to ComS with coefficients ranging from -.144 to .665, with 15 being higher than .40; items 120 to 194 highly correlated with MetaS with a coefficient range of -.155 to .705, with a third being higher than .30; items 195 to 207 highly positively related to AS with coefficients ranging from .000 to .369; and items 208 to 218 highly positively correlated with SS with a coefficient range of .000 to .522, with 8 being higher than .30. This signifies these six strategy categories were important subcomponents of the ELSI, which is further confirmed by the significantly high coefficients between the ELSI and its six components—MS (r = .736, p < .01), CogS (r = .866, p < .01), ComS (r = .617, p < .01), MetaS (r = .946, p < .01), AS (r = .777, p < .01) and SS (r = .729, p < .01), as presented in Table 4.18.

Table 4.18: Correlations among the ELSI and its Subscales
(WS) (N = 1203)

	CogS	ComS	MetaS	AS	SS	ELSI
MS	.669**	.383**	.603**	.481**	.431**	.736**
CogS	1	.465**	.724**	.604**	.562**	.866**
ComS		1	.497**	.434**	.358**	.617**
MetaS			1	.720**	.683**	.946**
AS				1	.628**	.777**
SS					1	.729**

Notes: WS = the whole sample; ** = p < .01

Moreover, Table 4.18 shows that these six components were also highly significantly related to one another. Alternatively, a more frequent user of one category of strategies tends to use other categories of strategies more frequently when learning English.

4.3.2 The whole sample's knowledge of English learning strategies

Of 215 journal participants, 84 TU, 31 BFU and 77 CUP students reported to know something about English learning strategies and have used some when learning English, as presented in Table 4.19.

Table 4.19: Students' Knowledge of
English Learning Strategies (the whole sample) (Source: journal)

TU	BFU	CUP
Memorize words (day by day)/expand vocabulary	Memorize words and grammar	Memorize words and phrases
Recite texts	Recite texts	Preview
Review frequently	Do exercise	Review
Remember important sentences	Listen to English	Recite texts
Read some passages/do lots of reading	Writing some articles	Listen to English
Take notes while listening to the teacher	Practice speaking	Repeat
Practice	Manage time	Read texts
Get the main idea of articles	Make a plan	Take notes
Make full use of the Internet and library		Practice
Listen to some radios		Read English books
Listen to English songs		
Listen to texts		Do exercises
Watch movie		Make good organization of time
Read newspapers		
Read the text, look up the new words		
Use English when having a chance		Make a plan
Study every day, in every place		Plan and revise
Listen carefully in class		
Do exercises after class		
Make a plan		
Make up for the weak points in study		
Have an open heart and energetic spirit		
Be brave and confident		
Keep a diary		
Stick to it, never give up		

Although quite a few strategies were listed here, memory strategies seemed to be predominant across universities: memorize words, recite sentences and texts, and (pre)review. In order to learn English better, these participants from all universities also made use of such cognitive strategies as repeated practice (e.g., doing exercises) and using resources for receiving and sending messages (e.g., listen to radio, watch movies,

67

read texts, etc.). Meanwhile, they planned their study and managed their time to serve for their study. In addition, the TU learners resorted to such affective strategies as writing diaries, remaining brave and confident, and never giving up.

In short, the three samples seemed to have some knowledge about English learning strategies, but not much. Comparatively, the TU participants knew more about English learning strategies and used more of them as well. At the same time, 65 TU, 31 BFU and 59 CUP students reflected that using these strategies was conducive to improving their English and enhancing their study efficiency.

4.3.3 Broad profile of English learning strategy use by the whole sample

When reporting frequency of use of English learning and test-taking strategies, we employ Oxford's (1990) key to understanding mean scores on SILL-based instruments whose scale range is 1 to 5:

— HIGH USE = 4.5 to 5.0 (always or almost always used) and 3.5 to 4.4 (usually used)

— MEDIUM USE = 2.5 to 3.4 (sometimes used)

— LOW USE = 1.5 to 2.4 (usually not used) or 1.0-1.4 (never or almost never used).

Based on the mean scores of English Learning Strategy Inventory (ELSI) items presented in Appendix II (total), items in different use ranges were summarized and reported in Table 4.20. Among the 184 ELSI items, 69 items were in the high use range, 102 in the medium use range and 13 in the low use range. That is, the majority of the strategies were sometimes used; around a fourth to a third of them were usually or always used; only a few were usually not used or even not used. The case was the same with each of the six strategy categories, as indicated in Table 4.20. A review of the ELSI mean scores reported in Appendix II further shows that mean scores for high use strategies never exceeded 4.00 and those for low use strategies never fell below 2.00. In another word, those high use strategies were just usually but not always used, while those low use strategies were just usually not used and none of them were never or almost never used. On the whole, all the strategies were employed by the students to different extents and the majority were sometimes or more often used.

Table 4.20: Number of English Learning
Strategy Items in Different Use Ranges (the whole sample)

English Learning Strategy categories	High use	Medium use	Low use
Memory Strategy (MS)	5	13	2
Cognitive Strategy (CogS)	10	33	1
Compensation Strategy (ComS)	14	6	1
Metacognitive Strategy (MetaS)	30	38	7
Affective Strategy (AS)	6	6	1
Social Strategy (SS)	4	6	1
English Learning Strategy Inventory (ELSI)	69	102	13

As reported in Table 4.21, the mean of overall strategy use was 3.23 on the 5-point Likert scale. This suggests "medium" strategy use (sometimes used) towards the upper end. Namely, the students reported having a quite frequent use of various strategies, which was close to high use but not to that extent, consistent with the analyses of the mean scores of different strategy items.

The mean scores for all the six strategy categories except compensation strategies which was in high use also fell in the medium-use range. Among the six categories, the most frequently used were compensation strategies with a mean of 3.51 (usually used), followed by metacognitive and social strategies with the same mean of 3.25, and then affective strategies with a mean of 3.24. Then came cognitive strategies with a mean of 3.14 and memory strategies were the least used with a mean of 3.06. The students reported having high use of compensation strategies, but only at the low end. That is, this category of strategies was more often used than "sometimes", whereas others were just sometimes used but at the middle (memory strategies) or the upper end (the other four categories) of the medium range. This indicates that students were fairly flexible in using various strategies when learning English.

Table 4.21: Means and Standard Deviations Indicating
English Learning Strategy Use (the whole sample) (N = 1203)

Strategy category (most used to least used)	Frequency of strategy use	
	Mean/range	Standard deviation
Compensation	3.51 (high use; low end)	.39
Metacognitive	3.25 (medium use; upper end)	.39
Social	3.25 (medium use; upper end)	.50
Affective	3.24 (medium use; upper end)	.46
Cognitive	3.14 (medium use; upper end)	.36
Memory	3.06 (medium use)	.43
ELSI	3.23 (medium use; upper end)	.33

This finding about the overall strategy use conforms to that of Bremner's (1999) study of Hong Kong university students though it is slightly different from that of Lan and Oxford's (2003) of Taiwanese students. Nevertheless, in all studies, participants were found not to use memory strategies frequently. This was surprising in that Chinese learners are generally believed to depend much on memory in learning (Yang & Weir, 1998; Zou, 1998, 2002). Nonetheless, this might suggest Chinese learners are changing in terms of strategy use, which adequately justifies further exploration of this issue.

4.3.4 The most and least used individual English learning strategies by the whole sample

As previously analyzed, the majority of the strategies were sometimes or usually used. Among these more often used strategies, twenty strategies were identified to be the most frequently used by the Chinese undergraduate EFL learners, as seen from Table 4.22.

Of the twenty most often used strategy items, most of them were compensation strategies and all were in the high-use range with a mean ranging from 3.73 to 3.98. The participants would usually use contextual clues to "understand unfamiliar English words" (mean = 3.98) and "make guesses when reading in English" (mean = 3.87); use background knowledge to make guesses when "reading in English" (mean = 3.81) and "listening to English" (mean = 3.74); "use visual aids to better understand English movies" (mean = 3.92); "use words or phrases similar in meaning as substitutes" (mean = 3.89); "use simple English words, expressions and sentence structures as substitutes" (mean = 3.88); and make guesses "on word formation to understand unfamiliar English words" (mean = 3.77) and "purposefully when listening to/reading English" (mean = 3.74). They also "look up frequently occurring words in dictionary" (mean = 3.87), and "read English without looking up every new word" (mean = 3.76). In addition, they tried to "link it with already known knowledge when reading or listening to English (mean = 3.79) and "link the topic with already known knowledge when speaking/writing in English" (mean = 3.75). When writing in English, these learners tried to "make it coherent" (mean = 3.86), "make as few grammatical mistakes as possible" (mean = 3.81) and "keep to the main idea" (mean = 3.79). Meanwhile, they "self-encourage not to lose heart when not doing well in English exams" (mean = 3.87) and "try to find out how to be a better learner of English" (mean = 3.75).

Though metacognitive strategies had the largest number of items in the present research, most of the most frequently used strategies belonged to the compensation category. The students would guess intelligently by using linguistic and other clues to help realize their goals. When deploying metacognitive strategies, the participants mainly depended on the strategy of centering one's learning by overviewing and linking with already known material and paying attention, as shown in Table 4.11. That only two affective strategies (encouraging oneself) were highly frequently used might be due to the fact that this category included many fewer items. It might also be because Chinese EFL learners seldom purposefully deploy any means to ease their anxiety, fear and/or doubt in English learning (Liu, 2009, 2006a). They seldom purposefully took their emotional temperature as well. The fact that no most frequently used strategies were included in the social category might be because students involved in the present research still did not have much access/exposure to spoken English in their daily life. It was surprising that only one memory and one cognitive strategies were highly frequently used by the participants though these two categories included quite a few strategy items. It was also contradictory to the journal participants' self-reports previously discussed.

On the whole, it was pleasant to find that these undergraduate non-English majors were accustomed to looking for clues, making guesses, and resorting to background knowledge in English learning.

Table 4.22: The Twenty Most Frequently and Twenty Least Used English Learning Strategies (the whole sample) (N = 1203)

The twenty most frequently used English learning strategies				
No.	Strategy	Mean	Category in which this strategy is classified	Comment
100	Make guesses based on	3.98	Compensation	H
108	Use visual aids to better	3.92	Compensation	H
119	Use words or phrases that	3.89	Compensation	H
117	Use simple English	3.88	Compensation	H
104	Use contextual clues to	3.87	Compensation	H
127	Look up the words in	3.87	Metacognitive	H
198	Self-encourage not to lose	3.87	Affective	H
135	Try to make it coherent	3.86	Metacognitive	H
105	Use background knowledge	3.81	Compensation	H
134	Try to make few	3.81	Metacognitive	H
48	Remember a new English....	3.79	Memory	H
120	Try to link it with what I	3.79	Metacognitive	H

136	Keep to the main idea when	3.79	Metacognitive	H
99	Make guesses based on	3.77	Compensation	H
77	Read English without looking	3.76	Cognitive	H
121	Try to link the topic with	3.75	Metacognitive	H
141	Try to find out how to be a	3.75	Metacognitive	H
106	Use background knowledge	3.74	Compensation	H
202	Purposefully make guesses	3.74	Affective	H
109	Try to predict the content	3.73	Compensation	H

The Twenty least frequently used English learning strategies				
No.	Strategy	Mean	Category in which this strategy is classified	Comment
78	Often read the transcript	2.22	Cognitive	L
51	Physically act out new	2.25	Memory	L
206	Write down feelings in	2.25	Affective	L
160	Try to write diaries and/or	2.29	Metacognitive	L
131	Pay attention to new	2.30	Metacognitive	L
118	Make up new words when	2.32	Compensation	L
168	Initiate to make friends	2.33	Metacognitive	L
169	Initiate to talk to teachers	2.36	Metacognitive	L
52	Use flashcards to remember	2.41	Memory	L
171	Actively take part in	2.45	Metacognitive	L
217	Care for what has to be said	2.45	Social	L
170	Often participate in various	2.46	Metacognitive	L
167	Initiate to greet and converse	2.47	Metacognitive	L
61	Often do really a lot of	2.51	Cognitive	M
161	Have a notebook ready for	2.51	Metacognitive	M
79	Read the transcript while	2.53	Cognitive	M
59	Practice pronunciation	2.56	Cognitive	M
159	Write emails and/or letter in	2.56	Metacognitive	M
176	Often search for various	2.57	Metacognitive	M
205	Often use a checklist to note	2.57	Affective	M

Notes: H = high use;   M = medium use;   L = low use

Among the twenty least often used strategies, 13 were in the low-use range at the upper end with a mean range from 2.22 to 2.47; 7 fell in the medium-use range at the low end with a mean range from 2.51 to 2.57, as presented in Table 4.12. For example, "often read the transcript before listening to English" (mean = 2.22); "physically act out new English words" (mean = 2.25); "try to write diaries and/or journals in English" (mean = 2.29); "make up new words when not knowing the right ones in English" (mean = 2.32); "use flashcards to remember new English words" (mean = 2.41); and "read the transcript while listening to English" (mean = 2.53).

4.3.5 Differences in English learning strategy use between male and female students and among those at different universities

According to Table 4.23, both male (with means ranging from 3.09 to 3.49) and female (with means ranging from 3.05 to 3.56) students had a medium or even high use of all the categories of English learning strategies whose means all exceeded 3.00. In addition, female students reported to use compensation and social strategies more frequently than their male peers. Their use of memory, cognitive and metacognitive strategies was less frequent, and the use of affective strategies was almost as frequent as that of their male peers'. But significant differences were found only in the use of compensation and social strategies, as proved by the results of Independent-samples t-tests reported in Table 4.23. Therefore, females utilized compensation and social strategies significantly more frequently than their male peers when learning English.

Table 4.23: Gender Differences in English Learning Strategy Use (the whole sample) (N = 1203)

		Mean	Standard Deviation	t-test results	
				t	p
MS	M (764)	3.09	.43	.83	.407
	F (439)	3.05	.43		
CogS	M (764)	3.15	.36	.42	.675
	F (439)	3.14	.34		
CompS	M (764)	3.49	.41	-3.00	.003
	F (439)	3.56	.35		
MetaS	M (764)	3.26	.40	1.12	.265
	F (439)	3.23	.38		
AS	M (764)	3.24	.46	-.02	.984
	F (439)	3.24	.45		
SS	M (764)	3.22	.52	-2.86	.004
	F (439)	3.30	.46		
ELSI	M (764)	3.23	.34	.11	.915
	F (439)	3.23	.32		

Notes: M = male; F = female

To explore differences in English learning strategy use among students from different universities, the analysis of one-way ANOVA was conducted. The results of which are presented in Table 4.24.

Table 4.24: ANOVA Results of English Learning Strategy Use
(the whole sample)

Measures	F	P	F*	University (Mean) TU = 451; BFU = 327; CUP = 425			Location of sig. difference (a = .05)
				TU	BFU	CUP	
MS	4.64*	.010	2.77	3.08	3.00	3.09	BFU & TU; BFU & CUP
CogS	.52	.596	2.77	3.15	3.13	3.15	/
ComS	1.48	.227	2.77	3.51	3.49	3.53	/
MetaS	3.91*	.020	2.77	3.28	3.20	3.25	TU & BFU
AS	2.34	.096	2.77	3.21	3.23	3.28	/
SS	.31	.733	2.77	3.24	3.25	3.26	/
ELSI	2.39	.092	2.77	3.25	3.20	3.25	/

Note: F* → Critical F value for Duncan's test at .05 level (Black, 1999).

As shown in Table 4.24, students from all universities had a medium use of the strategies except compensation strategies which were in the high use range. The CUP students reported using memory, cognitive, compensation, affective and social strategies the most frequently in learning English. The TU students self-reported to be the most frequent users of metacognitive strategies but the least frequent users of affective and social strategies; their BFU peers used memory, cognitive, compensation and metacognitive the least often and other strategies in between. However, the post-hoc tests revealed that significant differences occurred only in the use of memory and metacognitive strategies among students from different universities: the BFU students deployed significantly less frequently memory strategies than their TU and CUP counterparts; the TU students utilized significantly more frequently metacognitive strategies than their BFU peers.

Furthermore, as seen from Table 4.24, students from three universities all reported having a medium use of the overall strategies. The TU students used the strategies as frequently as did those from CUP, while their BFU counterparts had the least frequent use of the strategies. However, no significant differences were found.

4.3.6 Correlations between individual English learning strategy use and the whole sample's performance in English

To explore the relationship between the use of individual English learning strategies and students' performance in English, correlation analyses were conducted. The results are summarized in Table 4.25, which revealed 69 English learning strategy items significantly correlated with students' performance in English with coefficients ranging from -.147 to .149.

Table 4.25: Correlations between Individual English Learning Strategy Use and Students' Performance in English
(the whole sample) (N = 1203)

Items	P
37. Remember a new word by its formation (memory).	.075*
38. Think of relationships between what I already ... (memory).	.103**
39. Associate it with ... when learning a new word (memory).	.060*
40. Remember new English words by associating ... (memory).	.086*
45. Remember a new English word by making ... (memory).	.084*
49. Often review what I have learned in English (memory).	.062*
50. Copy down new English words in a special ... (memory).	.076**
54. Often recite English essays (memory).	-.071*
60. Try to imitate the pronunciation of ... (cognitive).	.077**
61. Often do really a lot of English listening exercises (cognitive).	.063*
63. Often practice reading English aloud (cognitive).	.067*
64. Often find out and deduce grammatical rules ... (cognitive).	.108**
68. Watch English language TV shows or English ... (cognitive).	.059*
69. Read for pleasure in English (cognitive).	.113**
70. Be much concerned with whether I understand ... (cognitive).	-.066*
75. Often try to enlarge my vocabulary by reading ... (cognitive).	.089**
76. Make sure of its meaning and learn how to ... (cognitive).	.077**
78. Often read the transcript before listening to English (cognitive).	-.133**
79. Read the transcript while listening to English (cognitive).	-.122**
80. Often turn to an English-Chinese or ... (cognitive).	.076**
81. Just pay attention to the meaning related to ... (cognitive).	-.116**
82. Often remember English grammatical rules ... (cognitive).	.108**
83. Try to deduce the author's opinion and ... (cognitive).	.113**
88. Often analyze the structure of complicated ... (cognitive).	.096**
90. Look for words in my own language that are ... (cognitive).	-.067*
91. Often translate what I learn in English into Chinese (cognitive).	-.144**
99. Make guesses based on word formation to ... (compensation).	.071*
101. Often use linguistic clues to make guesses if ... (compensation).	.105**

102. If I hear an unfamiliar English word, I often … (compensation).	.096**
106. Use background knowledge to make … (compensation).	.077**
107. Make guesses about the speaker's intention … (compensation).	.100**
108. Use visual aids to … English movies (compensation).	.059*
113. Use body language when I can't think of … (compensation).	.068*
114. Give it up if not understanding what is … (compensation).	-.122**
115. Often try to avoid using English (compensation).	-.147**
127. Look up the words in dictionary that … (metacognitive).	.078**
129. Look up in dictionary only those words that … (metacognitive).	.062*
132. Try to use a variety of sentence structures … (metacognitive).	.108**
133. Try to use a variety of words when writing … (metacognitive).	.149**
134. Try to make as few grammatical mistakes … (metacognitive).	.132**
135. Try to make it coherent when writing in … (metacognitive).	.072*
137. Pay attention to paragraphing when writing … (metacognitive).	.119**
141. Try to find out … better learner of English (metacognitive).	.088**
142. Have my own English learning plan … (metacognitive).	.136**
143. Plan my schedule in order to have enough … (metacognitive).	.072*
144. Organize my ideas quite logically … (metacognitive).	.112**
146. Have clear goals for improving my English … (metacognitive).	.082**
149. Often make a paragraph evolve around an … (metacognitive).	.103**
150. Often state the main idea in the first … (metacognitive).	.072*
152. Select different learning strategies … (metacognitive).	.065*
153. Often outline before starting to write in … (metacognitive).	.105**
159. Write emails and/or letter in English to my … (metacognitive).	.083**
165. Often speak English to myself (metacognitive).	.063*
166. Look for opportunities to read as much … (metacognitive).	.109**
167. Initiate to greet and converse with … (metacognitive).	.074*
172. Pay attention to the introduction in English … (metacognitive).	.063*
174. Pay attention to the English used in streets (metacognitive).	.063*
179. Don't pursue grammaticality so much … (metacognitive).	.069*
182. Note down the cases that I don't know how … (metacognitive).	-.065*
190. Pay attention to the feedback given by my … (metacognitive).	.101**
191. Repeatedly read and revise it after … (metacognitive).	.083**
192. Check spelling and grammatical mistakes … (metacognitive).	.088**
200. Often purposefully take chances to speak English … (affective).	.061*
202. Often purposefully … listening to/reading English (affective).	.064*
211. Ask English speakers to correct me when I talk (social).	-.066*
212. Ask my English teachers to correct my writing (social).	.066*
213. Practice English with other students outside class (social).	.076**
216. Try to learn about the culture of English speakers (social).	.065*

217. Just care for what I need to say and how to say it, … (social).	-.080**

Notes: ** = p < .01;   * = p < .05;   P = performance

According to Table 4.25, one memory, six cognitive, two compensation, one metacognitive, and two social strategies were significantly negatively correlated with students' performance in English. For example, strategy 54, "often recite English essays" (memory) (r = -.071); 78, "often read the transcript before listening to English" (cognitive) (r = -.133); 114, "give it up if not understanding what is heard and just listen to the English that I can understand" (compensation) (r = -.122); 182, "note down the cases that I don't know how to express myself in English for later improvement when writing in English" (metacognitive) (r = -.065); and 211, "ask English speakers to correct me when I talk" (social) (r = -.066). The more often students used these strategies when learning English, the less proficient they were in English. A careful review of these strategies indicates most of them would interfere the learning of English in a particular way, such as trying to avoid using English, looking for words in the mother tongue which are similar to new words in English, translating English into the mother tongue, reading the transcript before listening to English, and worrying about whether every sentence in English was understood. Therefore, it is no wonder they might exert a negative effect on students' performance in English. Surprisingly, the strategy "note down the cases that I don't know how to express myself in English for later improvement when writing in English" also negatively affected students' performance in English, though the relationship was not very strong.

The rest of the strategies were significantly positively related to students' performance in English. For example, strategy 37, "remember a new word by its formation" (memory) (r = .075); 60, "try to imitate the pronunciation of English native speakers" (cognitive) (r = .077); 99, "make guesses based on word formation to understand unfamiliar English words" (compensation) (r = .071); 133, "try to use a variety of words when writing in English" (metacognitive) (r = .149); 200, "often purposefully take chances to speak English even if I may not speak it well" (affective) (r = .061); and 212, "ask my English teachers to correct my writing" (social) (r = .066). The more frequently students deployed these strategies in English learning, the higher they achieved in English.

Moreover, among these strategies, the majority belonged to the metacognitive (27) category, followed by cognitive (18), compensation (9), memory (8), social (5) and affective (2) categories. More strategy items fell into metacognitive and cognitive categories may be because these two categories included a larger number of items. As Table 4.25 shows, most of the metacognitive strategies were concerned with paying attention, planning, organizing, and seeking practice opportunities. The cognitive strategies were mainly related to practicing, deducing and reasoning, creating resources for sending and receiving messages, translating and transferring.

4.4 English test-taking strategy use by the whole sample

4.4.1 Factor analysis of the ETSI of the whole sample

A factor analysis with varimax rotation was conducted on the English Test-taking Strategy Inventory (ETSI) to investigate if the statements formed clusters matching different hypothesized views. The analysis yielded six factors—(a) test-taking memory strategies (TMS), (b) test-taking cognitive strategies (TCogS), (c) test-taking compensation strategies (TComS), (d) test-taking metacognitive strategies (TMetaS), (e) test-taking affective strategies (TAS), and (f) test-taking social strategies (TSS) (Table 4.26), which is consistent with the view held by the researchers based on Oxford's (1990) model.

Six items (219-224) were included in interpreting the first ETSI component—TMS, which accounted for 35.47% of the total variance; seventeen items (225-241) were included in interpreting the second ETSI component—TCogS, which explained 23.03% of the total variance. Twelve items (242-253) were included in interpreting the third ETSI component—TComS, which accounted for 11.49% of the total variance; forty-eight items (254-301) were included in the forth ETSI component—TMetaS, which explained 28.63% of the total variance. The fifth ETSI factor—TAS included four items (302-305), which accounted for 1.32% of the total variance; and the last ETSI factor—TSS included four items (306-309), which explained 1.06% of the total variance. The results are reported in Table 4.26.

78

Table 4.26: Varimax Rotated Loadings for Factor Analysis of the ETSI (the whole sample) (N = 1203)

	1	2	3	4	5	6
219. I review a lot before English ...	.203	.184	.187	.596		
220. ..., I keep up my homework	.333	.195	.118	.475	.154	
221. I use high technology to help	.528	-.108		.136	.116	
222. I create flashcards ... exam.	.543	-.144		.176	.182	
223. I memorize model texts/essays	.490	-.117		.244	.101	
224. I often dump information on the	.570		-.186		.128	
225. I practice a lot before English tests.	.348	.404		.256		
226. I practice speaking English in	.421	.215				.212
227. I practice writing answers to	.468	.288	.153	.134		
228. I practice translating English	.163	.551		.149		
229. I practice writing by modeling	.212	.522			.158	
230. I analyze past test papers to	.180	.319	.184	.345	.158	.117
231. I take good notes as my English			.284	.494	.138	
232. I create summary notes and	.559		-.107		.154	
233. I look for the central idea of	.196	.326	.200		.197	.180
234. I directly get to the point		.425	.125	.183		.102
235. I use both general and specific		.395	.212		.114	.150
236. I eliminate certain answers		.613	.142	.188		
237. I analyze the sentence structure		.248	.438		.158	.134
238. I break up run-on sentences into		.504	.151	.121	.204	.116
239. I jot down information in the		.373			.288	
240. ..., I jot down important ideas	.214	.375			.370	.102
241. I highlight some sentences or		.513		.152	.250	
242. I exchange with English	.537	.109			.119	
243. I ask the instructor what to	.483					
244. I use my linguistic knowledge			.647			
245. I make guesses based on			.723	.115		
246. I use my linguistic knowledge			.708			
247. I use my background knowledge....			.746			
248. I use my background knowledge....			.731			
249. I use my background knowledge....			.689			
250. I use Chinese when I don't	.478		-.181			
251. I use body language	.368		.178	-.136		.247
252. I try to translate the main idea			.323	.176		.196
253. I attend class when the	.213		.153	.191		.283
254. I attend 100% of my English	-.198		.432	.415		
255. I look for main topics and key ...		.300	.322	.275	.170	.126
256. I avoid speaking with other	.466	.109	-.108			
257. I pay particular attention to ...!	.388		.187	.428		
258. I pay particular attention	.342		.265	.557		.116
259. I pay particular attention to	.254		.167	.326	-.142	
260. I develop a timetable for exam ...	.521	.162		.214		
261. I estimate the time I'll need to	.316	.174	.240		.269	.112

262. I finish my studying the day	.237	.292				.150
263. I get familiar with the test room	.285	.332		.123	.136	
264. I gather and organize all the		.257	.272	.400		.124
265. I always arrive at the test room	-.181	.142	.374	.428		.123
266. I set a goal for myself	.275			.346		
267. I read old exam papers before	.188	.580	.180	.164		
268. I know exactly the format and		.160	.200	.465		
269. I try to predict examination	.554	.327	-.106		.137	
270. I test myself in similar oral	.485	.323		-.233		.162
271. I create study checklists before	.626	.251	-.104	-.170		
272. I test ... before an English test.	.429			.478		
273. I use whatever information	.156		.437	-.118		.386
274. I try to better understand the		.150		.595		.243
275. I make a good use of my past	.264		.314	.495		
276. I listen to instructions carefully	.142		.433	.501		
277. I read test directions carefully			.505	.113		.326
278. I listen to directions carefully			.496	.131		.349
279. I listen to keywords when			.658	.160		.307
280. I listen to clues				.607		.291
281. I listen to questions carefully			.556	.285		.222
282. I look for keywords			.594	.214		.197
283. I look for clues			.633	.171		.185
284. I read questions carefully			.477	.253	.107	.261
285. I write legibly during tests.			.287	.254	.262	.239
286. I answer easy questions first	.164			.212	.453	
287. I scan the test first and then	.286			.111	.516	
288. I outline my answers to	.264		.144	.605		
289. I plan and organize my ideas	.284		.127	.617		
290. I select a title for each question ...	.215	.196	.241	.456		
291. I paragraph my writing during		.173		.400	.278	.194
292. I write a topic sentence for each	.204	.175	.186		.393	.221
293. I make a good use of the	.176		.272		.214	.472
294. I try to make my writing		.140	.211	.509	.140	.311
295. I try to make as few mistakes as	-.116	.146	.227	.449	.138	.297
296. I try to make my translation		.226	.137			.149
297. I double-check my answers			.157	.372	.207	.206
298. ..., I list what did not work for	.140	.100		.300	.157	.405
299. I forget ... after an English test.	.112	-.136	.154			-.103
300. I summarize my performance	.239	.218		.385	.218	.161
301. ..., I list what worked and hold	.214	.165	.119	.382	.232	.161
302. ... I try to get a good night's sleep.		.143	.256		.458	.118
303. I breathe deeply to calm down	.109	.187	.245	.142	.262	.127
304. I approach the exam with	.110	.179	.177		.284	.381
305. ..., I often reward myself	.176			.115	.418	
306. I exchange with fellow students	.405		.181	.111		.142
307. I form a study group with other	.567	.112				
308. I listen to my partner carefully			.327			.577

309. I support and help my partner ….			.407	.117		.534

Notes: Loadings of less than .10 are excluded from the Table.

Factor 1 (TMS) = Test-taking memory strategies

Factor 2 (TCogS) = Test-taking cognitive strategies

Factor 3 (TComS) = Test-taking compensation strategies

Factor 4 (TMetaS) = Test-taking metacognitive strategies

Factor 5 (TAS) = Test-taking affective strategies

Factor 6 (TSS) = Test-taking social strategies

The loadings presented in Table 4.26 indicate the majority of the items within a subcomponent of the ETSI was highly correlated with that subcomponent: items 219-to 224 were highly positively related to TMS with coefficients ranging from .203 to .570, with 4 being higher than .40; items 225 to 241 were highly positively correlated with TCogS with a coefficient range of .00 to .613, with a majority being higher than .30; items 242 to 253 highly related to TComS with coefficients ranging from .00 to .746, with 7 being higher than .30; items 254 to 301 highly correlated with TMetaS with a coefficient range of .00 to .617, with a half being higher than .30; items 302 to 305 highly positively related to TAS with coefficients ranging from .262 to .458; and items 306 to 309 highly positively correlated with TSS with a coefficient range of .000 to .577, with 2 being higher than .50. This signifies these six strategy categories were important subcomponents of the ETSI, which is further supported by the significantly high coefficients between the ETSI and its six components—TMS ($r = .580$, p < .01), TCogS ($r = .872$, p < .01), TComS ($r = .783$, p < .01), TMetaS ($r = .964$, p < .01), TAS ($r = .643$, p < .01) and TSS ($r = .636$, p < .01), as presented in Table 4.27.

Table 4.27: Correlations among the ETSI and its Subscales (WS)

	TCogS	TComS	TMetaS	TAS	TSS	ETSI
TMS	.479**	.339**	.471**	.314**	.354**	.580**
TCogS	1	.637**	.783**	.513**	.506**	.872**
TComS		1	.707**	.470**	.482**	.783**
TMetaS			1	.592**	.567**	.964**
TAS				1	.414**	.643**
TSS					1	.636**

Notes: WS = the whole sample; N = 1203; ** = p < .01

Moreover, Table 4.27 shows that these six components were also highly significantly related to one another. Alternatively, a more frequent

81

user of one category of strategies tends to use other categories of strategies more frequently when taking English tests.

4.4.2 The whole sample' knowledge of English test-taking strategies

Of 215 journal participants, 51 TU, 23 BFU and 44 CUP students reported using some strategies when taking English exams, as presented in Table 4.28.

Table 4.28: Students' Knowledge of English
Test-taking Strategies (the whole sample) (Source: journal)

TU	BFU	CUP
Review notes and texts	Memorize words and phrases	Review notes, texts, words, grammar and all that have
Memorize words and phrases		been learned
Never do special things	Review notes, texts and mistakes	Memorize words
Review the mistakes		Recite texts
Prepare one month before	Do some simulated exam papers	Have a good sleep before the exam
Do some exercises		
Read some English articles before the exams	Breathe deeply	Do some simulated tests
Listen to some English conversations	Close eyes	Do exercises
Listen to the tape	Look out of window	Listen to the tape
Do a similar test to check myself	Tell themselves to 'believe yourself'	Read some English articles before the exams
Do reading first (good at it)	Read first and then scan	Do reading and listening comprehension
Work out the problems one by one	Do the easy first (from easy to difficult)	Have a deep breath
Highlight important or difficult parts	Arrange the time properly	Control the writing time
Listen to and read instructions carefully	Concentrate on the exam	Do the easy first, from easy to difficult
Do the easy questions first	Review their performance in the exam	Be concentrated
Guess sometimes according to the context		Treat it carefully
Write carefully		Guess the meaning of new words
Face exams bravely		Try my best
To be calm during the test		Review my performance during the test
Reflect on what has been done well or bad during the test		

According to Table 4.28, the participants from each university would prepare for a coming exam (carefully) by reviewing notes and even mistakes, memorizing words and phrases, doing exercises, reading articles and self-testing on certain materials. The TU and CUP learners would also listen to some English in order to be better prepared. The CUP correspondents would try to have a good sleep before the exam. During the test, these students from all universities would start with the easy questions and then move on to difficult ones. The BFU and CUP learners would concentrate on the exam and plan the testing time carefully. At the same time, the TU participants would work out the problems one by one, write carefully, highlight the important or difficult parts, listen to and read instructions carefully, and guess sometimes according to the context. The BFU respondents would use the strategy of scanning; and their CUP peers would deal with the questions carefully and guess the meanings of new words. In order to deal with the exam more effectively, these students would try to stay calm during the exam by facing it bravely (TU), breathe deeply (BFU and CUP), closing eyes (BFU), looking out of the window (BFU), and/or telling themselves to 'believe yourself' (BFU). After finishing the exam, each sample would reflect on it to see where they had done well or poorly so that they could perform better in future exams.

As such, it is clear that these participants at different universities would utilize some memory, cognitive, metacognitive and affective strategies when taking an English exam. The TU participants seemed to use more types of strategies than their BFU and CUP peers; the BFU students seemed to employ more affective strategies but fewer other types of strategies. Moreover, most of these participants reported that using these strategies could help them perform better in exams.

4.4.3 Broad profile of English test-taking strategy use by the whole sample

Based on the mean scores of English Test-taking Strategy Inventory (ETSI) items presented in Appendix II, items in different use ranges were summarized and reported in Table 4.29 (please refer to section 4.3.3 for the analyzing key). Among the 91 ETSI items, 42 items were in the high use range, 46 in the medium use range and 3 in the low use range. That is, around half of the strategies were sometimes or usually/always used; only three were usually not used or even not used. The case was the same with each of the six strategy categories, as shown in Table 4.29. A review of the ETSI mean scores reported in Appendix II further shows that mean scores for high use strategies hardly exceeded 4.00 and those for low use strategies never fell below 2.00. In another word, those high use strategies were just usually but not always used; while those low use strategies were just not usually used and none of them were never or almost never used, as were English learning strategies. In conclusion, all the strategies were employed by the students to different extents during English tests and the majority were sometimes or more often used.

Table 4.29: Number of Test-taking

Strategy Items in Different Use Ranges (the whole sample)

Test-taking Strategy categories	High use	Medium use	Low use
Memory Strategy (TMS)	1	4	1
Cognitive Strategy (TCogS)	8	9	0
Compensation Strategy (TComS)	7	4	1
Metacognitive Strategy (TMetaS)	22	25	1
Affective Strategy (TAS)	2	2	0
Social Strategy (TSS)	2	2	0
English Test-Taking Strategy Inventory (ETSI)	42	46	3

As reported in Table 4.30, the mean of overall strategy use was 3.41 on the 5-point Likert scale. This suggests "medium" strategy use (sometimes used) towards the upper end. Alternatively, the respondents reported having quite frequent use of various strategies during English tests, close to high use but not to that extent, consistent with the analyses of mean scores of different English test-taking strategy items.

The mean scores for all the six test-taking strategy categories also fell in the medium-use range. Among the six categories, the most frequently used were affective strategies with a mean of 3.49, followed by metacognitive and compensation strategies with a mean of 3.47 and 3.46 respectively, and then cognitive strategies with a mean of 3.41. The next came in the social strategies with a mean of 3.29 and memory strategies were the least frequently used with a mean of 2.87. That is, strategies of all categories were just sometimes used but at the middle (memory strategies) or the upper end (the other five) of the medium range.

Table 4.30: Means and Standard Deviations Indicating

Test-taking Strategy Use (the whole sample) (N = 1203)

Strategy category (most used to least used)	Frequency of strategy use	
	Mean/range	Standard deviation
Affective	3.49 (medium use; upper end)	.61
Metacognitive	3.47 (medium use; upper end)	.41
Compensation	3.46 (medium use; upper end)	.48
Cognitive	3.41 (medium use; upper end)	.47
Social	3.29 (medium use; upper end)	.62
Memory	2.87 (medium use; low end)	.67
ETSI	3.41 (medium use; upper end)	.39

This finding about the overall test-taking strategy use conforms to that of previous studies either situated in Beijing (Zhang & Liu, 2008), Hong Kong (Bremner, 1999) or Taiwan (Lan & Oxford, 2003). Nevertheless, in all studies, participants were found not to use memory strategies frequently. This was unexpected in that Chinese learners are generally believed to depend much on memory in learning and taking tests (Yang & Weir, 1998; Zou, 1998, 2002). Nonetheless, this might be because English tests often did not target a specific textbook, sentence structure or word use; thus memory could not help much. Yet, it might also be because memory strategies in the present study covered a small number of items. It might also indicate Chinese learners are changing in terms of test-taking strategy use, which adequately justifies further exploration of this issue.

4.4.4 The most and least used individual test-taking strategies by the whole sample

As previously analyzed, most of the test-taking strategies were sometimes or usually used. Among these more often used strategies, twenty were identified to be the most frequently used by the Chinese undergraduate EFL learners during English tests, as presented in Table 4.31.

Of these twenty most often used test-taking strategy items, all were in the high-use range with a mean ranging from 3.83 to 4.36. The participants would usually "attend 100% of my English classes" (mean = 4.36) to be better prepared for English tests. When there was a test, they would "try to get a good night's sleep" (mean = 3.93); "gather and organize all the supplies needed" (mean = 3.85) and "arrive at the test room on time" (mean = 4.21). During the test, they would "look for keywords" (mean = 3.97) and "clues" (mean = 3.95) while reading; "listen to keywords when doing listening comprehension" (mean = 3.94); "read and listen to questions carefully" (mean = 3.94 and 3.85 respectively). When writing, they would try to make it coherent and cohesive (mean = 3.91) and "make as few mistakes as possible" (mean = 3.89). Meanwhile, the participants would use background knowledge of the topic to help guess and deduce "while reading" (mean = 3.92) and "complete the cloze test" (mean = 3.89), and linguistic knowledge to help "complete the cloze test" (mean = 3.88) and "guess and deduce what the speaker says while doing listening comprehension" (mean = 3.85).

Table 4.31 also indicates that the most frequently used strategies were of metacognitive (12) category, followed by compensation (5),

85

cognitive (2) and affective (1) categories. The high mean scores show that these undergraduate non-English majors were accustomed to arriving at the test room on time, looking for clues, guessing from the context, and resorting to background knowledge during an English test. When in an oral test, they were also aware of the importance of cooperation between partners by listening to them carefully, as proved by the strategy item means reported in Appendix II. On the whole, the students were able to employ various strategies to better their performance in an English test.

Table 4.31: The Twenty Most Frequently and Twenty Least Used Individual Test-taking Strategies (the whole sample) (N = 1203)

No.	Strategy	Mean	Category in which this strategy is classified	Comment
	The twenty most frequently used strategies			
254	Attend 100% of English classes.	4.36	Metacognitive	H
265	Always arrive at the test room	4.16	Metacognitive	H
282	Look for keywords while reading	3.97	Metacognitive	H
283	Look for clues while reading	3.95	Metacognitive	H
236	Eliminate certain answers when	3.94	Cognitive	H
279	Listen to keywords when	3.94	Metacognitive	H
284	Read questions carefully	3.94	Metacognitive	H
248	Use background knowledge of	3.92	Compensation	H
302	Try to get a good night's sleep	3.93	Affective	H
294	Try to make writing coherent	3.91	Metacognitive	H
245	Make guesses based on different	3.90	Compensation	H
247	Use background knowledge of	3.89	Compensation	H
295	Try to make as few mistakes as	3.89	Metacognitive	H
246	Use my linguistic knowledge	3.88	Compensation	H
280	Listen to clues	3.88	Metacognitive	H
244	Use linguistic knowledge to help ...	3.85	Compensation	H
264	Gather and organize all	3.85	Metacognitive	H
274	Try to better understand	3.85	Metacognitive	H
281	Listen to questions carefully	3.85	Metacognitive	H
238	Break up run-on sentences	3.83	Cognitive	H
	The Twenty least frequently used strategies			
No.	Strategy	Mean	Category in which this strategy is classified	Comment
224	Often dump information	2.25	Memory	L
250	Use Chinese when not knowing	2.42	Compensation	L
271	Create study checklists	2.48	Metacognitive	L
221	Use high technology to help	2.56	Memory	M
307	Form a study group with	2.61	Social	M
269	Try to predict examination	2.65	Metacognitive	M
222	Create flashcards for words, ...	2.70	Memory	M
232	Create summary notes	2.71	Cognitive	M

256	Avoid speaking with other	2.73	Metacognitive	M
270	Self-test in similar oral	2.81	Metacognitive	M
242	Exchange with English teachers	2.88	Compensation	M
243	Ask the instructor what to	2.90	Compensation	M
272	Self-test on the material	2.94	Metacognitive	M
223	Memorize model texts/essays	2.97	Memory	M
260	Develop a timetable	2.98	Metacognitive	M
263	Get familiar with the test room	2.99	Metacognitive	M
228	Practice translating English	3.02	Cognitive	M
226	Practice speaking English in	3.04	Cognitive	M
229	Practice writing by modeling	3.06	Cognitive	M
266	Set a goal before an English test.	3.07	Metacognitive	M

Notes: H = high use;   M = medium use;   L = low use

Among the twenty least often used strategies, all were distinctly in the medium-use range except the first three with a mean range of 2.25 to 3.07, as presented in Table 4.31. For example, "dump information on the back of the English test paper" (mean = 2.25); "create study checklists before an English test" (mean = 2.48); "use high technology to help review materials before English tests" (mean = 2.56); "try to predict examination questions and then outline answers" (mean = 2.65); "created flashcards" (mean = 2.07); "developed a timetable" (mean = 2.70); "memorize model texts/essays before an English essay test" (mean = 2.97); "get familiar with the test room before an English test" (mean = 2.99); "practice speaking English in different situations before an oral test" (mean = 3.04); and "practice writing by modeling good essays before an English essay test" (mean = 3.06).

As seen from Table 4.31, the least often used strategies included metacognitive (8), cognitive (4), memory (4), compensation (3) and social (1) strategies. During an English test, the students would not self evaluate, pay attention or organize so often; they would not often depend on such cognitive strategies as using resources for receiving and sending messages and summarizing; and they would not employ action much either. That the students did not get help and/or cooperate with peers much during English tests might be because most of the tests required independent work.

In conclusion, it should be noted that though these strategies were the least frequently employed, the majority fell in the medium-use range. This clearly suggests the students were very flexible in taking various strategies to help complete English tests, which might also account for why Chinese EFL learners could often achieve high marks in English exams.

4.4.5 Differences in test-taking strategy use between male and female students and among those from different universities

Table 4.32 shows that both male (with means ranging from 2.85 to 3.49) and female (with means ranging from 2.90 to 3.48) students had a medium use of all the six categories of English learning strategies. Their ETSI means (3.40 and 3.41 for males and females respectively) also fell in the medium use range. Moreover, female students reported to use compensation and affective strategies less frequently but all the other categories of strategies more often than their male peers during English exams. But no significant difference was found in the use of the strategy categories, as indicated by the results of Independent-samples t-tests reported in Table 4.32.

Table 4.32: Gender Differences in English Test-taking Strategy Use (the whole sample) (N = 1203)

		Mean	Standard Deviation	t-test results	
				t	p
TMS	M (764)	2.85	.70	-1.43	.154
	F (439)	2.90	.63		
TCogS	M (764)	3.40	.49	-.79	.431
	F (439)	3.42	.44		
TCompS	M (764)	3.47	.47	.73	.465
	F (439)	3.45	.41		
TMetaS	M (764)	3.46	.43	-.38	.703
	F (439)	3.47	.37		
TAS	M (764)	3.49	.62	.34	.735
	F (439)	3.48	.59		
TSS	M (764)	3.29	.62	.18	.857
	F (439)	3.29	.63		
ETSI	M (764)	3.40	.41	-.28	.780
	F (439)	3.41	.36		

Notes: M = male; F = female

To investigate differences in test-taking strategy use among students from different universities, the analysis of one-way ANOVA was conducted, the results of which are reported in Table 4.33.

Table 4.33: ANOVA Results of English Test-taking Strategy Use (WS)

Measures	F	P	F*	University (Mean) TU = 451; BFU = 327; CUP = 425			Location of sig. difference (a = .05)
				TU	BFU	CUP	
TMS	3.18	.042	2.77	2.81	2.89	2.91	TU & CUP
TCogS	3.66	.026	2.77	3.44	3.35	3.41	TU & BFU
TComS	2.60	.075	2.77	3.50	3.42	3.46	TU & BFU
TMetaS	2.66	.070	2.77	3.46	3.43	3.50	BFU & CUP
TAS	2.47	.085	2.77	3.49	3.43	3.53	BFU & CUP
TSS	3.29	.038	2.77	3.30	3.22	3.33	BFU & CUP
ETSI	2.74	.065	2.77	3.41	3.36	3.43	BFU & CUP

Notes: WS = the whole sample

F* → Critical F value for Duncan's test at .05 level (Black, 1999).

As seen from Table 4.33, students from all universities generally had a medium use of test-taking strategies in all categories. The CUP students reported using memory, metacognitive, affective and social strategies the most frequently when taking English exams. The TU students self-reported to be the most frequent users of cognitive and compensation strategies but the least frequent users of memory strategies; their BFU peers used memory strategies in between and other strategies the least often during English exams. The post-hoc tests revealed that the differences in the use of all categories of strategies were statistically significant; but the differences occurred only between students from two universities. The TU students employed memory strategies significantly less frequently than their CUP peers, cognitive and compensation strategies significantly more frequently than their BFU counterparts. The BFU students deployed metacognitive, affective and social strategies significantly less frequently than those from CUP during English exams.

Furthermore, as shown in Table 4.33, students from three universities all reported having a medium use of the overall test-taking strategies. The CUP students used the strategies the most frequently, whereas their BFU peers had the least frequent use of the strategies; and the difference was statistically significant. The TU students used the strategies in between, and no significant difference was found between the TU students and those from the other two universities.

4.4.6 Correlations between individual English test-taking strategy use and the whole sample's performance in English

To address this question, correlation analyses were conducted. The results were reported in Table 4.34, which reveals 37 English learning strategy items significantly correlated with the whole sample' performance in English with coefficients ranging from -.069 to .123.

Among these 37 strategy items, two memory and one metacognitive strategies were significantly negatively correlated with students' performance in English: strategy 223, "memorize model texts/essays before an English essay test" ($r = -.062$); 224, "often dump information on the back of the English test paper upon receiving it" ($r = -.067$); and 286, "answer easy questions first during an English test" ($r = -.069$). The more frequently students turned to these three strategies during English exams, the less they achieved in English.

The rest of the test-taking strategy items were significantly positively related to students' performance in English. For example, strategy 220, "keep up my homework and review my notes regularly to prepare for English exams" ($r = .071$); 233, "look for the central idea of each question" ($r = .103$); 244, "use linguistic knowledge to help guess and deduce what the speaker says while doing listening comprehension" ($r = .067$); 279, "listen to keywords when doing listening comprehension" ($r = .067$); and 304, "approach the exam with confidence" ($r = .107$). The more frequently the participants utilized these test-taking strategies during English exams, the higher they achieved in the exams.

In addition, among these 37 test-taking strategy items, the majority belonged to the metacognitive (17) category, followed by cognitive (10), compensation (6), memory (3), and affective (1) categories. As shown in Table 4.34, most of the metacognitive strategies were related to planning, organizing, paying attention, and self-evaluating. The majority of the cognitive strategies involved practicing, deducing, reasoning and analyzing, taking notes, and highlighting.

Table 4.34: Correlations between Individual English Test-taking Strategy Items and Students' Performance in English (WS) (N = 1203)

Items	P
220. Keep up my homework and review my notes regularly … (memory).	.071*
223. Memorize model texts/essays before an English essay test (memory).	-.062*
224. Often dump information on the back of the English … (memory).	-.067*
226. Practice speaking English in different situations … (cognitive).	.087**
230. Analyze past test papers to determine how to improve … (cognitive).	.059*

231. Take good notes as my English teacher tells what … (cognitive).	.090*
233. Look for the central idea of each question (cognitive).	.103**
235.Use both general and specific information … (cognitive).	.099**
237. Analyze the sentence structure before translating … (cognitive).	.121**
238. Break up run-on sentences into smaller parts to … (cognitive).	.104**
239. Jot down information in the margin while listening … (cognitive).	.103**
240. Jot down important ideas that come to mind … (cognitive).	.092**
241. Highlight some sentences or phrases while reading … (cognitive).	.085**
242. Exchange with English teachers about how and … (compensation).	.071*
244. Use linguistic knowledge to help guess and … (compensation).	.067*
246. Use linguistic knowledge to help complete … (compensation).	.072*
248. Use background knowledge of the topic to help … (compensation).	.091**
249. Use background knowledge of the topic to help … (compensation).	.061*
253. Attend class when the instructor reviews … (compensation).	.084**
254. Attend 100% of my English classes (metacognitive).	.067*
263. Get familiar with the test room before … (metacognitive).	.060*
267. Read old exam papers before English tests (metacognitive).	.072*
272. Self-test on the material before an English test (metacognitive).	.088**
274. Try to better understand the sentence … (metacognitive).	.117**
279. Listen to keywords when doing listening … (metacognitive).	.067*
280. Listen to clues while doing listening comprehension (metacognitive).	.078**
285. Write legibly during tests (metacognitive).	.066*
286. Answer easy questions first during an English test (metacognitive).	-.069*
288. Outline my answers to questions during an essay test (metacognitive).	.123**
289. Plan and organize my ideas before answering … (metacognitive).	.102**
291. Paragraph my writing during English tests (metacognitive).	.112**
292. Write a topic sentence for each paragraph … (metacognitive).	.095**
294. Try to make my writing coherent and cohesive (metacognitive).	.064*
295. Try to make as few mistakes as possible … (metacognitive).	.066*
296. Try to make my translation more like Chinese … (metacognitive).	.077**
297. Double-check my answers when completing … (metacognitive).	.120**
304. Approach the exam with confidence (affective).	.107**

Notes: WS = the whole sample;

   ** = p < .01;   * = p < .05;   P = performance

4.5 Correlations among measured variables and the whole sample's performance in English

To explore the relationships among the measured variables and the whole sample' performance in English, correlation analyses were conducted, the results of which are summarized in Table 4.35.

Table 4.35: Correlations among Measured Variables and Students' Performance in English (WS) (N = 1151~1203)

	ELM	InSM	InsM	ELMS	MS	CogS	CompS	MetaS	AS	SS	ELSI	TMS	TCogS	TCompS	TMetaS	TAS	TSS	ETSI	Performance
CAS	-.33**	-.08**	-.21**	-.23**	-.29**	-.27**	-.23**	-.35**	-.25**	-.26**	-.36**	-.04	-.19**	-.23**	-.24**	-.18**	-.18**	-.23**	-.07*
ELM	1	.04	.21**	.32**	.23**	.25**	.25**	.31**	.21**	.24**	.32**	.06	.26**	.19**	.23**	.18**	.13**	.23**	.17**
InsM		1	.24**	.72**	.14**	.19**	.19**	.15**	.19**	.16**	.20**	.18**	.18**	.17**	.22**	.17**	.13**	.23**	-.07*
InsM			1	.83**	.37**	.44**	.23**	.41**	.36**	.33**	.46**	.17**	.24**	.22**	.28**	.26**	.21**	.30**	.09**
ELMS				1	.36**	.44**	.29**	.40**	.38**	.35**	.46**	.22**	.30**	.28**	.35**	.30**	.23**	.36**	.05
MS					1	.67**	.38**	.60**	.48**	.43**	.74**	.29**	.42**	.31**	.41**	.32**	.32**	.44**	.07*
CogS						1	.47**	.72**	.60**	.56**	.87**	.33**	.48**	.34**	.49**	.35**	.35**	.51**	.04
CompS							1	.50**	.43**	.36**	.62**	.17**	.39**	.39**	.40**	.26**	.27**	.42**	.03
MetaS								1	.72**	.68**	.95**	.36**	.56**	.43**	.61**	.41**	.45**	.62**	.11**
AS									1	.63**	.78**	.39**	.46**	.40**	.49**	.43**	.40**	.54**	.01
SS										1	.73**	.32**	.46**	.37**	.47**	.32**	.41**	.51**	.03
ELSI											1	.38**	.59**	.46**	.62**	.44**	.46**	.65**	.08**
TMS												1	.48**	.34**	.47**	.31**	.35**	.58**	.01
TCogS													1	.64**	.78**	.51**	.51**	.87**	.13**
TCompS														1	.71**	.47**	.48**	.78**	.10**
TMetaS															1	.59**	.57**	.96**	.07*
TAS																1	.41**	.64**	.06*
TSS																	1	.64**	-.03
ETSI																		1	.08**

Notes: WS = the whole sample; **. p < .01; *. p < .05

92

As shown in Table 4.35, the measured variables were highly correlated with one another and most of them significantly correlated with students' performance in English as well.

The Classroom Anxiety Scale (CAS) was significantly negatively correlated with English Learning Motivation Scale (ELMS) and its three subscales (ELM, InsM and IntM), English Learning Strategy Inventory (ELSI) and its six categories (MS, CogS, CompS, MetaS, AS and SS), English Test-taking Strategy Inventory (ETSI) and its six categories (TMS, TCogS, TCompS, TMetaS, TAS and TSS). Namely, the more anxious the students were in English classrooms, the less motivated they were to learn English, the less frequently they used strategies when learning English and taking English exams.

The ELMS and its three subscales also significantly positively correlated with one another. The more instrumentally motivated students tended to be more integratively motivated and generally more motivated to learn English. Meanwhile, the ELMS and its subscales were all significantly positively correlated with the ELSI and the ETSI and their subcategories. The more (instrumentally/ integratively) motivated the students were to learn English, the more frequently they deployed different categories of strategies when learning English and taking English exams.

The ELSI and the ETSI and their subcategories all significantly positively correlated with one another. For example, the more frequent user of memory strategies (MS) tended to use cognitive, compensation, metacognitive, affective and social strategies more frequently in English learning. S/he also tended to be a more frequent user of the six categories of test-taking strategies during English exams.

Finally, these measured variables generally significantly correlated with the students' performance in English. Among these variables, the CAS and the InsM were significantly inversely related to students' performance in English ($r = -.073$ and $-.065$ respectively); the test-taking social strategies (TSS) were insignificantly inversely correlated with students' performance in English; the ELMS, English learning cognitive, compensation, affective and social strategies, and test-taking memory strategies (TMS) insignificantly positively correlated with the students' performance in English. Alternatively, the more frequent user of English learning memory and metacognitive strategies, English test-taking cognitive, compensation, metacognitive, affective and social strategies tended to be more proficient in English.

4.6 The structural model of the measured variables and performance of the whole sample

The statistical analyses of the data discussed above reveal that the data satisfied the statistical assumptions of structural equation modeling (SEM). In specifying a general model of the relationships between reported degree or use of the measured variables and the students' performance in English for the whole sample, we argued for a one-factor model of classroom anxiety (CAS), a three-factor model of motivation (ELMS), and a six-factor model of English learning and test-taking strategy use respectively, as detailed in previous sections.

Of the numerous models tested, the baseline model of the measured variables and performance for the whole sample, presented in Figure 4.1, seemed to fit the data well from both a statistical and substantive perspective. The model produced a CFI of .962, a TLI of .950, an IFI of .963, a RFI of .935, and a NFI of .951, indicating a fairly good representation of the sample data. All parameter estimates in the model were substantively plausible and statistically significant at the .000 level.

As shown in the structural model, classroom anxiety exerted a significant, negative effect (-1.79) on the students' performance in English, while motivation (.50), English learning strategy use (.40) and English test-taking strategy use (.06) produced a significant, positive effect on the latter.

Concerning the effect of the measured variables on one another, motivation displayed a significant, negative effect on classroom anxiety (-.85) and English test-taking strategy use (-1.04); classroom anxiety yielded a significant, negative effect on English learning strategy use (-1.33) and English test-taking strategy use (-1.07). Finally, the model shows that English learning strategy use significantly positively affected English test-taking strategy use (3.05).

Then, what concerns us is (1) whether the multidimensional constructs of the measured variables and the students' performance in English are equivalent across universities (ability levels) and (2) whether the effects of the measured variables on the students' performance in English are equivalent across the three groups. Finally, if the models are not equivalent, how are they different, and what implications might this have for our understanding of how these variables affect these participants' learning of English?

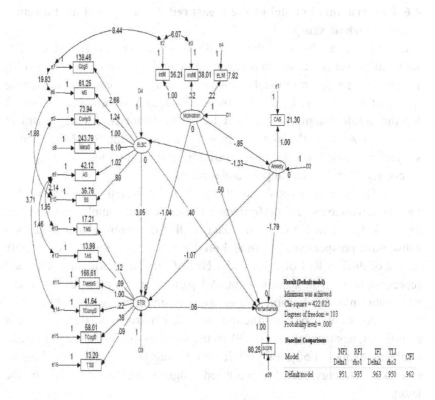

Figure 4.1: The Whole Sample Analysis—Measured Variables and Performance

4.7 Summary

According to the results of factor analyses, English learning motivation (ELM), instrumental motivation (InsM) and integrative motivation (IntM) are three important components of the English Learning Motivation Scale (ELMS); the English Learning Strategy Inventory (ELSI) has six important factors—memory strategies (MS), cognitive strategies (CogS), compensation strategies (ComS), metacognitive strategies (MetaS), affective strategies (AS), and social strategies (SS); and test-taking memory strategies (TMS), test-taking cognitive strategies (TCogS), test-taking compensation strategies (TComS), test-taking metacognitive strategies (TMetaS), test-taking affective strategies (TAS), and test-taking social strategies (TSS) were six important subscales of the English Test-taking Strategy Inventory (ETSI).

As revealed by the analyses of the data, around a third of the students of the whole sample as well as of each university suffered anxiety to varying degrees in English language classrooms due to various reasons such as low English proficiency, lack of practice, lack of vocabulary, lack of confidence, lack of preparation and personality. Meanwhile, they were motivated to learn English and considered it worthwhile to learn the language for a variety of instrumental and integrative reasons such as going abroad, higher education, improving English abilities in four basic skills, the good feeling of doing better in class, and the satisfaction of finding out new things. And they were significantly more instrumentally than integratively motivated to learn English.

With some knowledge of English learning and test-taking strategies, the participants reported having a medium use of the overall learning and test-taking strategies and their six categories. Among the six categories of English learning strategies, the most frequently used were compensation strategies, followed by metacognitive, social, affective, cognitive, and memory strategies. Among the six categories of English test-taking strategies, the most frequently used were affective strategies, followed by metacognitive, compensation, cognitive, social, and memory strategies.

Concerning gender differences in the measured variables, female respondents were significantly more motivated to learn English both instrumentally and integratively than their male peers. They also utilized compensation and social strategies significantly more frequently when learning English.

As to differences in the measured variables among different university groups, the TU students were significantly less instrumentally motivated than their BFU and CUP counterparts; the BFU correspondents deployed significantly less frequently memory strategies than their TU and CUP peers, while the TU participants utilized significantly more frequently metacognitive strategies than their BFU peers when learning English. Regarding English test-taking strategies, the TU learners employed memory strategies significantly less frequently than their CUP peers, but cognitive and compensation strategies significantly more frequently than their BFU counterparts. The BFU participants deployed metacognitive, affective and social strategies significantly less frequently than those from CUP during English exams.

And the CUP students used the overall test-taking strategies the most frequently, whereas their BFU peers had the least frequent use of the strategies; and the difference was statistically significant.

Regarding the relationship between the measured variables and the students' performance in English, statistical analyses revealed that the measured variables were highly correlated with one another and most of them significantly correlated with the students' performance in English as well. Classroom anxiety exerted a significantly negative effect while motivation, English learning and test-taking strategy use produced a significantly positive effect on the students' performance in English. As to the interaction of these measured variables, motivation displayed a significantly negative effect on classroom anxiety and English test-taking strategy use; classroom anxiety significantly negatively affected English learning and test-taking strategy use, and English learning strategy use significantly positively affected English test-taking strategy use.

Chapter 5   Results of the TU Sample

This chapter reports the results of the TU (Tsinghua University) sample. For each measured variable, descriptive analysis and analysis of ANOVA (Duncan's) were conducted. Subsequently, correlation coefficients were computed to determine the associations among the measured variables and performance in English. Finally, SEM was run to further explore these relationships.

5.1 English language classroom anxiety of the TU sample

5.1.1 General picture of English language classroom anxiety of the TU sample

5.1.1.1 Item analysis of the CAS of the TU sample

Table 5.1 summarizes the TU students' responses (the first number means the real number and the second percentage) to the CAS (Classroom Anxiety Scale) items. All percentages refer to the number of students who (strongly) disagreed, neither disagreed nor agreed, or (strongly) agreed with the statements (percentages were rounded to the nearest whole number).

Table 5.1: CAS Items with Numbers and
Percentages of TU Students Selecting Each Alternative (N = 451)

SD/D	N	A/SA
1. I don't usually get anxious when I have to respond to a question ….		
156/34.6	53/11.8	242/53.7
2. I am always afraid that other students would laugh at me if I speak….		
304/67.4	70/15.5	77/17.1
3. I always feel that other students are more at ease than I am in ….		
188/41.7	123/27.3	140/31.1
4. I am never embarrassed to volunteer answers in English class.		
178/39.5	112/24.8	161/35.7
5. I am generally tense whenever participating in English class.		
327/72.5	68/15.1	56/12.4
6. I never understand why other students are so nervous in English class.		

210/46.6   133/29.5   108/24.0

7. I usually feel relaxed and confident when active participation takes ….

131/29.0   124/27.5   196/43.5

8. Whenever I have to answer a question, out loud, I get nervous ….

274/60.8   79/17.5   98/21.7

Notes: SD → Strongly disagree;   D → Disagree

N → Neither disagree nor agree   A → Agree;   SA → Strongly agree

As presented in Table 5.1, consistent with the mean scores of CAS items presented in Appendix II and the results of the whole participant sample, most TU students rejected statements reflective of speech anxiety such as "whenever I have to answer a question, out loud, I get nervous and confused in English class" (item 8) (60.8%); "I am always afraid that other students would laugh at me if I speak up in English class" (item 2) (67.4%); "I am generally tense whenever participating in English class" (item 5) (72.5%). This suggests many students did not feel anxious or even feel confident and relaxed in English class. Nevertheless, more than 30% of them (strongly) disagreed with CAS items indicative of confidence when speaking in English class such as "I usually feel relaxed and confident when active participation takes place in English class" (item 7) (29.0%); "I don't usually get anxious when I have to respond to a question in English class" (item 1) (34.6%); "I am never embarrassed to volunteer answers in English class" (item 4) (39.5%); and "I never understand why other students are so nervous in English class" (item 6) (46.6%). This indicates at least a third of the TU students experienced anxiety to different degrees in English language classrooms, as found in previous studies (Gardner & MacIntyre, 1992; Horwitz et al., 1986; Horwitz, 2001; Liu, 2006a, 2006b, 2007b). These students were afraid to speak or became anxious when speaking English in class.

This finding generally conforms to the result of the journal data. Of 95 TU journal participants, 77 reported that they were (a little) anxious in English classrooms, especially when speaking English publicly in class. The principal reasons were: low English proficiency, lack of practice, lack of vocabulary, lack of confidence, lack of preparation, personality, and so on, as detailed in Table 5.5.

5.1.1.2 General tendency of the CAS of the TU sample

In order to know the general tendency of the TU students' anxiety in English class, the total score, mean, standard deviation, median, mode, maximum and minimum of the CAS were computed, as did with the whole participant sample (please refer to section 4.1.1.2 for the computing and interpreting scheme). The results are shown in Table 5.2.

Table 5.2: Statistical Analyses of the CAS of TU Students

	Mean	Standard deviation	Median	Mode	Range
Male (336)	21.91	5.43	22.00	20.00	8.00-37.00
Female (115)	20.59	5.20	20.00	24.00	8.00-34.00
Total (451)	21.57	5.40	22.00	20.00	8.00-37.00

As shown in Table 5.2, though some TU students (with a score of 37.00) felt extremely nervous, a mean of 21.57, a median of 22.00 and a mode of 20.00 on the CAS, all below the average score of 24.00, imply the majority felt relaxed and that only around a third experienced anxiety in English class. These findings are consistent with the results of item analysis of the CAS and the mean scores of CAS items of the TU correspondents presented in Appendix II.

In addition, as seen from Table 5.2, female students with a mean of 20.59 seemed to be less anxious than males with a mean of 21.91 in English class. And the difference was statistically significant, as proved by the Independent-samples t Test result: $t = 2.27$, $p = .02$.

5.1.2 Differences in English language classroom anxiety among TU students at different proficiency levels

In order to know the differences in English language classroom anxiety among the TU students at different proficiency levels, the total scores, means, standard deviations, medians, modes, maximums and minimums of the CAS were computed, as done in section 4.2.1.2. The results and further analyses are presented in the following Tables.

Table 5.3: Statistical Analyses of the CAS across Levels (TU)

	Mean	Standard Deviation	Median	Mode	Range
Band 1 (113)	22.28	5.30	22.00	25.00	8.00-36.00
Band 2 (205)	21.33	5.67	21.00	23.00	8.00-37.00
Band 3 (133)	21.35	5.04	21.00	20.00	10.00-36.00

Table 5.4: ANOVA Results of the CAS (TU)

Measure	F	P	F*	Level (Mean) 1 = 113; 2 = 205; 3 = 133			Location of sig. difference
				1	2	3	
CAS	1.31	.271	2.77	22.28	21.33	21.35	/

Note: F* → Critical F value for Duncan's test at .05 level (Black, 1999).

As presented in Table 5.3, although some students (with a mean of 36.00 or 37.00) reported to be extremely anxious and nervous in English class, the mean score, median and mode, all below 24.00, of each band group indicate the majority at each band level did not feel nervous in English classrooms. Nevertheless, these scores also reveal at least a third of the students from each band group suffered anxiety in English class, consistent with the finding in previous studies (Chen, 2002; Kitano, 2001; Saito, Horwitz & Garza, 1999; Liu, 2006a, 2006b; Wang & Ding, 2001).

According to Table 5.3, the band 1 students scored the highest while their band 2 peers scored the lowest on the CAS. The band 1 students not only had the highest mean (22.28) but also the highest median (22.00) and mode (25.00); the band 2 group had a higher mode (23.00) and maximum (37.00) than did the band 3 group, but their other scores were lower or the same as the band 3 group's. It seems that the band 1 students felt the most anxious while their band 2 counterparts felt the least in English class. Namely, students at the lowest proficiency level suffered anxiety the most in English class. However, as shown in Table 5.3, those at the highest level did not necessarily experience the least anxiety. This is still surprising though the difference was statistically insignificant, as indicated by the ANOVA results summarized in Table 5.4.

This finding again is consistent with that of the journal data, as reported in Table 5.5.

Table 5.5: Student Anxiety Reported in Journals (TU)

	Total No.	(Very) Nervous N/%	A little nervous N/%	Sometimes nervous N/%	Not nervous N/%
Band 1	34	20/58.8%	8/23.5%	0	6/17.6%
Band 2	33	17/51.5%	7/21.2%	2/6.1%	7/21.2%
Band 3	28	15/53.6%	7/25%	1/3.6%	5/17.9%
Total	95	52/54.7%	22/23.2%	3/3.2%	18/18.9%

As seen from Table 5.5, more than half of the TU journal participants admitted that they felt (very/a little) nervous in English class due to various reasons. A closer comparison of the three groups reveals that more band 1 students (82.3%) self-reported to be anxious than their band 2 (78.8%) and 3 (82.1%) peers, while the fewest band 2 learners self-reported to be anxious in English class in their reflective journals. It confirmed the statistical result that the band 2 students seemed to be the least anxious while their band 1 counterparts felt the most anxious in English classrooms.

5.1.3 Causes for and consequences of language classroom anxiety of the TU sample

As discussed above, the majority of the TU students in three band groups reported feeling anxious in English class. Nevertheless, the reasons for anxiety might be different, as summarized in Table 5.6.

Table 5.6: Causes for Language Classroom Anxiety (TU)
(Source: journals)

	Band 1 (Total N = 34) N/%	Band 2 (Total N = 33) N/%	Band 3 (Total N = 28) N/%
Personality	3/8.8%	9/27.3%	7/25%
Other students' wonderful performance	1/2.9%	5/14.7%	8/28.6%
Lack of /limited vocabulary	6/17.6%	5/15.2%	2/7.1%
Low English proficiency	16/47.1%	2/6.1%	1/3.6%
Poor oral English	6/17.6%	2/6.1%	2/7.1%
Lack of confidence	1/2.9%	3/9.1%	5/17.9%
Fear of being the center of attention	0	1/3%	3/10.7%
Being unable to find appropriate words to express myself	0	3/9.1%	1/3.6%
English being a foreign language	0	2/6.1%	1/3.6%
Lack of practice	2/5.9%	1/3%	0
Inadequate grammatical knowledge	3/8.8%	0	0
Having never spoken English before so many people	2/5.9%	1/3%	0
Different teaching method	2/5.9%	0	0
Not understanding what the teacher is saying	0	1/3%	1/3.6%
Lack of preparation	1/2.9%	1/3%	0
Teaching and learning tradition	0	1/3%	1/3.6%
Poor/Bad pronunciation	2/5.9%	0	0
Not liking speaking English	2/5.9%	0	0
Fear of speaking	0	0	1/3.6%
Slow progress	0	0	1/3.6%
Taking speaking seriously	0	0	1/3.6%
Hating being required to write down a word that I can't spell	0	0	1/3.6%
Coming from the countryside where English teaching is poor	0	0	1/3.6%

Inability to organize speech when speaking	0	0	1/3.6%
Lack of familiarity with classmates	1/2.9%	0	0
Fear of being unable to understand the teacher	1/2.9%	0	0
Poor listening	1/2.9%	0	0
Not knowing the keys to questions	1/2.9%	0	0

As shown in Table 5.6, the three main factors contributing to the TU students' anxiety in English class were personality (mainly introversion and shyness based on their own description) (8.8%, 27.3%, and 25% respectively), other students' wonderful performance (2.9%, 14.7%, and 28.6% respectively), and lack of/limited vocabulary (17.6%, 15.2%, and 7.1% respectively).

To these TU students, especially band 2 and 3 groups, personality constituted a big obstacle to their learning of English. Because of introverted personality, they would easily become anxious, especially when speaking English in class. Another great contributor to their anxiety was other students' wonderful performance. Probably because they had been top students before entering the University, they might be more prone to compare their own performance with others', which put them under (serious) pressure. Consequently, they were driven anxious when using the target language in class. This can be illustrated by what a band 3 student reported in her journal, "I really feel nervous in university English classrooms—especially when the class is a 'strong' one. I think my classmates' English is perfect and excellent. And my personality makes me easy to be anxious when speaking and writing English. I don't do well in putting English into practice; especially, my speaking and writing English are weak" (Guo, female).

Another big problem was the lack of vocabulary, which easily made the students anxious when using English in class, because he "doesn't know how to express himself" (Zhen, male, band 2). What's worse, lack of adequate vocabulary drove the students more and more nervous.

The next three important reasons were low English proficiency, poor oral English and lack of confidence. As students in a top 1 or 2 university in China, these respondents should be fairly good at each subject, including English. However, just because of the lack of confidence, some students became anxious when using the language in class. The other factors ranged from fear of being the focus of attentions, to inadequate grammatical knowledge, to lack of preparation, etc., with varying weights assigned to them by different band students.

Since quite many TU students felt anxious in English class, did anxiety have any effect on their performance in English? When asked if so, 64 of 95 journal participants held the belief that the relationship was negative, 7 maintained that anxiety exerted a positive effect, 5 regarded anxiety as something both good and bad, 10 believed that anxiety could produce no effect, and 8 didn't give any comment. The results are presented in Table 5.7.

Table 5.7: Impact of Anxiety on TU Students' Learning of English
(Source: journal)

	Bad	Good	Good and bad	No effect	No comment
Band 1 (34)	22/64.7	1/2.9%	1/2.9%	7/20.6%	3/8.8%
Band 2 (33)	20/60.6%	3/9.1%	3/9.1%	3/9.1%	4/12.1%
Band 3 (28)	22/78.6%	3/10.7%	2/7.1%	0	1/3.6%
Total (95)	64/67.4%	7/7.4%	6/6.3%	10/10.5%	8/8.4%

As noted from Table 5.7, the band 3 students had a very distinctive view of the effect of anxiety on their performance in English. 78.6% believed anxiety to be something bad to their learning of English in that anxiety made them perform worse, lowered their English proficiency, work slowly, progress slowly and decrease their passion for learning English. This is best illustrated by the quote from a student's journal, "if one is afraid of English, he will probably try to avoid using English, which will definitely leads to even lower English proficiency (Jiang, male, band 3). 10.7% of the band 3 students took anxiety to be a facilitator, which, according to them, served as a motivation and urged them to work harder. Similarly, 7.1% of the students viewed anxiety as something both good and bad to their learning of English, because "anxiety can motivate me to work harder, yet too much anxiety negatively affect my English proficiency" (Liu, male, band 3).

For the same reason, 1 band 1 student believed anxiety to be a facilitator and 1 took it to be both good and bad. And more than 60% of the band 1 learners reported that anxiety negatively affect their learning of English. According to them, anxiety made them forget how to read, write, speak, or listen well, become diffident, forget answers, distract from study and make unnecessary mistakes. Consequently, their English became poorer or performance in English was worsened. Surprising, 20.6% thought that anxiety could produce no effect on their learning of English because "there is no need to be anxious, English is a must" (Jian, male, band 1) and "I just try my best to study English" (Mao, male, band 1).

Compared with the other two groups, fewer band 2 students (60.6%) believed that anxiety negatively affected their learning of English, and more of them (9.1%) regarded it as something conducive.

Although the majority of each group viewed anxiety as a debilitator, only a few had intentionally taken some measures to cope with anxiety, such as breathing deeply, telling oneself to be brave and/or thinking of the content of the speech rather than the scene and audience. Most of them seemed to be helpless while hoping more contact with the target language could reduce their anxiety. Nevertheless, they offered a number of suggestions for language learners and teachers to help reduce/overcome anxiety, as summarized in Table 5.8.

Table 5.8: TU Students' Suggestions to Cope with Anxiety for Language Learners and Teachers (Source: journal)

Suggestions for teachers	Common to all the Ss	Create a relaxing and comfortable classroom environment.
		Organize some interesting activities.
		Choose interesting topics.
		Encourage students to speak more.
		Give students more chances to express themselves.
		Be friendly and helpful.
		Ask students to answer questions.
		Slow down speech.
		Smiling and nodding.
	Common to band 1 & 2 Ss	Often praise students.
		Give students some time to prepare the answers.
	Common to band 2 & 3	Give more chances to nervous students.
		Help students with examples.
	Particular to band 1 Ss	Encourage Ss to be more confident by playing English games or by asking easy questions.
		Let students talk in pairs.
		Treat students equally.
	Particular to band 2 Ss	Arrange consistent meetings for students to gather and practice oral English.
	Particular to band 3 Ss	Teach according to students' English proficiency and personality, etc.
		Help students discover the beauty of English.
		Develop students' interest in English.
		Explain difficult words.
	Common to all the Ss	More practice.
		Be more self-confident.
		Don't be afraid of making mistakes.
		Improve English.

Suggestions for students	Common to band 1 & 2 Ss	Be braver.
		Enlarge vocabulary.
	Common to band 1 & 3 Ss	Study harder.
	Common to band 2 & 3 Ss	Change personality.
		Believe in yourself.
	Particular to band 1 Ss	Be more prepared.
		Care little about marks.
		Improve grammatical knowledge.
		Make a study plan.
		Love English.
		Focus on the teachers' lessons.
	Particular to band 2 Ss	Fix several groups.
		Read English as often as possible.
		Don't fear being laughed at.
		Speak to themselves.
	Particular to band 3 Ss	Don't lose heart.
		Don't give up.
		Communicate with classmates with the same problem and experience.
		Telling yourself "it's a good chance to show yourself".
		Don't laugh at others.
		Be optimistic.
		Develop positive attitudes toward English learning.

Note: Ss → students.

According to Table 5.8, all the students suggested that they would become less nervous when using/speaking English in class if the teachers could prepare more interesting topics, create a relaxing classroom environment, encourage them more and give them more chances for practicing the target language in class. Many students believed that they would feel more at ease and freer to use/speak English to others if the topic was interesting, the class was friendly, and/or the teacher didn't speak fast but often smiled and nodded to them. Band 1 and 2 students also hoped English teachers could praise their students more and give them more thinking time before answering a question. Band 2 and 3 students suggested English teachers give more chances to nervous students and help students with examples. Generally speaking, all the students relied on the teachers to help build up and enhance their self-confidence. Nevertheless, band 1 and 2 students wished to receive more help from the teachers, while their band 3 counterparts were more demanding in that they wanted teachers to develop their interest in English, help them discover the beauty of the language, and teach them differently depending on their individual characteristics.

As far as the students were concerned, all the participants, as suggested by previous researchers (Donley, 1998; Jackson, 2002; Tsui, 1996), commented that they should have more practice, be more confident, improve English and not fear making mistakes in order to become more confident when speaking English in class.

Apart from the common suggestions, the students from different band groups suggested other ways to overcome anxiety in English class. In spite of differences in wording, the essence lay in improving English, having more contact with and practice of English, and supporting each other in the classroom. Some students also pointed out the fact that English was only a foreign language and thus they should feel natural to speak it with some mistakes. This, however, was unbearable to many of these top students, who thought that they should speak English fluently, as found in Liu's (2006a) study.

5.2 English learning motivation of the TU sample

5.2.1 General picture of English learning motivation of the TU sample

5.2.1.1 Item analysis of the ELMS of the TU sample

Table 5.9 presents the TU students' responses (the first number means the real number and the second percentage) to the ELMS (English Learning Motivation Scale) items, in the same way as the presentation of their responses to CAS items.

Table 5.9: ELMS Items with Numbers and Percentages of TU Students Selecting Each Alternative (N = 451)

SD/D	N	A/SA
9. Honestly, I don't know whether I am motivated to learn English.		
278/61.6	74/16.4	99/21.9
10. I have the impression that I am wasting my time in studying English.		
380/84.3	44/9.8	27/6.0
11. I study English in order to get a good job later on.		
219/48.6	83/18.4	149/33.0
12. I study English in order to earn more money later on.		
243/53.9	95/21.1	113/25.1

13. I study English for higher education later on.
     76/16.9   61/13.5   314/69.6
14. I study English in order to go abroad later on.
     104/23.3   70/15.5   276/61.2
15. I study English because I think it is important for my future work.
     62/13.7   65/14.4   324/71.8
16. I study English because I want to get high marks in English exams.
     235/52.1   93/20.6   123/27.2
17. I study English because it is required with credits at my university.
     255/56.5   87/19.3   109/24.2
18. I study English because I want to have ….
     298/66.1   82/18.2   71/15.8
19. … I have to pass English exams; otherwise, I would not learn it.
     357/79.2   52/11.5   42/9.3
20. … I am good at English listening, … and thus interested in it.
     179/39.7   118/26.2   154/34.1
21. I study English because I want to improve my English abilities ….
     67/14.9   54/12.0   330/73.2
22. I study English because I would feel guilty if I didn't know English.
     231/51.2   120/26.6   100/22.2
23. I study English because I would feel ashamed if I couldn't speak to ….
     203/45.0   99/22.0   149/33.0
24. … I think it is important for my personal development.
     31/6.9   34/7.5   387/85.6
25. … I choose to be the kind of person who can … one language.
     79/17.5   78/17.3   294/65.2
26. … I choose to be the kind of person who can speak English.
     58/12.9   98/21.7   295/65.4
27. I study English for the satisfied feeling I get in finding out new things.
     90/20.0   141/31.3   220/48.8
28. I study English for the pleasure that I experience in … literature.
     122/27.1   167/37.0   162/35.9
29. I study English because I enjoy the feeling of learning about ….
     135/29.9   130/28.8   186/41.2
30. I study English for the enjoyment … a difficult idea in English.
     197/43.7   165/36.6   89/19.7
31. … I feel when I am doing difficult exercises in English.
     277/61.4   116/25.7   58/12.9

32. I study English for the good feeling …I do better than I thought in ….
153/33.9   154/34.1   144/31.9
33. I study English for the excitement that I get while speaking English.
200/44.3   138/30.6   113/25.0
34. I study English for the excitement … speaking a foreign language.
242/53.7   112/24.6   98/21.7

Notes: SD → Strongly disagree;   D → Disagree
N → Neither disagree nor agree   A → Agree;   SA → Strongly agree

As shown in Table 5.9, more than 60% of the respondents vetoed such ELMS items implicative of little English learning motivation as "Honestly, I don't know whether I am motivated to learn English (item 9)" (61.6%) and "I have the impression that I am wasting my time in studying English (item 10)" (84.3%). This strongly suggests the TU students were motivated to learn English and considered learning the language was worthwhile.

The frequencies and percentages of responses to items 9 to 21 presented in Table 5.9 and ELMS item mean scores reported in Appendix II also indicate the TU students were highly instrumentally motivated to learn English. They reported being motivated to learn the language for various instrumental reasons such as going abroad (item 14) (61.2%); higher education (item 13) (69.6%); future career (item 15) (71.8%); improving English abilities in four basic skills (item 21) (73.2%); and personal development (item 24) (85.6%), as found in Liu's (2009) study. Meanwhile, they rejected statements expressing learning English for certificates and passing exams, as demonstrated by their responses to items 18 (66.1%) and 19 (79.2%).

Concerning integrative reasons, most students attributed their motivation to learn English to such reasons as the good feeling of learning about English-speaking people and their way of life (item 29) (41.2%); the satisfaction of finding out new things (item 27) (48.8%); choosing to speak more than one language (item 25) (65.2%) and English (item 26) (65.4%). Meanwhile, they denied being motivated to learn English for such reasons as excitement of speaking English (item 33) (44.3%); feeling guilty (item 22) (51.2%); excitement of hearing someone speaking English (item 34) (53.7%); and satisfaction of doing difficult exercises in English (item 31) (61.4%). These clearly indicate that the students' integrative motivation was more concerned with their school performance than their liking for the language, as supported by the mean scores of ELMS items presented in Appendix II as well.

This finding was also in conformity with the results of the journal data. Of 95 TU journal participants, 85 reported to be motivated to learn English in university because of a range of reasons, as shown in Table 5.10.

Table 5.10: Reasons for TU Students' Motivation to Learn English
(Source: Journal)

		Band 1 (34)	Band 2 (33)	Band 3 (28)
No Motivation	Number	4/11.8%	5/15.2%	1/3.6%
	Reason	Don't like English So many new words and hard texts	Don't like English No pressure	Not use English outside the classroom
Motivation	Number	30/88.2 %	28/84.8%	27/96.4%
	Reason	To do things for the Olympic Games 2008 To find a good job To improve English To study abroad To get more knowledge from English books Pass the TEPT 1 English being useful English being not so hard now To be a postgraduate Admire those who can speak well To talk with foreigners To change the present situation To feel very proud	To go abroad To find a better job To communicate with foreigners For further study To improve English English being useful English being important Being interested in English English being a beautiful language To be a volunteer for the Olympic Games 2008	English being important To go abroad For further study English being a useful tool To have more better opportunities To find a better job Being interested in English To communicate with foreign people To communicate with others easily To enhance English proficiency English being charming and attractive To become a serious English speaker Passion and curiosity Learning English being fun

According to Table 5.10, the common reasons for the TU learners' motivation to learn English across levels were to find a good/better job, to go abroad, to pursue further study, to improve English, and to communicate with foreigners. English being a useful tool was also a common motivation. Band 2 and 3 students were motivated also because they were interested in English and because English was important and beautiful. Because of the desire to contribute to the Olympic Games 2008, some band 1 and 2 students studied English hard. On the whole, the three band groups were motivated to learn English both instrumentally and integratively, though there seemed to have more instrumental reasons.

5.2.1.2 General tendency of the ELMS of the TU sample

In order to know the general tendency of the TU students' English learning motivation, the total score, mean, and standard deviation of the ELMS and its three subscales were computed, as done in section 4.2.1.3 (please refer to section 4.2.1.3 for the computing and interpreting scheme). The results are summarized in Table 5.11.

Table 5.11: Statistical Analyses of
the ELMS and its Subscales of TU Students

		Mean	Standard Deviation	Median	Mode	Range
ELMS	M (336)	79.07	10.34	79.00	81.00	43.00-123.00
	F (115)	83.02	9.52	83.00	82.00	55.00-107.00
	T (451)	80.08	10.27	80.00	81.00	43.00-123.00
ELM	M (336)	7.71	1.75	8.00	8.00	2.00-10.00
	F (115)	8.26	1.45	8.00	8.00	5.00-10.00
	T (451)	7.85	1.69	8.00	8.00	2.00-10.00
InsM	M (336)	36.23	6.34	36.00	36.00	15.00-56.00
	F (115)	36.99	5.43	36.00	34.00	25.00-54.00
	T (451)	36.42	6.12	36.00	36.00	15.00-56.00
IntM	M (336)	35.13	6.81	36.00	37.00	12.00-57.00
	F (115)	37.77	6.45	38.00	39.00	20.00-54.00
	T (451)	35.80	6.81	36.00	37.00	12.00-57.00

Notes: M = male; F = female;   T = total

As reported in Table 5.11, though some TU students (with a score of 43.00) had little motivation to learn English, a mean of 80.08, a median of 80.00 and a mode of 81.00, all above the average score of 78.00, indicate the majority were (highly) motivated to learn the language, as found with the whole participant sample. In addition, a mean of 7.85, a median and a mode of 8.00 on the ELM imply the majority had moderate or strong motivation to learn English. Likewise, a mean of 36.42, a median of 36.00 and a mode of 36.00 on the InsM, all scarcely above the average 36.00, are implicative of moderate instrumental motivation. And their IntM mean (35.80), median (36.00) and mode (37.00) reported in Table 5.11 show the TU students were moderately integratively motivated as well, as was the whole participant sample.

Moreover, as shown by the InsM and IntM mean scores reported in Table 5.11, the TU students reported to be more instrumentally than integratively motivated to learn English. But the difference was statistically insignificant, as supported by the results of paired samples t Test: t = 1.60, p = .110.

Further, according to Table 5.11, female students were generally more motivated to learn English both instrumentally and integratively than their male peers; and their motivation was stronger as well. Differences in the ELMS, the ELM and the IntM were statistically significant, as proved by the results of Independent-samples t tests reported in Table 5.12.

Table 5.12: Independent-samples t Test Results
for Gender Differences in ELMS and its Subscales (TU)

	ELM	InsM	IntM	ELMS
t	-.3.03	.1.15	-3.63	-3.60
p	.003	.250	.000	.000
t*	3.291	3.291	3.291	3.291

Note: t* → Critical t value at .001 level (Black, 1999).

5.2.2 Differences in English learning motivation among TU students at different proficiency levels

In order to know the differences in English learning motivation among the TU students at different proficiency levels, the total scores, means, standard deviations, medians, modes, maximums and minimums of the ELMS and its subscales were computed, as done in section 4.2.1.3 (please refer to section 4.2.1.3 for the computing and interpreting scheme). The results and further analyses are presented in Tables 5.13 and 5.14.

Table 5.13: Statistical Analyses of
the ELMS and its Subscales across Levels (TU)

Measure	Level	Mean	Standard Deviation	Median	Mode	Range
ELMS	1 (113)	78.11	9.89	79.00	88.00	50.00-105.00
	2 (205)	80.70	10.30	81.00	81.00	55.00-123.00
	3 (133)	80.80	10.40	81.00	82.00	43.00-107.00
ELM	1 (113)	7.18	1.69	7.00	8.00	2.00-10.00
	2 (205)	8.05	1.64	8.00	8.00	3.00-10.00
	3 (133)	8.12	1.64	8.00	10.00	2.00-10.00
InsM	1 (113)	36.98	5.88	37.00	34.00	19.00-51.00
	2 (205)	36.30	6.25	36.00	36.00	20.00-56.00
	3 (133)	36.14	6.15	36.00	34.00	15.00-54.00

112

IntM	1 (113)	33.95	7.01	35.00	35.00	12.00-49.00
	2 (205)	36.36	6.98	37.00	37.00	12.00-57.00
	3 (133)	36.53	6.09	37.00	39.00	20.00-52.00

Table 5.14: ANOVA Results of the ELMS and its Subscales (TU)

Measures	F	P	F*	University (Mean) 1 = 113; 2 = 205; 3 = 133			Location of sig. difference ($a = .05$)
				1	2	3	
ELMS	2.81*	.061	2.77	78.11	80.70	80.80	1 & 2; 1 & 3
ELIM	12.67*	.000	2.77	7.18	8.05	8.12	1 & 2; 1 & 3
InsM	.65	.521	2.77	36.98	36.30	36.14	/
IntM	5.76*	.003	2.77	33.95	36.36	36.53	1 & 2; 1 & 3

Note: F* → Critical F value for Duncan's test at .05 level (Black, 1999).

As shown in Table 5.13, the mean scores, medians and modes of the three band groups on the ELMS and its subscales clearly indicate the majority of each band group had moderate or even strong motivation to learn English. They were also moderately or even strongly instrumentally/ integratively motivated to learn the language.

As seen from Table 5.13, the band 1 students had the lowest mean scores on the ELMS, the ELM and the IntM but the highest mean score on the InsM; the band 3 students had the highest mean scores on the ELMS, the ELM and the IntM but the lowest mean score on the InsM; their band 2 peers had all the mean scores in between. It seems that the band 1 students had the lowest overall motivation while their band 3 counterparts had the highest overall motivation to learn English. However, the band 1 students were the most instrumentally but the least integratively motivated when learning English. Conversely, their band 3 peers were the least instrumentally but the most integratively motivated. Alternatively, students at the highest proficiency level were the most motivated to learn English, whereas those at the lowest proficiency level were the least motivated. And the differences were generally statistically significant, as evidenced by the ANOVA results summed up in Table 5.14. The band 1 students achieved significantly lower mean scores than their band 2 and 3 peers on the ELMS, the ELM and the IntM; but no significant difference was found on the InsM.

5.3 English learning strategy use by the TU sample

5.3.1 TU students' knowledge of English learning strategies

Of 95 TU journal participants, 34 band 1, 27 band 2, and 23 band 3 students reported to know something about English learning strategies and have used some when learning English, as summarized in Table 5.15.

**Table 5.15: TU Students' Knowledge
of English Learning Strategies** (Source: journal)

Band 1	Band 2	Band 3
Memorize words (day by day)	Practice	Practice more
Recite texts	Read text book carefully	Expand vocabulary
Read some passages/do lots of reading	Do exercises every day	Take notes while
Get the main idea of articles	Make full use of the	listening to the
Remember important sentences	Internet and library	teacher
Listen to some radios	Recite	Listen to English
Study every day, in every place	Read novels	songs
Listen carefully in class	Make a good plan	Watch movie
Do exercises after class	Take notes while	Read newspapers
Make a plan	listening to the teacher	Keep a diary
Make up for the weak points in study	Use English	Review frequently
Have an open heart and energetic spirit	Be courageous	Plan
Stick to it, never give up	Review more	Use English when
Read the text, look up the new words		having a chance
Listen to texts		Be brave and confident

Though quite a few strategies were listed here, memory strategies seemed to be predominant across levels: recite (words, sentences and texts) and review. In order to learn English better, the three groups also resorted to repeated practice by doing exercises, and using resources for receiving and sending messages (e.g., listen to radio, watch movies, read texts, etc.). Band1 and 2 students also paid attention by listening or reading carefully. Meanwhile, band 2 and 3 students also reported using affective strategies such as keeping a diary and being brave and confident and metacognitive strategies such as planning and using English. On the whole, it seems that the three groups knew consciously only a little about English learning strategies, though students at the higher level reported knowing more types of strategies. Nevertheless, 27 band 1, 20 band 2 and 18 band 3 students reflected that using these strategies was conducive to improving their English and studying more effectively.

114

5.3.2 Broad profile of English learning strategy use by the TU sample

Based on TU mean scores of English Learning Strategy Inventory (ELSI) items presented in Appendix II, items in different use ranges were summarized and reported in Table 5.16 (please refer to section 4.3.3 for the analyzing key). Among the 184 ELSI items, 65 items were in the high use range, 110 in the medium use range and 9 in the low use range. In other words, the majority of the strategies were sometimes used; around a fourth to a third of them were usually or always used; only a few were usually not used or even not used. That is, all the strategies were employed by the students to different extents and the majority were sometimes or more often used. The case was the same with each of the six strategy categories, as shown in Table 5.16. A review of the ELSI mean scores presented in Appendix II further indicates that mean scores for high use strategies never exceeded 4.00 and those for low use strategies never fell below 2.00. Namely, those high use strategies were just usually but not always used, while those low use strategies were just usually not used and none of them were never or almost never used.

Table 5.16: Number of English Learning
Strategy Items in Different Use Ranges (TU)

English Learning Strategy categories	High use	Medium use	Low use
Memory Strategy (MS)	5	14	1
Cognitive Strategy (CogS)	9	33	2
Compensation Strategy (ComS)	15	5	1
Metacognitive Strategy (MetaS)	27	45	3
Affective Strategy (AS)	5	7	1
Social Strategy (SS)	4	6	1
English Learning Strategy Inventory (ELSI)	65	110	9

As reported in Table 5.17, the mean of overall strategy use was 3.25 on the 5-point Likert scale. This signifies "medium" strategy use (sometimes used) towards the upper end. That is, the TU respondents had a quite frequent use of various strategies in English learning, close to high use but not to that extent, in conformity with the analyses of mean scores of different strategy items.

The mean scores for all the six strategy categories except compensation strategies which were in high use were also in the medium-use range. Among the six categories, the most frequently used were compensation strategies with a mean of 3.51 (usually used), followed by metacognitive (mean = 3.28), social (mean = 3.24), and affective (mean = 3.21) strategies, and then cognitive (3.15) and memory (mean = 3.08)

115

strategies. The TU students reported having high use of compensation strategies, but only at the low end. In another word, this category of strategies was more often used than "sometimes", whereas, others were just sometimes used but at the middle (memory strategies) or the upper end (the other four categories) of the medium range.

Table 5.17: Means and Standard Deviations
Indicating English Learning Strategy Use (TU) (N = 451)

Strategy category (most used to least used)	Frequency of strategy use	
	Mean/range	Standard deviation
Compensation	3.51 (high use; low end)	.4
Metacognitive	3.28 (medium use; upper end)	.41
Social	3.24 (medium use; upper end)	.53
Affective	3.21 (medium use; upper end)	.48
Cognitive	3.15 (medium use; upper end)	.36
Memory	3.08 (medium use)	.44
ELSI	3.25 (medium use; upper end)	.35

This finding about the overall strategy use conforms to that of the whole participant sample discussed in Chapter four, though contradictory to the results of the journal data reported in Table 5.15.

5.3.3 The most and least used individual learning strategies by the TU sample

As discussed above, the majority of the strategies were sometimes or usually used. Among these strategies, twenty were identified to be the most frequently used by Tsinghua undergraduate EFL learners, as shown in Table 5.18.

Of twenty most often used strategy items, all were in the high-use range with a mean range of 3.73 to 3.97. Most of these highly frequently used strategies fell into compensation (10) and metacognitive (10) categories; a few belonged to affective (2), memory (1) and cognitive (1) categories. The TU respondents would usually use contextual clues to "understand unfamiliar English words" (mean = 3.97) and "make guesses about English reading" (mean = 3.86); use background knowledge to make guesses when "reading in English" (mean = 3.82) and "listening to English" (mean = 3.75); make guesses "on word formation to understand unfamiliar English words" (mean = 3.77), "on linguistic clues when not understanding what had been heard in English" (mean = 3.73), "about the speaker's intention according to his/her tone, intonation and pause" (mean

= 3.75) and "purposefully when listening to/reading English" (mean = 3.73). They also "use visual aids to better understand English movies" (mean = 3.92); "use words or phrases similar in meaning as substitutes" (mean = 3.82); and "use simple English words, expressions and sentence structures as substitutes" (mean = 3.83). In addition, they "look up frequently occurring words in dictionary" (mean = 3.90), and "read English without looking up every new word" (mean = 3.77). Moreover, they tried to "link it with already known knowledge when reading or listening to English (mean = 3.78) and "select English learning materials based on English proficiency" (mean = 3.74). When writing in English, these TU learners tried to "make it coherent" (mean = 3.85), "make as few grammatical mistakes as possible" (mean = 3.82); "keep to the main idea" (mean = 3.76); "use a variety of words" (mean = 3.73); and made "a summary and restate the main idea in the concluding paragraph(s) (mean = 3.73). Meanwhile, they "self-encourage not to lose heart when not doing well in English exams" (mean = 3.79) and "try to find out how to be a better English learner" (mean = 3.77).

On the whole, the TU students would guess intelligently by using linguistic and other clues and resort to background knowledge to help realize their goals in English learning. When employing metacognitive strategies, they mainly depended on the strategy of centering one's learning by overviewing and linking with already known material and paying attention, as shown in Table 5.18. It is also worth noting that only two affective strategies were highly frequently used by the TU learners. This might also be because these EFL learners seldom purposefully deployed any means such as writing diaries and talking about feelings to ease their anxiety, fear and/or doubt in English learning (Liu, 2009, 2006a). It might be due to the same reason that few memory, cognitive and social strategies were highly frequently employed by the TU learners.

**Table 5.18: The Twenty Most Frequently and
Twenty Least Used English Learning Strategies** (TU) (N = 451)

The twenty most frequently used English learning strategies				
No.	Strategy	Mean	Category in which this strategy is classified	Comment
100	Make guesses based on contextual	3.97	Compensation	H
108	Use visual aids to help better	3.92	Compensation	H
127	Look up frequently occurring	3.90	Metacognitive	H
104	Use contextual clues to make	3.86	Compensation	H
135	Try to make it coherent when	3.85	Metacognitive	H
117	Often use simple words, expressions	3.83	Compensation	H

No.	Strategy	Mean	Category in which this strategy is classified	Comment
105	Use background knowledge to ….	3.82	Compensation	H
119	Use words or phrases similar in ….	3.82	Compensation	H
134	Try to make as few grammatical ….	3.82	Metacognitive	H
198	Self-encourage not to lose heart ….	3.79	Affective	H
120	Often try to link it with already ….	3.78	Metacognitive	H
77	Read English without looking up ….	3.77	Cognitive	H
99	Make guesses based on word ….	3.77	Compensation	H
141	Try to find out how to be a better ….	3.77	Metacognitive	H
136	Keep to the main idea when ….	3.76	Metacognitive	H
106	Use background knowledge to ….	3.75	Compensation	H
107	Make guesses about the ….	3.75	Compensation	H
155	Select English learning materials ….	3.74	Metacognitive	H
48	Remember a new English word ….	3.73	Memory	H
101	Often use linguistic clues to make ….	3.73	Compensation	H
130	Pay attention when someone is ….	3.73	Metacognitive	H
133	Try to use a variety of words ….	3.73	Metacognitive	H
151	Often make a summary and ….	3.73	Metacognitive	H
202	Often purposefully make guesses ….	3.73	Affective	H
The Twenty least frequently used English learning strategies				
No.	Strategy	Mean	Category in which this strategy is classified	Comment
78	Often read the transcript before ….	2.14	Cognitive	L
206	Write down my feelings in ….	2.18	Affective	L
51	Physically act out new English words.	2.24	Memory	L
118	Make up new words when not ….	2.27	Metacognitive	L
217	Just care for what I need to say and ….	2.38	Social	L
168	Initiate to make friends with ….	2.40	Metacognitive	L
79	Read the transcript while ….	2.45	Cognitive	L
171	Actively take part in various ….	2.48	Metacognitive	L
161	Have a notebook ready for writing ….	2.49	Metacognitive	L
52	Use flashcards to remember new ….	2.50	Memory	M
169	Initiate to talk to teachers in English.	2.50	Metacognitive	M
160	Try to write diaries and/or journals ….	2.51	Metacognitive	M
170	Often participate in various ….	2.52	Metacognitive	M
54	Often recite English essays.	2.54	Memory	M
61	Often do really a lot of English ….	2.56	Cognitive	M
59	Practice pronunciation ….	2.59	Cognitive	M
205	Often use a checklist to note my ….	2.61	Affective	M
167	Initiate to greet and converse ….	2.63	Metacognitive	M
115	Often try to avoid using English.	2.65	Metacognitive	M
176	Often search for various English ….	2.65	Metacognitive	M

Among the twenty least often used strategies, 9 were in the low-use range at the upper end with a mean range from 2.14 to 2.49; 11 fell in the medium-use range at the low end with means ranging from 2.50 to 2.65, as presented in Table 5.12. For example, "write down my feelings in language learning diaries" (mean = 2.18); "often read the transcript before listening to English" (mean = 2.14); "physically act out new English words" (mean = 2.24); "make up new words when not knowing the right ones in English" (mean = 2.27); "read the transcript while listening to English" (mean = 2.45); "actively take part in various English contests" (mean = 2.48); "try to write diaries and/or journals in English" (mean = 2.51); and "practice pronunciation according to English phonological rules" (mean = 2.59).

5.3.4 Differences in English learning strategy use between TU male and female students and among those at different proficiency levels

As seen from Table 5.19, TU male and female students scored 3.23 and 3.30 respectively on the 5-point Likert ELSI, which suggests medium use of the strategies. They both had a medium or even high use of all the six categories of strategies (mean range of 3.06 to 3.50 and 3.14 to 3.56 for males and females respectively). In addition, TU female students reported to use all the categories of English learning strategies more frequently than their male counterparts. But significant difference existed only in the use of social strategies, as supported by the results of Independent-samples t-tests presented in Table 5.19. Therefore, females employed social strategies significantly more frequently than their male peers in English learning.

Table 5.19: TU Gender Differences in English Learning Strategy Use (N = 451)

		Mean	Standard Deviation	t-test results		
				t	p	t*
MS	M (336)	3.06	.46	-1.70	.091	1.96
	F (115)	3.14	.38			
CogS	M (336)	3.13	.38	-1.91	.057	1.96
	F (115)	3.20	.32			
CompS	M (336)	3.50	.42	-1.52	.129	1.96
	F (115)	3.56	.32			
MetaS	M (336)	3.26	.42	-1.28	.200	1.96
	F (115)	3.32	.37			
AS	M (336)	3.19	.49	-1.51	.131	1.96
	F (115)	3.27	.46			
SS	M (336)	3.19	.55	-3.08	.002	3.291

	F (115)	3.37	.47			
ELSI	M (336)	3.23	.36	-1.94	.053	1.96
	F (115)	3.30	.31			

Notes: M = male; F = female

T* → Critical t values at .05 and .001 levels respectively (Black, 1999)

To explore differences in English learning strategy use among the TU students at three different proficiency levels, the analysis of one-way ANOVA was conducted. The results are summed up in Table 5.20.

Table 5.20: ANOVA Results of English Learning Strategy Use (TU)

Measures	F	P	F*	Level (Mean) 1 = 113; 2 = 205; 3 = 133			Location of sig. difference (a = .05)
				Band 1	Band 2	Band 3	
MS	3.51*	.031	2.77	2.99	3.12	3.08	Bands 1 & 2
CogS	5.27*	.005	2.77	3.05	3.19	3.17	Bands 1 & 2; Bands 1 & 3
ComS	5.67	.004	2.77	3.41	3.56	3.53	Bands 1 & 2; Bands 1 & 3
MetaS	9.37*	.000	2.77	3.14	3.34	3.30	Bands 1 & 2; Bands 1 & 3
AS	4.76*	.009	2.77	3.13	3.28	3.17	Bands 2 & 1; Bands 2 & 3
SS	3.24*	.040	2.77	3.13	3.26	3.29	Bands 1 & 2; Bands 1 & 3
ELSI	8.57*	.000	2.77	3.13	3.30	3.26	Bands 1 & 2; Bands 1 & 3

Note: F* → Critical F value for Duncan's test at .05 level (Black, 1999).

According to Table 5.20, students at all proficiency levels had a medium use of the strategies; band 2 and 3 students even had a high use of compensation strategies. The band 3 students reported using social strategies the most frequently in learning English; the band 2 learners self-reported to be the most frequent users of memory, cognitive, compensation, metacognitive and affective strategies, they also scored the highest on the ELSI; their band 1 peers employed all categories of strategies the least often. And the post-hoc tests revealed that significant differences were found in all categories of strategies among students at different proficiency levels. The band 1 students employed cognitive, compensation, metacognitive, social and the overall strategies significantly less frequently than their band 2 and 3 counterparts; the band 1 learners also used memory strategies significantly less frequently than their band 2 peers; the band 2 group had significantly more frequent use of affective strategies than band 1 and 3 groups.

It can be concluded that the band 2 students were generally the most frequent users of English learning strategies, whereas their band 1 peers were the least frequent users. It is surprising that the band 3 students were not the most frequent users of the strategies, but they did not differ significantly from their band 2 peers in the use of the strategies either. This might be because band 2 and 3 students did not really differ from each other in terms of English proficiency while both were significantly better at English than their band 1 counterparts.

5.3.5 Correlations between individual English learning strategy use and TU students' performance in English

To address this question, correlation analyses were conducted, which revealed 35 English learning strategy items significantly correlated with the TU students' performance in English with coefficients ranging from -.132 to .160, as reported in Table 5.21.

Table 5.21: Correlations between Individual English Learning Strategies and TU Students' Performance in English (N = 451)

Items	P
40. Remember new English words by associating them … (memory).	.160**
41. Use new English words in a sentence so I can … (memory).	.098*
49. Often review what I have learned in English (memory).	.105*
50. Copy down new English words … them regularly (memory).	.100*
62. Try to talk like native English speakers (cognitive).	.097*
63. Often practice reading English aloud (cognitive).	.094*
64. Often find out and deduce grammatical rules … (cognitive).	.127**
76. Make sure of its meaning … word in a dictionary (cognitive).	.110*
82. Often remember English grammatical … memory (cognitive).	.136**
92. Try not to translate word-for-word when … (cognitive).	.126**
98. Highlight certain phrases or sentences … (cognitive).	.100*
102. If I hear an unfamiliar English word, … (compensation).	.099*
104. Use contextual clues to make guesses about … (compensation).	.112*
105. Use background knowledge to make … (compensation).	.120*
106. Use background knowledge to make … (compensation).	.133**
107. Make guesses about the speaker's intention … (compensation).	.094*
115. Often try to avoid using English (compensation).	-.132**
127. Look up the words in dictionary that … (metacognitive).	.106*
129. Look up in dictionary only those words … (metacognitive).	.112*

130. Pay attention when someone is speaking … (metacognitive).	.102*
136. Keep to the main idea when writing in English (metacognitive).	.100*
137. Pay attention to paragraphing when writing … (metacognitive).	.094*
142. Have my own English learning plan … (metacognitive).	.097*
143. Plan my schedule in order to have enough … (metacognitive).	.102*
144. Organize my ideas quite logically when … (metacognitive).	.108*
146. Have clear goals for improving my English … (metacognitive).	.098*
149. Often make a paragraph evolve … in English (metacognitive).	.117*
154. Often try to list the ideas related to the topic … (metacognitive).	.116*
165. Often speak English to myself (metacognitive).	.097*
166. Look for opportunities to read as much as … (metacognitive).	.112*
173. Pay attention to the English used in various … (metacognitive).	.120*
174. Pay attention to the English used in streets (metacognitive).	.120*
187. Assess my English learning strategies … (metacognitive).	.132**
203. Give myself a reward or treat when doing well in … (affective).	.101*
204. Notice if I am tense or nervous when studying … (affective).	.153**

Notes: ** = p < .01;   * = p < .05;   P = performance

According to Table 5.21, one compensation strategy significantly negatively correlated with the TU students' performance in English: strategy 115, "often try to avoid using English" (r = -.132). The more often the TU students tried to avoid using English in the process of learning the language, the less proficient they were in English.

The remaining strategies all had a significantly positive relationship with the TU students' performance in English. For example, 40, "remember new English words by associating them with others" (r = .160); 82, "often remember English grammatical rules based on understanding rather than rote memory" (r = .136); 104, "104. Use contextual clues to make guesses about English reading" (r = .112); 130, "pay attention when someone is speaking English" (r = .102); and 203, "give myself a reward or treat when doing well in English" (r = .101). The more frequently the TU students resorted to these strategies in English learning, the more proficient they were in English.

Moreover, among these strategies, the majority belonged to the metacognitive (16) category, followed by cognitive (7), compensation (6), memory (4), and affective (2) categories. More strategy items fell into metacognitive and cognitive categories maybe because these two categories included a larger number of items. Among the memory strategies, most were concerned with remembering words and reviewing what had been learned. Similarly, most of the compensation strategies were related to guessing by using different clues. Though only 7 cognitive strategies proved to be significantly related to the TU students' performance in English, they covered all aspects such as practicing, receiving and sending messages, analyzing and reasoning, and creating structure for input and output. It was the same with metacognitive strategies.

5.4 English test-taking strategy use by the TU sample

5.4.1 TU students' knowledge of English test-taking strategies

Of 95 TU journal participants, 15 band 1, 17 band 2, and 19 band 3 students reported using some strategies when taking English exams, as presented in Table 5.22.

Table 5.22: TU Students' Knowledge of English Test-taking Strategies (Source: journal)

Band 1	Band 2	Band 3
Memorize notes and texts	Read some English articles before the exams	Review notes and texts
Never do special things		Memorize words and phrases
Review notes and texts	Review before exams	Be calm during the test
Memorize words and phrases	Memorize all the words	Work out the problems one by one
Do some exercises	Do exercises to warm up	
Prepare one month before	Listen to some English conversations	Highlight important or difficult parts
Review the mistakes	Review the questions that were done wrong before	Listen to and read instructions carefully
From easy to difficult		
Do it one by one	Listen to the tape	Do the easy questions first
Do reading first (good at it)	Do a similar test to check myself	Guess sometimes according to the context
Be calm	Review my performance during the test	
Write carefully		Reflect what I have done well or bad during the test
Face exams bravely		

As shown in Table 5.22, the TU students at all levels would prepare for a coming exam (carefully) by reviewing notes, memorizing words and phrases, doing exercises and reading articles. Band 1 and 2 students even review the mistakes they had made. The band 2 students also tested their own proficiency by doing some simulated tests. During the test, band 1 and 3 students would stay calm, work out the problems one by one, or do the easy problems or those they were good at first. Meanwhile, the band 1 students would write carefully, and the band 3 learners would highlight important or difficult parts, listen to and read instructions carefully, and guess sometimes according to the context. After the exam, band 2 and 3 would reflect on it to see where they had done well or poorly so that they could perform better in the future.

As such, it is clear that these TU students at different proficiency levels would employ some memory, cognitive, metacognitive and affective strategies when taking an English exam. Band 1 and 3 participants seemed to use more types of strategies than their band 2 peers. Nevertheless, the number of each category of strategies deployed by each group was small, as listed in Table 5.22. Moreover, 17 band 1, 19 band 2 and 19 band 3 participants believed using these strategies helped them perform better in exams.

5.4.2 Broad profile of English test-taking strategy use by the TU sample

Based on TU mean scores of English Test-taking Strategy Inventory (ETSI) items presented in Appendix II, items in different use ranges were summarized and presented in Table 5.23 (please refer to section 4.3.3 for the analyzing key). Among the 91 ETSI items, 43 items were in the high use range, 45 in the medium use range and 3 in the low use range. Namely, the majority of the strategies were sometimes or usually/always used; only three were usually not used or even not used. It was the same with each of the six strategy categories, as shown in Table 5.23. A review of the ETSI mean scores reported in Appendix II further illustrates that mean scores for high use strategies rarely exceeded 4.00 and those for low use strategies never fell below 2.00. That is, those high use strategies were just usually but not always used; while those low use strategies were just not usually used and none of them were never or almost never used, as were English learning strategies. On the whole, all the strategies were employed by the TU students to different extents during English tests, the majority of which were sometimes or more often used.

Table 5.23: Number of Test-taking Strategy Items in Different Use Ranges (TU)

Test-taking Strategy categories	High use	Medium use	Low use
Memory Strategy (TMS)	0	4	2
Cognitive Strategy (TCogS)	9	8	0
Compensation Strategy (TComS)	7	4	1
Metacognitive Strategy (TMetaS)	23	25	0
Affective Strategy (TAS)	2	2	0
Social Strategy (TSS)	2	2	0
English Test-Taking Strategy Inventory (ETSI)	43	45	3

As reported in Table 5.24, the mean of overall test-taking strategy use was 3.41 on the 5-point Likert scale. This signifies "medium" strategy use (sometimes used) towards the upper end. That is, the TU participants reported to employ quite frequent use of various strategies during English tests, close to high use but not to that extent, consistent with the analyses of the mean scores of different English test-taking strategy items.

The mean scores for all the six test-taking strategy categories generally fell in the medium-use range. Among the six categories, the most frequently used was compensation strategies with a mean of 3.50, followed by affective, metacognitive, cognitive and social strategies with a mean of 3.49, 3.46, 3.44 and 3.30 respectively. The least frequently used were memory strategies with a mean of 2.81. In a word, the TU students were able to deploy various strategies when taking English exams to better their performance.

Table 5.24: Means and Standard Deviations
Indicating Test-taking Strategy Use (TU) (N = 451)

Strategy category (most used to least used)	Frequency of strategy use	
	Mean/range	Standard deviation
Compensation	3.50 (medium use; upper end)	.47
Affective	3.49 (medium use; upper end)	.60
Metacognitive	3.46 (medium use; upper end)	.42
Cognitive	3.44 (medium use; upper end)	.48
Social	3.30 (medium use; upper end)	.62
Memory	2.81 (medium use; low end)	.68
ETSI	3.41 (medium use; upper end)	.41

This finding about the overall test-taking strategy use basically conforms to that of the whole participant sample. Likewise, the TU participants also reported to use memory strategies the least frequently during English exams; however, these learners used compensation strategy the most frequently. This was contradictory to what the journal participants reported in their reflective journals, as listed in Table 5.22.

5.4.3 The most and least used individual test-taking strategies by the TU sample

As demonstrated above, most of the test-taking strategies were sometimes or usually used. Among these more often used strategies, twenty were identified to be the most frequently used by TU undergraduate EFL learners during English tests, as shown in Table 5.25.

Of these twenty most often used test-taking strategy items, all were in the high-use range with means ranging from 3.80 to 4.28. The TU students would usually "attend 100% of my English classes" (mean = 4.28) to be better prepared for English tests. When a test was coming, they would "try to get a good night's sleep" (mean = 3.94) and "arrive at the test room on time" (mean = 4.09). During the test, they would "look for clues" (mean = 3.91) and "keywords" (mean = 3.88) while reading; "listen to keywords" (mean = 3.93), "clues" (mean = 3.90) and "directions carefully" (mean = 3.80) when doing listening comprehension"; and "read questions and test directions carefully" (mean = 3.87 and 3.80 respectively). When writing, they would "make as few mistakes as possible" (mean = 3.90) and try to make it coherent and cohesive (mean = 3.86). To better their performance, these learners would "eliminate certain answers when answering multiple-choice questions" (mean = 3.93); use background knowledge of the topic to help guess and deduce "while reading" (mean = 3.92) and "complete the cloze test" (mean = 3.86), and linguistic knowledge to help "complete the cloze test" (mean = 3.91) and "guess and deduce what the speaker says while doing listening comprehension" (mean = 3.86) during the exam.

Table 5.25 also indicates that most of the most frequently used strategies were of metacognitive category (12), followed by compensation (5), cognitive (2) and affective (1) categories. The high means indicate these TU learners were used to arriving at the test room on time, looking for clues, guessing from the context, and resorting to background and linguistic knowledge during an English test. During an oral test, they were also aware of the importance of cooperation between partners by listening to them carefully, as illustrated by the strategy item means summarized in Appendix II. In a word, these students were able to employ various strategies to better their performance in an English test.

Table 5.25: The Twenty Most Frequently and Twenty Least Used Test-taking Strategies (TU) (N = 451)

The twenty most frequently used strategies				
No.	Strategy	Mean	Category in which this strategy is classified	Comment
254	Attend 100% of my English classes.	4.28	Metacognitive	H
265	Always arrive at the test room on time.	4.09	Metacognitive	H
302	Try to get a good night's sleep	3.94	Affective	H
236	Eliminate certain answers	3.93	Cognitive	H
279	Listen to keywords	3.93	Metacognitive	H

245	Make guesses based on	3.92	Compensation	H
248	Use my background knowledge of	3.92	Compensation	H
246	Use linguistic knowledge to	3.91	Compensation	H
283	Look for clues while reading	3.91	Metacognitive	H
280	Listen to clues	3.90	Metacognitive	H
295	Try to make as few mistakes	3.90	Metacognitive	H
282	Look for keywords while	3.88	Metacognitive	H
274	Try to better understand	3.87	Metacognitive	H
284	Read questions carefully	3.87	Metacognitive	H
244	Use linguistic knowledge to help	3.86	Compensation	H
247	Use background knowledge of the	3.86	Compensation	H
294	Try to make writing coherent and	3.86	Metacognitive	H
238	Break up run-on sentences into	3.84	Cognitive	H
277	Read test directions carefully	3.80	Metacognitive	H
278	Listen to directions carefully	3.80	Metacognitive	H
The Twenty least frequently used strategies				
No.	Strategy	Mean	Category in which this strategy is classified	Comment
224	Often dump information	2.28	Memory	L
250	Use Chinese when not knowing	2.42	Compensation	L
221	Use high technology to help	2.48	Memory	L
271	Create study checklists	2.56	Metacognitive	M
222	Create flashcards for words, ...	2.71	Memory	M
256	Avoid speaking with other students	2.71	Metacognitive	M
232	Create summary notes and	2.72	Cognitive	M
269	Try to predict	2.73	Metacognitive	M
223	Memorize model texts/essays	2.85	Memory	M
260	Develop a timetable for exam	2.92	Metacognitive	M
270	Self-test in similar oral English	2.94	Metacognitive	M
228	Practice translating English	2.96	Cognitive	M
242	Exchange with English teachers	3.01	Compensation	M
263	Get familiar with the test room	3.01	Metacognitive	M
266	Set a goal for myself	3.04	Metacognitive	M
243	Ask the instructor what to	3.05	Compensation	M
287	Scan the test first and then develop	3.07	Metacognitive	M
272	Self-test on the material	3.09	Metacognitive	M
305	Often self-reward if having done	3.10	Affective	M
220	Keep up homework and my notes	3.12	Memory	M

Notes: H = high use;   M = medium use;   L = low use

Among the twenty least often used strategies, all were distinctly in the medium-use range except the first three with a mean range of 2.28 to 3.12, as reported in Table 5.25. For example, "dump information on the back of the English test paper" (mean = 2.28); "use Chinese when not knowing how to express myself in English during English tests" (mean = 2.42); "use high technology to help review materials before English tests" (mean = 2.48); "create study checklists before an English test" (mean = 2.56); "create flashcards" (mean = 2.71); "try to predict examination questions and then outline answers" (mean = 2.73); "memorize model texts/essays before an English essay test" (mean = 2.85); "developed a timetable" (mean = 2.92); "get familiar with the test room before an English test" (mean = 3.01); and "self-test on the material before an English test" (mean = 3.09).

According to Table 5.25, the least often used strategies mainly belonged to metacognitive (9) category, followed by memory (5), compensation (3), cognitive (2) and affective (1) categories. To prepare and/or during an English test, these TU learners would not use much such metacognitive strategies as creating study checklists, predicting, self testing, developing a preparation timetable, and scanning. They would not often depend on such memory strategies as dumping information, using high technology, memorization and review of homework and notes. They would not employ such compensation strategies as using the mother tongue and talking with their English teachers or instruction about exam preparation either. This finding was generally in conformity with the results of the journal data reported in Table 5.22, except the use of memorization and review of homework and notes, which were reported to be an important strategy for exams by the journal participants at all levels.

However, it is worth noting that although these strategies were the least frequently employed, the majority were in the medium-use range (sometimes used). This clearly indicates these students were highly flexible in utilizing various strategies to help complete and/or better their performance in English tests. This might be part of the reasons why these learners often did better than most of their peers in other universities in the country.

5.4.4 Differences in test-taking strategy use between TU male and female students and among those at different proficiency levels

To explore differences in English test-taking strategy use between TU male and female students, the means and standard deviations were computed, and the Independent-samples t-tests were conducted. The results are shown in Table 5.26. With mean ranges of 2.80 to 3.50 and of 2.82 to 3.53 for male and female students respectively, they both had a medium or even high use of all the categories of strategies. Moreover, TU female students reported to be more frequent users of memory, cognitive, compensation, metacognitive, affective and the overall strategies when learning English, and use social strategies as frequently as did their male peers. However, no statistically significant difference was found in the use of any of the strategies, as evidenced by t-test results presented in Table 5.26.

Table 5.26: TU Gender Differences in English Learning Strategy Use (N = 451)

		Mean	Standard Deviation	t-test results	
				t	p
TMS	M (336)	2.80	.71	-.26	.795
	F (115)	2.82	.59		
TCogS	M (336)	3.44	.51	-.55	.584
	F (115)	3.47	.38		
TCompS	M (336)	3.50	.49	-.02	.983
	F (115)	3.50	.39		
TMetaS	M (336)	3.45	.45	-1.21	.227
	F (115)	3.51	.35		
TAS	M (336)	3.48	.63	-.74	.462
	F (115)	3.53	.56		
TSS	M (336)	3.30	.61	.01	.992
	F (115)	3.30	.64		
ETSI	M (336)	3.40	.43	-.80	.424
	F (115)	3.44	.34		

Notes: M = male; F = female

To address the question whether there was any difference in the English test-taking strategy use among students at different proficiency levels, the analysis of one-way ANOVA was conducted. The results are reported in Table 5.27.

Table 5.27: ANOVA Results of English Test-taking Strategy Use (TU)

Measures	F	P	F*	Level (Mean) 1 = 113; 2 = 205; 3 = 133			Location of sig. difference (a = .05)
				Band 1	Band 2	Band 3	
TMS	18.46*	.000	2.77	2.83	2.97	2.53	Bands 3 & 1 Bands 3 & 2
TCogS	9.24*	.000	2.77	3.28	3.52	3.47	Bands 1 & 2 Bands 1 & 3

129

TComS	7.29*	.001	2.77	3.35	3.54	3.56	Bands 1 & 2
							Bands 1 & 3
TMetaS	4.31*	.014	2.77	3.37	3.52	3.46	Bands 1 & 2
TAS	5.32*	.005	2.77	3.34	3.57	3.49	Bands 1 & 2
							Bands 1 & 3
TSS	2.96*	.053	2.77	3.18	3.34	3.35	Bands 1 & 2
							Bands 1 & 3
ETSI	6.23*	.002	2.77	3.31	3.47	3.40	Bands 1 & 2
							Bands 1 & 3

Note: F* → Critical F value for Duncan's test at .05 level (Black, 1999).

As reported in Table 5.27, the TU students at all proficiency levels generally had a medium or high use of test-taking strategies in all categories. The band 3 students reported using compensation and social strategies the most frequently, memory strategies the least frequently and other categories of strategies in between when taking English exams. The band 2 learners self-reported to be the most frequent users of memory, cognitive, metacognitive and affective strategies; their band peers used memory strategies in between and other categories of strategies the least often during English exams. The post-hoc tests indicated differences in the use of all categories of strategies were statistically significant. The band 1 students deployed cognitive, compensation, affective, social and the overall strategies significantly less frequently than their band 2 and 3 counterparts. Their use of metacognitive strategies was also significantly less than that of their band 2 peers. The band 3 students employed memory strategies significantly less frequently than band 1 and 2 groups.

5.4.5 Correlations between individual English test-taking strategy use and TU students' performance in English

To explore the relationship between the use of individual English test-taking strategies and the TU students' performance in English, correlation analyses were conducted. The results, summarized in Table 5.28, show that 22 English test-taking strategy items were significantly correlated with the TU students' performance in English with coefficients ranging from .096 to .141. All of these 22 strategy items had a significantly positive relationship with the TU students' performance in English. For instance, strategy 219, "review a lot before English exams" (r = .096); 235, "use both general and specific information when answering an essay question" (r = .113); 242, "exchange with English teachers about how and what to prepare before English tests" (r = .100); 259, "pay particular attention to clues that indicate an instructor might test for a particular idea" ($r = .109$); 288, "outline my answers to questions during an essay test" ($r = .117$); and 304, "approach the exam with confidence" ($r = .099$). The more frequently the TU learners turned to these test-taking strategies during English exams, the higher they achieved in the exams.

In addition, among these 22 test-taking strategy items, the majority belonged to the metacognitive (9) category, followed by cognitive (7), compensation (2), memory (2), and affective (2) categories. As listed in Table 5.27, most of the metacognitive strategies were related to planning and paying attention; most of the cognitive strategies were concerned with analyzing and creating structure for input and output.

Table 5.28: Correlations between Individual English Test-taking Strategies and TU Students' Performance in English (N = 451)

Items	P
219. Review a lot before English exams (memory).	.096*
220. Keep up my homework and review my notes ... (memory).	.122*
229. Practice writing by modeling good essays before ... (cognitive).	.104*
231. Take good notes as my English teacher tells ... (cognitive).	.098*
235. Use both general and specific information when ... (cognitive).	.113*
237. Analyze the sentence structure before translating ... (cognitive).	.098*
238. Break up run-on sentences into smaller parts to ... (cognitive).	.102*
240. Jot down important ideas that come to mind ... (cognitive).	.120*
241. Highlight some sentences or phrases ... (cognitive).	.112*
242. Exchange with English teachers about ... (compensation).	.100*
248. Use my background knowledge of ... (compensation).	.119*
254. Attend 100% of my English classes (metacognitive).	.111*
259. Pay particular attention to clues that ... (metacognitive).	.109*
264. Gather and organize all the supplies I need ... (metacognitive).	.100*
280. Listen to clues while doing listening ... (metacognitive).	.141**
284. Read questions carefully during an English test (metacognitive).	.123**
288. Outline my answers to questions ... (metacognitive).	.117*
289. Plan and organize my ideas before ... (metacognitive).	.108*
292. Write a topic sentence for each paragraph ... (metacognitive).	.126**
301. List what worked and hold onto those ... (metacognitive).	.098*
303. Breathe deeply to calm down when I became ... (affective).	.132**
304. Approach the exam with confidence (affective).	.099*

Notes: ** = $p < .01$;   * = $p < .05$;   P = performance

5.5 Correlations between measured variables and TU students' performance in English

To explore the relationships among the measured variables and the TU students' performance in English, correlation analyses were conducted. The results are presented in Table 5.29.

Table 5.29: Correlations between Measured Variables and TU Students' Performance in English (N = 438~451)

	ELM	InSM	IntM	ELMS	MS	CogS	CompS	MetaS	AS	SS	ELSI	TMS	TCogS	TCompS	TMetaS	TAS	TSS	ETSI	Performance
CAS	-.30**	-.04	-.17**	-.18**	-.27**	-.24**	-.20**	-.37**	-.27**	-.28**	-.35**	.01	-.13**	-.18**	-.19**	-.16**	-.16**	-.18**	-.08
ELM	1	.01	.10*	.23**	.21**	.28**	.28**	.34**	.24**	.24**	.34**	.02	.23**	.20**	.21**	.19**	.11*	.21**	.23**
InsM		1	.20**	.73**	.10*	.19**	.19**	.15**	.18**	.17**	.19**	.21**	.18**	.18**	.21**	.12*	.15**	.22**	-.02
IntM			1	.80**	.42**	.50**	.15**	.39**	.34**	.34**	.45**	.20**	.20**	.19**	.28**	.22**	.20**	.28**	.05
ELMS				1	.37**	.49**	.26**	.41**	.37**	.37**	.47**	.26**	.28**	.27**	.34**	.24**	.24**	.35**	.06
MS					1	.69**	.42**	.61**	.47**	.44**	.74**	.32**	.33**	.23**	.33**	.24**	.23**	.35**	.08
CogS						1	.52**	.73**	.61**	.59**	.87**	.34**	.47**	.33**	.46**	.30**	.31**	.48**	.08
CompS							1	.53**	.51**	.38**	.65**	.16**	.36**	.30**	.34**	.22**	.22**	.35**	.07
MetaS								1	.75**	.71**	.95**	.39**	.54**	.41**	.57**	.36**	.41**	.58**	.12**
AS									1	.69**	.80**	.43**	.45**	.42**	.50**	.38**	.42**	.54**	.08
SS										1	.75**	.30**	.42**	.36**	.48**	.27**	.45**	.49**	.04
ELSI											1	.40**	.55**	.42**	.57**	.37**	.41**	.59**	.11*
TMS												1	.50**	.35**	.48**	.35**	.34**	.59**	.11*
TCogS													1	.69**	.80**	.54**	.53**	.88**	.17**
TCompS														1	.77**	.51**	.55**	.83**	.13**
TMetaS															1	.61**	.58**	.97**	.13**
TAS																1	.47**	.66**	.12*
TSS																	1	.65**	.03
ETSI																		1	.15**

Notes: **. p < .01; *. p < .05

133

According to Table 5.29, the measured variables were highly correlated with one another and most of them significantly correlated with the TU respondents' performance in English.

The Classroom Anxiety Scale (CAS) was negatively correlated with English Learning Motivation Scale (ELMS) and its three subscales (ELM, InsM and IntM), English Learning Strategy Inventory (ELSI) and its six categories (MS, CogS, CompS, MetaS, AS and SS), English Test-taking Strategy Inventory (ETSI) and its six categories (TMS, TCogS, TCompS, TMetaS, TAS and TSS). All the correlations were statistically significant except those between the CAS and the InsM and TMS. Namely, the more anxious student tended to be less motivated to learn English and use strategies less frequently when learning English and taking English exams.

The ELMS and its three subscales significantly positively correlated with one another except the ELM and the InsM whose relationship was positive but insignificant. The more instrumentally motivated a student was, the more integratively motivated s/he was to learn English. In addition, the ELMS and its subscales were all significantly positively correlated with the ELSI and the ETSI and their subcategories except the correlation between the ELM and the TMS which was positive but insignificant. The more (instrumentally/ integratively) motivated student was generally also the more frequent user of different categories of strategies when learning English and taking English exams.

The ELSI and the ETSI and their subcategories all highly positively correlated with one another. For instance, the more frequent user of cognitive strategies (CogS) tended to use memory, compensation, metacognitive, affective and social strategies more frequently in English learning. S/he also tended to deploy the six categories of test-taking strategies more frequently during English exams.

Finally, these measured variables generally significantly correlated with the TU participants' performance in English. Among these variables, the CAS and the InsM were insignificantly negatively correlated with students' performance in English ($r = -.08$ and $-.02$ respectively); the IntM, the ELMS, MS, CogS, CompS, SS, and the TSS were insignificantly positively related to students' performance in English. All the other measurements significantly positively correlated with the students' performance in English. Namely, the more frequent user of English learning metacognitive strategies and English test-taking strategies tended to achieve higher in English.

5.6 The structural model of the measured variables and performance of the TU sample

The statistical analyses of the data discussed above demonstrate that the data satisfied the statistical assumptions of SEM. In specifying a general model of the relationships between reported degree or use of the measured variables and the students' performance in English for the whole sample, we argued for a one-factor model of classroom anxiety (CAS), a three-factor model of motivation (ELMS), and a six-factor model of English learning and test-taking strategy use respectively, as did with the whole sample.

Of the numerous models tested, the baseline model of the measured variables and performance for the whole sample, presented in Figure 5.1, seemed to fit the data well from both a statistical and substantive perspective. The model produced a CFI of .951, a TLI of .936, a IFI of .951, a RFI of .902, and a NFI of .924, indicating a fairly good representation of the sample data. All parameter estimates in the model were substantively plausible and statistically significant at the .000 level.

As seen from the structural model, classroom anxiety yielded a significant, negative effect (-.80) on the students' performance in English, while motivation (.18), English learning strategy use (.28) and English test-taking strategy use (.07) exerted a significantly positive effect on the latter.

When it comes to the effect of the measured variables on one another, motivation displayed a significant, negative effect on classroom anxiety (-1.57) and English test-taking strategy use (-1.73); classroom anxiety showed a significantly negative effect on English learning strategy use (-1.53) but a significant and positive effect on English test-taking strategy use (.21). Finally, the model reveals that English learning strategy use significantly positively affected English test-taking strategy use (3.50).

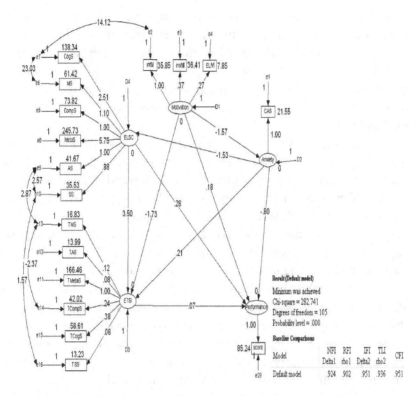

Figure 5.1: TU Group Analysis—Measured Variables and Performance

5.7 Summary

As revealed by the analyses, around a third of the TU students experienced anxiety to different degrees in English language classrooms due to a variety of reasons such as low English proficiency, lack of practice, lack of vocabulary, lack of confidence, lack of preparation, and personality. Though being strongly motivated to learn English for such reasons as going abroad, improving English and pursuing further study, they were only moderately instrumentally and integratively motivated.

Although knowing a little about English learning and test-taking strategies, the TU learners had a medium use of the overall English learning and test-taking strategies. Among the six categories of English learning strategies, the most frequently used were compensation strategies, followed by social, affective, metacognitive, cognitive, and memory strategies. Among the six categories of English test-taking strategies, the

136

most frequently used were metacognitive strategies, followed by affective strategies, compensation, cognitive, social, and memory strategies.

As to gender differences in the measured variables, female TU students reported o be significantly less anxious, more integratively motivated than males in English class., employed cognitive, social and overall strategies significantly more frequently than their male peers in English learning.

In terms of differences in the measured variables among different proficiency groups, the band 1 students had the lowest overall motivation while their band 3 counterparts had the highest overall motivation to learn English, they were the most instrumentally but the least integratively motivated as well; while their band 3 peers were the least instrumentally but the most integratively motivated. The band 1 students also employed cognitive, compensation, metacognitive, social and the overall English learning strategies significantly less frequently than their band 2 and 3 counterparts; and the band 2 group had significantly more frequent use of affective strategies than band 1 and 3 groups. Likewise, the band 1 students deployed cognitive, compensation, affective, social and the overall test-taking strategies significantly less frequently than their band 2 and 3 counterparts, whereas, their band 3 peers employed memory strategies significantly less frequently than band 1 and 2 groups.

Regarding the relationship between the measured variables and the TU students' performance in English, statistical analyses revealed that all the measured variables were highly correlated with one another and most of them significantly correlated with the students' performance in English. Classroom anxiety yielded a significant, negative effect on the students' performance in English, while motivation, English learning and test-taking strategy use exerted a significantly positive effect on the latter. Motivation displayed a significant, negative effect on classroom anxiety and English test-taking strategy use; classroom anxiety showed a significantly negative effect on English learning strategy use but a significantly positive effect on English test-taking strategy use; and English learning strategy use significantly positively affected English test-taking strategy use.

Chapter 6   Results of the BFU Sample

This chapter reports the results of the BFU (Beijing Forestry University) sample. For each measured variable, descriptive analysis and analysis of ANOVA (Duncan's) were conducted. Subsequently, correlation coefficients were computed to determine the associations among the measured variables and performance in English. Finally, SEM was run to further explore these relationships.

6.1 English language classroom anxiety of the BFU sample

6.1.1 General picture of English language classroom anxiety of the BFU sample

6.1.1.1 Item analysis of the CAS of the BFU sample

Table 6.1 summarizes the BFU learners' responses (the first number means the real number and the second percentage) to the CAS (Classroom Anxiety Scale) items. All percentages refer to the number of students who (strongly) disagreed, neither disagreed nor agreed, or (strongly) agreed with the statements (percentages were rounded to the nearest whole number).

Table 6.1: CAS Items with Numbers and Percentages of BFU Students Selecting Each Alternative (N = 327)

SD/D	N	A/SA
1. I don't usually get anxious when I have to respond to a question		
128/39.1	39/11.9	160/48.9
2. I am always afraid that other students would laugh at me if I speak		
246/75.2	38/11.6	43/13.1
3. I always feel that other students are more at ease than I am in		
183/56.0	74/22.6	70/21.4
4. I am never embarrassed to volunteer answers in English class.		
163/49.9	74/22.6	90/27.5
5. I am generally tense whenever participating in English class.		
268/82.0	33/10.1	26/7.9
6. I never understand why other students are so nervous in English class.		

139/42.5　　　　109/33.3　　　　79/24.2

7. I usually feel relaxed and confident when active participation takes ….
　127/38.8　　　　80/24.4　　　　120/36.7

8. Whenever I have to answer a question, out loud, I get nervous and ….
　199/60.9　　　　61/18.6　　　　67/20.4

Notes: SD → Strongly disagree;　　　D → Disagree

N → Neither disagree nor agree;　A → Agree;　　SA → Strongly agree

As seen from Table 6.1, like their TU peers, more than 60% of the BFU students vetoed statements implicative of speech anxiety such as "whenever I have to answer a question, out loud, I get nervous and confused in English class" (item 8) (60.9%); "I am always afraid that other students would laugh at me if I speak up in English class" (item 2) (75.2%); "I am generally tense whenever participating in English class" (item 5) (82.0%). Moreover, 56.0% of the BFU participants always felt "other students are more at ease than I am in English class" (item 3). It is clear most BFU students did not feel anxious when speaking English in class, they might even feel confidant and relaxed. Surprisingly, more than a third of them (strongly) disagreed with CAS items expressing confidence when speaking English in class such as "I usually feel relaxed and confident when active participation takes place in English class" (item 7) (38.8%); "I don't usually get anxious when I have to respond to a question in English class" (item 1) (39.1%); "I never understand why other students are so nervous in English class" (item 6) (42.5%); and "I am never embarrassed to volunteer answers in English class" (item 4) (49.9%). This suggests at least a third of the BFU respondents experienced anxiety to different degrees in English language classrooms, as did their TU counterparts. They were also afraid to speak or became anxious when speaking English in class.

This finding is generally consistent with the result of the journal data. Of 37 journal participants, 21 reported that they were anxious in English class. The reasons were: poor (spoken) English, not understanding the teacher, not listening clearly, lack of vocabulary, poor pronunciation, fear of being asked, fear of being laughed at, personality, lack of practice, and lack of confidence, with low English proficiency being identified by most of the participants.

6.1.1.2 General tendency of the CAS of the BFU sample

In order to know the general tendency of the BFU correspondents' anxiety in English class, the total score, mean, standard deviation, median, mode, maximum and minimum of the CAS were computed (please refer to section 4.1.1.2 for the computing and interpreting scheme). The results are shown in Table 6.2.

Table 6.2: Statistical Analyses of the CAS of BFU Students

	Mean	Standard Deviation	Median	Mode	Range
Male (116)	21.59	5.31	22.00	20.00	36.00-10.00
Female (211)	21.45	4.69	22.00	22.00	33.00-9.00
Total (327)	21.50	4.91	22.00	22.00	36.00-9.00

As can be seen in Table 6.2, a mean score of 21.50, a median of 22.00 and a mode of 22.00 on the CAS, all below the average score of 24.00, suggest only around a third of the BFU students felt anxious in English class while the majority were relaxed. This finding is consistent with the results of frequency analysis of CAS items and the mean scores of CAS items of TU students presented in Appendix II.

Moreover, Table 6.2 indicates female students with a mean of 21.45 reported to be less anxious than males with a mean of 21.59 in English class. But the difference was statistically insignificant, as proved by the Independent-samples t Test result: $t = .239$, $p = .811$.

6.1.2 Causes for and consequences of language classroom anxiety of the BFU sample

Surprisingly, analyses of the journal data revealed that the majority of the students felt (a little) anxious in English class. Among 37 BFU journal participants, 31 reported feeling anxious in English classrooms, only 5 thought they didn't feel nervous or anxious. The reasons varied from person to person. The results are presented in Table 6.3.

Table 6.3: Student Anxiety Reported in Journals (BFU) (N = 327)

Anxiety	Reasons
Yes (31)	Poor English proficiency (16/51.6%)
	Lack of practice of oral English (13/41.9%)
	Lack of vocabulary (10/32.2%)
	Being not able to understand what is said/the teacher (9/29%)
	Being afraid of being laughed at (5/16%)
	Being not confident (5/16%)
	Being not able to listen clearly (4/12.9%)
	Being not good at speaking/Poor spoken English (4/12.9%)
	Personality (4/12.9%)

	Poor/bad pronunciation (3/10%)
	Teachers always speaking English in the whole class (1/3.2%)
	Being afraid of being asked (1/3.2%)
	Coming from a small city (1/3.2%)
	Having not finished homework (1/3.2%)
No (5)	Enjoying/Liking English (3/60%)
	Good teacher (2/40%)
	Good teaching method (2/40%)
	Class being interesting (2/40%)
	Having not much stress (1/20%)
	Being able to get the meaning (1/20%)
	Relaxing classroom environment (1/20%)
	The teacher being humorous (1/20%)
	Classroom being the right place to speak out and communicate with others (1/20%)
	Being not bad at English (1/20%)
	Outgoing personality (1/20%)

Apparently, a multitude of factors contributed to the BFU students' anxiety in English class, such as poor English proficiency, lack of vocabulary, lack of practice, lack of confidence, and being unable to understand what was heard. As shown in Table 6.3, the majority of the 31 anxious students attributed their anxiety to poor English proficiency (51.6%), followed by lack of practice (41.9%), lack of vocabulary (32.2%), being unable to understand what was said/the teacher (29%), being afraid of being laughed at (16%), and lack of confidence (16%). Some students also became nervous if they had not finished the homework, or just because they feared being asked to answer questions or speak out opinions. Some students came from a small city, where there was little opportunity to speak English. This also drove them anxious, especially when speaking the target language, in English class.

Contrarily, liking English (60%), being able to get the meaning (1/20%), being not bad at English (1/20%), and outgoing personality (1/20%) empowered the five students not to feel anxious in English class. Their little/no anxiety was also attributed to their good teacher (40%), good teaching method (40%), interesting class (40%). Meanwhile, having not much stress (10%) and a relaxing classroom environment (10%) also enabled them to feel easy in English class. Some students didn't feel anxious just because they believed classroom to be the right place to speak out and communicate with others.

Since so many students felt anxious in English class, would anxiety negatively affect their performance in English? When asked if so, 32 of the 37 participants reported that anxiety exerted a negative effect on them, 2 regarded anxiety as a facilitator, 2 believed anxiety had no effect, and 1 didn't give any comment, as shown in Table 6.4.

Table 6.4: Impact of Anxiety on BFU Students' Learning of English
(N = 327) (Source: journal)

Impact of anxiety	Reasons
Good (2)	Making me study harder/learn better
Bad (32)	Making me afraid of /dare not to speak English and my spoken English in turn becomes poorer (21/65.6%) Preventing me speaking fluently (5/15.6%) Making me feel blind-minded when speaking (5/15.6%) Being nervous made me unable to listen clearly or understand precisely (4/12.5%) Making me feel discouraged/frightened and give up English learning (3/9.4%) Discouraging me (3/9.4%) Making me unable to listen clearly and miss important points (3/9.4%) Making it difficult to express myself (well) (3/9.4%) Making me lose interest in English (2/6.3%) Making me feel inferior to others (1/3.1%) Making me unable to read fluently (1/3.1%) Making me unable to answer questions, thus I feel ashamed and afraid to speak English in class (1/3.1%) Making me unable to understand simple words (1/3.1%) Making me forget what I want to say (1/3.1%) Making me only dare read and talk when left alone (1/3.1%) Making me study more slowly (1/3.1%) Making me shier and shier and unable to communicate with others smoothly (1/3.1%) Making me not confident (1/3.1%)
No (2)	Enjoying English
Not mentioned (1)	

As seen from Table 6.4, two students regarded anxiety as something good because it urged them to study/learn better; two students didn't think anxiety had any effect on them because they enjoyed learning English.

Nevertheless, to those who believed anxiety to be debilitating to their learning of English, they suffered much from anxiety. To most of them (65.6%), anxiety made them afraid of speaking English or dare not speak the language and thus their spoken English in turn became poorer. As a student reported, "because of anxiety, my voice becomes strange and I feel embarrassed and speak less. So my spoken English gets poorer". Anxiety also either prevented 15.6% of them from speaking fluently or made them (12.5%) unable to listen clearly or understand precisely. Because of anxiety, 15.6% of the participants became blind-minded when speaking the target language in class, 9.4% felt discouraged or frightened and then even gave up learning English, 6.3% lost interest in English. Meanwhile, some students studied more slowly or became diffident, and so on, due to anxiety.

Although anxiety negatively affected their learning of English, 93% the journal participants admitted that they just let it be rather than be proactive. They hoped that anxiety would gradually decrease or even disappear as they had more access to English and more opportunities to use the language. Only a few students reflected that they sometimes breathed deeply or encouraged themselves by saying that "you are good, you can do it". Meanwhile, these students offered several suggestions for other learners and hoped English teachers could take some measures to help them overcome anxiety, as summarized in Table 6.5.

Table 6.5: BFU Students' Suggestions to Cope with Anxiety for Language Learners and Teachers (Source: journal)

Suggestions for language learners	Practice more (e.g., listen to English songs, watch E movies, talk with others in English, take part in English corner).
	Do not give up.
	Recite useful sentences and paragraphs.
	Be confident and relaxed, don't be shy.
	Don't worry and work hard.
	Do not laugh at others.
	Prepare well.
	Have passion.
	Spend more time on it.
	Believe yourself.
	Read English novels.
	Take part in psychological lessons.
	Read more and loudly.
	Be brave.
	Expand the vocabulary.
	Improve oral English.

	Don't be afraid of making mistakes.
	Communicate with the teachers.
Suggestions for language teachers	Make class funny and interesting.
	Encourage students and help them.
	Help students to pronounce correctly.
	Ask students to read more, write more and speak more.
	Give more chances for students to use or speak English.
	Organize more activities in class.
	Teach useful things.
	Communicate with/ pay more attention to shy students.
	Have patience and love for students.
	Make simple conversations in class.
	Cancel exams.
	Be humorous.
	Speak slowly.
	Use Chinese sometimes.
	Be friends with students.
	Solve the problem together with students.
	Ask students to answer questions frequently in class.
	Make students feel confident.
	Play games in class.
	Correct students' mistakes.
	Introduce new ways of study.
	Smile more.

As noted from Table 6.5, in order to reduce or overcome anxiety, these BFU participants suggest language learners do the following: practice more by listening to English songs, watching English movies, and talking to others in English, recite useful sentences and paragraphs, be confident, relaxed and brave, do not laugh at others, prepare well, don't be afraid of making mistakes, and work harder to improve English.

At the same time, they hoped language teachers to help them become less anxious by doing such things as making the class funny and interesting, encouraging students and giving them suggestions, asking students to do more practice, communicating with or paying more attention to shy students, speaking slowly, and smiling more in class. Some students believed that a humorous teacher could help students become less nervous; and using Chinese sometimes in class could also be helpful.

6.2 English learning motivation of the BFU sample

6.2.1 Item analysis of the ELMS of the BFU sample

Table 6.6 sums up the BFU students' responses to the ELMS (English Learning Motivation Scale) items, in the same way as the presentation of their responses to CAS items.

Table 6.6: ELMS Items with Numbers and
Percentages of BFU Students Selecting Each Alternative (N = 327)

SD/D	N	A/SA
9. Honestly, I don't know whether I am motivated to learn English.		
214/65.4	46/14.1	67/20.5
10. I have the impression that I am wasting my time in studying English.		
256/78.3	19/5.8	52/15.9
11. I study English in order to get a good job later on.		
96/29.4	52/15.9	179/54.7
12. I study English in order to earn more money later on.		
114/34.9	63/19.3	150/45.9
13. I study English for higher education later on.		
55/16.8	54/16.5	218/66.6
14. I study English in order to go abroad later on.		
67/20.5	55/16.8	205/62.7
15. I study English because I think it is important for my future work.		
49/15.0	40/12.2	238/72.8
16. I study English because I want to get high marks in English exams.		
116/35.5	58/17.7	153/46.8
17. I study English because it is required with credits at my university.		
125/38.2	41/12.5	161/49.3
18. I study English because I want to have different kinds ….		
157/48.0	70/21.4	100/30.6
19. … I have to pass English exams; otherwise, I would not learn it.		
248/75.8	41/12.5	38/11.7
20. I study English because I am good at English listening, speaking, ….		
145/44.3	79/24.2	103/31.5
21. I study English because I want to improve my English abilities in ….		
61/18.7	38/11.6	228/69.7
22. I study English because I would feel guilty if I didn't know English.		
184/56.3	53/16.2	90/27.5

145

23. I study English because I would feel ashamed if I couldn't speak to ....
    149/45.6   70/21.4   108/33.0
24. ... I think it is important for my personal development.
    28/8.6   21/6.4   278/85.0
25. ... I choose to be the kind of person who can speak more ....
    56/17.1   46/14.1   225/68.8
26. ... I choose to be the kind of person who can speak English.
    56/17.1   55/16.8   216/66.1
27. I study English for the satisfied feeling I get in finding out new things.
    83/25.4   82/25.1   162/49.5
28. I study English for the pleasure that I experience in knowing more ....
    99/30.3   101/30.9   127/38.9
29. I study English because I enjoy the feeling of learning about ....
    115/35.2   89/27.2   123/37.6
30. I study English for the enjoyment I experience when I ....
    127/38.8   107/32.7   93/18.5
31. ... satisfaction I feel when I am doing difficult exercises in English.
    170/52.0   71/21.7   86/26.3
32. I study English for the good feeling I get when I do better ....
    93/28.4   84/25.7   150/45.9
33. I study English for the excitement that I get while speaking English.
    150/45.9   80/24.5   97/29.7
34. I study English for the excitement I feel when I hear someone ....
    173/52.9   82/25.1   72/21.0

Notes: SD → Strongly disagree;   D → Disagree
N → Neither disagree nor agree;   A → Agree;   SA → Strongly agree

According to Table 6.6, more than 60% of the BFU respondents disagreed with ELMS items expressing little English learning motivation: "Honestly, I don't know whether I am motivated to learn English (item 9)" (65.4%) and "I have the impression that I am wasting my time in studying English (item 10)" (78.3%). This implies the BFU participants were motivated to learn English and considered it worthwhile to learn the language.

According to Table 6.6, most BFU students were highly instrumentally motivated to learn English. Some of the instrumental reasons highly popular among the BFU students were: earning more money (item 12) (45.9); getting a good job in the future (item 11) (54.7); going abroad (item 14) (62.7%); higher education (item 13) (66.6%); improving English abilities in four basic skills (item 21) (69.7%); future career (item 15) (72.8%); and personal development (item 24) (85.0%), as found in Liu's (2005) study. Like their TU peers, more than 70% of them denied learning English to pass exams, as shown by their responses to item 19 (75.8%).

Students' responses to items 22-34 reported in Table 6.6 indicate they were also integratively motivated to learn English. The reasons also varied, but the most popular ones were: the good feeling of learning about English-speaking people and their way of life (item 29) (37.6%) and of doing better than expected (item 32) (45.9); the satisfaction of finding out new things (item 27) (49.5%); choosing to speak English (item 26) (66.1%) and more than one language (item 25) (68.8%). Meanwhile, they rejected such integrative reasons as excitement of speaking English (item 33) (45.9%) and hearing someone speaking English (item 34) (52.9%); feeling guilty (item 22) (56.3%); and satisfaction of doing difficult exercises in English (item 31) (52.0%). It seems that the BFU students' integrative motivation was more concerned with their school performance than their liking for English, as proved by the mean scores of ELMS items presented in Appendix II.

This finding, again, conforms to the results of the journal data. Of 37 journal participants, 36 reported to be motivated to learn English in university because of a range of reasons, as shown in Table 6.7.

Table 6.7: Reasons for BFU Students' Motivation to Learn English
(Source: Journal)

To find a better/good job (27/75%)	To enjoy the new learning environment (1/2.8%)
To go abroad (13/36.1%)	
To pass CET band 4 (4/11.1%)	To learn more for graduation (1/2.8%)
Being interested in English (4/11.1%)	To see English movies (1/2.8%)
To communicate with foreigners (4/11.1%)	To play computer games (1/2.8%)
	To improve English (1/2.8%)
To become graduate students (4/11.1%)	To do something for the Olympic Games 2008 (1/2.8%)
English being a requirement for computer majors (2/5.6%)	College English being more interesting (1/2.8%)
To listen to English (1/2.8%)	Being envious of those who can speak
To speak good English (1/2.8%)	English smoothly (1/2.8%)
To understand the difference between	English being very important/useful (1/2.8%)
dreams and reality (1/2.8%)	English being helpful in understanding

For a beautiful future (1/2.8%)	foreigners (1/2.8%)
American movies being funny (1/2.8%)	English being important for learning foreign knowledge and customs, etc. (1/2.8%)
Teachers being interesting and not stiff (1/2.8%)	English being funny (1/2.8%)
Realizing what has been learned is limited (1/2.8%)	English being an important tool in work (1/2.8%)

Among these motivational reasons, to find a better/good job was identified by 27 (75%) of the participants, followed by to go abroad (13/36.1%), to pass CET band 4 (4/11.1%), being interested in it (4/11.1%), to communicate with foreigners (4/11.1%), and to become graduate students (3/8.3%). Other reasons were very varying, ranging from American movies being funny, to realizing what has been learned was limited, to being envious of those who could speak English smoothly, to English being important for learning foreign knowledge and customs, to English being funny. Nevertheless, it is obvious that the learning of English was closely related to the BFU respondents' personal needs for a better future.

Unexpectedly, the student self-reported to have no motivation to learn English just because there were "so many new words and hard texts" (Qiao, male).

6.2.2 General tendency of the ELMS of the BFU sample

In order to know the general tendency of the BFU students' English learning motivation, the total score, mean, and standard deviation of the ELMS and its three subscales were computed, as done in section 4.2.1.3 (please refer to section 4.2.1.3 for the computing and interpreting scheme). The results are presented in Table 6.8.

Table 6.8: Statistical Analyses of the ELMS and its Subscales of BFU Students

		Mean	Standard Deviation	Median	Mode	Range
ELMS	M (116)	81.77	11.52	81.00	75.00	56.00-117.00
	F (211)	83.78	11.36	83.00	75.00	50.00-122.00
	T (327)	83.07	11.44	82.00	75.00	50.00-122.00
ELM	M (116)	7.32	2.04	8.00	8.00	2.00-10.00
	F (211)	7.86	1.74	8.00	10.00	2.00-10.00
	T (327)	7.67	1.86	8.00	8.00	2.00-10.00
InsM	M (116)	39.10	5.94	38.50	38.00	16.00-54.00

	F (211)	38.82	5.92	39.00	37.00	23.00-55.00
	T (327)	38.92	5.92	39.00	37.00	16.00-55.00
IntM	M (116)	35.34	7.25	35.00	33.00	16.00-53.00
	F (211)	37.10	7.13	37.00	36.00	20.00-59.00
	T (327)	36.48	7.21	36.00	36.00	16.00-59.00

Notes: M = male; F = female;   T = total

As seen from Table 6.8, like their TU peers, the majority of the BFU learners were (highly) motivated to learn English, as supported by their ELMS mean (83.07), median (82.00) and mode (75.00) which were generally much more than the average 78.00. In addition, a mean of 7.67, a median and a mode of 8.00 on the ELM indicate the majority had moderate or strong motivation to learn English. Likewise, a mean of 38.92, a median of 39.00 and a mode of 37.00 on the InsM, all above the average 36.00, are indicative of moderate or even strong instrumental motivation. Meanwhile, these students seemed to be only moderately integratively motivated as well, as implied by their IntM mean (36.48), median (36.00) and mode (36.00).

Moreover, according to Table 6.8, the BFU participants reported to be more instrumentally than integratively motivated to learn English. And the difference was statistically significant, as proved by the results of paired samples t Test: $t = 5.87$, $p = .000$. This is further confirmed by the reported reasons for motivation to learn English presented in Table 6.7.

Furthermore, as reported in Table 6.8, girl students seemed to be more integratively while less instrumentally motivated to learn English than their male peers; and their motivation was stronger as well. But the differences were generally statistically insignificant except in IntM, as proved by the results of Independent-samples t Tests reported in Table 6.9. Namely, girl students were only significantly more integratively motivated to learn English than were their male peers.

**Table 6.9: Independent-samples t Test Results
for Gender Differences in ELMS and its Subscales** (BFU)

	ELM	InsM	IntM	ELMS
t	-.2.55	.41	-2.12	-1.53
p	.011	.679	.035	.128
t*	2.576	2.576	1.96	1.96

Note: t* → Critical t values at .01 and .05 levels respectively (Black, 1999).

6.3 English learning strategy use by the BFU sample

6.3.1 Broad profile of English learning strategy use by the BFU sample

Analysis of the journal data revealed that the BFU participants knew little about English learning strategies except for the following: memorizing words and grammar, reciting texts, doing exercise, listening to English, writing some articles, making a plan, practicing speaking, and managing time. This knowledge, according to them, mainly came from their English teachers, senior students and their own learning experience. Even so, they reported to have a medium use of various specific strategies listed in the survey, as detailed below. They (31/83.8%) also generally believed that using learning strategies was conducive to their learning of English. They reflected that using learning strategies enhanced their English proficiency, enabled them to study English effectively and even begin to love English. They also avoided wasting time on useless work and had a clear aim when doing exercises with the help of learning strategies.

Based on BFU mean scores of English Learning Strategy Inventory (ELSI) items reported in Appendix II, items in different use ranges were summarized and shown in Table 6.10 (please refer to section 4.3.3 for the analyzing key). Among the 184 ELSI items, 51 items fell in the high use range, 120 in the medium use range and 13 in the low use range. That is, more than 60% of the strategies were sometimes used; around a third of them were usually or always used; only a few were usually not used or even not used. Thus, it is clear that all the strategies were employed by the students to different degrees and the majority were sometimes or more often used. The case was the same with each of the six strategy categories, as presented in Table 6.10. A review of the ELSI mean scores summarized in Appendix II further reveals that mean scores for high use strategies never exceeded 4.00 and those for low use strategies seldom fell below 2.00. Alternatively, those high use strategies were just usually but not always used; while those low use strategies were just usually not used and few of them were never or almost never used.

Table 6.10: Number of English Learning Strategy Items in Different Use Ranges (BFU)

English Learning Strategy categories	High use	Medium use	Low use
Memory Strategy (MS)	2	16	2
Cognitive Strategy (CogS)	6	36	2
Compensation Strategy (ComS)	13	7	1
Metacognitive Strategy (MetaS)	21	48	6

Affective Strategy (AS)	4	8	1
Social Strategy (SS)	5	5	1
English Learning Strategy Inventory (ELSI)	51	120	13

As seen from Table 6.11, the mean of overall strategy use was 3.20 on the 5-point Likert scale, which represents "medium" strategy use (sometimes used) towards the upper end. Namely, the BFU students had quite frequent use of various strategies in English learning, consistent with the analyses of mean scores of different strategy items.

The mean scores for all the six categories of strategies also fell in the medium-use range. Among the six categories, the most frequently used were compensation strategies with a mean of 3.49, followed by social (mean = 3.25), affective (mean = 3.23), and metacognitive (mean = 3.20) strategies. Next came cognitive (3.13) and memory (mean = 3.00) strategies. It seems that the BFU students preferred to guess by using linguistic/background knowledge, seek help and self-encourage to overcome difficulties or obstacles in English learning.

Table 6.11: Means and Standard Deviations
Indicating English Learning Strategy Use (BFU) (N = 327)

Strategy category (most used to least used)	Frequency of strategy use	
	Mean/range	Standard deviation
Compensation	3.49 (high use; low end)	.40
Social	3.25 (medium use; upper end)	.45
Affective	3.23 (medium use; upper end)	.42
Metacognitive	3.20 (medium use; upper end)	.37
Cognitive	3.13 (medium use; upper end)	.36
Memory	3.00 (medium use)	.42
ELSI	3.20 (medium use; upper end)	.32

6.3.2 The most and least used individual learning strategies by the BFU sample

As did in sections 4.4.2 and 5.4.2, twenty strategies most frequently used by BFU undergraduates were identified, as shown in Table 6.12.

Of twenty most often used strategy items, all were in the high-use range with a mean range of 3.70 to 3.91. Most of these highly frequently used strategies fell into compensation (10) and metacognitive (6) categories; a few belonged to cognitive (2), affective (1), memory (1) and Social (1) categories. Like their TU counterparts, the BFU learners would also usually use contextual clues to "understand unfamiliar English words" (mean = 3.91) and "make guesses about English reading" (mean = 3.80); use background knowledge to make guesses when "reading in English" (mean = 3.72) and "listening to English" (mean = 3.70); make guesses "on word formation to understand unfamiliar English words" (mean = 3.72), and "about the speaker's intention according to his/her tone, intonation and pause" (mean = 3.70). They also "use visual aids to better understand English movies" (mean = 3.91); "use words or phrases similar in meaning as substitutes" (mean = 3.90); and "use simple English words, expressions and sentence structures as substitutes" (mean = 3.86). In addition, they "look up frequently occurring words in dictionary" (mean = 3.80), and "read English without looking up every new word" (mean = 3.73). Moreover, they tried to "link it with already known knowledge when reading or listening to English (mean = 3.77) and "link the topic with known knowledge when speaking/writing in English (3.74). When writing in English, these BFU learners tried to "make it coherent" (mean = 3.82); "keep to the main idea" (mean = 3.77); and "make as few grammatical mistakes as possible" (mean = 3.76). When reading in English, they would "highlight certain phrases or sentences" (mean = 3.73) and "try to predict the content according to the title" (mean = 3.70). When not doing well in English exams they "self-encourage not to lose heart" (mean = 3.86).

In conclusion, the BFU correspondents would use certain strategies fairly highly to help better their English learning. When utilizing compensation strategies, they would make guesses by using context clues, background and linguistic knowledge to overcome/reduce difficulty in English learning. When employing metacognitive strategies, they mainly relied on the strategy of centering one's learning by overviewing and linking with already known material and paying attention especially when writing in English. As did their TU peers, these BFU learners seldom deployed affective, memory and social strategies very frequently. The reasons might be the same, as explained in section 5.4.2.

Table 6.12: The Twenty Most Frequently and Twenty Least Used English Learning Strategies (BFU) (N = 327)

The twenty most frequently used English learning strategies				
No.	Strategy	Mean	Category in which this strategy is classified	Comment
100	Make guesses based on	3.91	Compensation	H
108	Use visual aids to help better	3.91	Compensation	H
119	Use a word or phrase that means	3.90	Compensation	H
117	Use simple words, expressions	3.86	Compensation	H
198	Self-encourage not to lose heart	3.86	Affective	H

135	Try to make it coherent when	3.82	Metacognitive	H
104	Use contextual clues to make	3.80	Compensation	H
127	Look up frequently occurring	3.80	Metacognitive	H
120	Often try to link it with known	3.77	Metacognitive	H
136	Keep to the main idea when	3.77	Metacognitive	H
134	Try to make as few grammatical	3.76	Metacognitive	H
121	Often try to link the topic with	3.74	Metacognitive	H
48	Remember a new English word	3.73	Memory	H
77	Read English without looking up	3.73	Cognitive	H
98	Highlight certain phrases or	3.73	Cognitive	H
99	Make guesses based on word	3.72	Compensation	H
105	Use background knowledge to	3.72	Compensation	H
209	Ask the other person to slow	3.72	Social	H
106	Use background knowledge to	3.70	Compensation	H
107	Make guesses about the speaker's	3.70	Compensation	H
109	Try to predict the content	3.70	Compensation	H
The Twenty least frequently used English learning strategies				
No.	Strategy	Mean	Category in which this strategy is classified	Comment
160	Try to write diaries and/or	1.88	Metacognitive	L
51	Physically act out new English	2.20	Memory	L
78	Often read the transcript	2.26	Cognitive	L
89	Often pay attention to the	2.30	Cognitive	L
168	Initiate to make friends	2.33	Metacognitive	L
169	Initiate to talk to teachers in English.	2.33	Metacognitive	L
206	Write down my feelings in	2.34	Affective	L
52	Use flashcards to remember	2.36	Memory	L
171	Actively take part in various	2.38	Metacognitive	L
118	Make up new words when not ...	2.40	Compensation	L
167	Initiate to greet and converse	2.42	Metacognitive	L
170	Often participate in various	2.45	Metacognitive	L
217	Just care for what I need to say	2.46	Social	L
159	Write emails and/or letter in	2.50	Metacognitive	M
176	Often search for various	2.50	Metacognitive	M
205	Often use a checklist to note	2.52	Affective	M
54	Often recite English essays.	2.53	Memory	M
164	Try to voluntarily seek chances	2.53	Metacognitive	M
178	Often surf various English	2.54	Metacognitive	M
61	Often do really a lot of	2.56	Cognitive	M
79	Read the transcript while	2.56	Cognitive	M

Among the twenty least often used strategies, 13 were in the low-use range at the upper end with a mean range from 1.88 to 2.46; 7 fell in the medium-use range at the low end with means ranging from 2.50 to 2.56, as seen from Table 6.12. For example, "try to write diaries and/or journals in English" (mean = 1.88); "physically act out new English words" (mean = 2.20); "often read the transcript before listening to English" (mean = 2.26); "write down my feelings in language learning diaries" (mean = 2.34); "use flashcards to remember new English words" (mean = 2.36); "actively take part in various English contests" (mean = 2.38); and "make up new words when not knowing the right ones in English" (mean = 2.40).

6.3.3 BFU Gender differences in English learning strategy use

According to Table 6.13, male and female students scored 3.22 and 3.19 on the 5-point Likert ELSI respectively, which suggests medium use of the strategies. They also had a medium or even high use of the six categories of strategies (means ranging from 3.04 to 3.42 and from 2.98 to 3.52 for males and females respectively). Moreover, BFU male students reported to use only compensation strategies less frequently but all the other five categories of strategies more often than their female peers when learning English. However, significant difference was found only in the use of compensation strategies, as revealed by the results of Independent-samples t-tests presented in Table 6.13. It is thus clear that BFU females utilized compensation strategies significantly more frequently than their male peers in English learning.

Table 6.13: BFU Gender Differences in English Learning Strategy Use (N = 327)

		Mean	Standard Deviation	t-test results		
				t	p	t*
MS	M (116)	3.04	.45	1.16	.247	2.326
	F (211)	2.98	.40			
CogS	M (116)	3.17	.40	1.62	.106	2.326
	F (211)	3.10	.34			
CompS	M (116)	3.42	.45	-2.36	.019	2.326
	F (211)	3.52	.37			
MetaS	M (116)	3.23	.39	1.02	.308	2.326
	F (211)	3.18	.36			
AS	M (116)	3.27	.44	1.34	.181	2.326
	F (211)	3.21	.41			
SS	M (116)	3.27	.51	.62	.534	2.326
	F (211)	3.24	.42			
ELSI	M (116)	3.22	.35	.93	.355	2.326
	F (211)	3.19	.30			

Notes: M = male; F = female

t* → Critical t value at .02 level (Black, 1999).

6.3.4 Correlations between individual English learning strategies and BFU students' Performance in English

Correlation analyses revealed 53 English learning strategy items significantly correlated with students' performance in English with coefficients ranging from -.194 to .226, as shown in Table 6.14.

Table 6.13: Correlations between Individual English learning Strategies and BFU Students' Performance in English (N = 327)

Items	P
35. Remember English words by grouping them together … (memory).	.129*
36. Remember English words according to pronunciation … (memory).	.141*
38. Think of relationships between what I already know and … (memory).	.126*
39. Associate it with those I already know when learning … (memory).	.114*
43. Connect the sound of a new English word and an image …. (memory).	.136*
45. Remember a new English word by making a … (memory).	.165**
49. Often review what I have learned in English (memory).	.144*
58. Practice the sounds of English (cognitive).	.146**
63. Often practice reading English aloud (cognitive).	.157**
64. Often find out and deduce grammatical rules myself when (cognitive).	.120*
69. Read for pleasure in English (cognitive).	.141*
77. Read English without looking up every new word (cognitive).	.114*
78. Often read the transcript before listening to English (cognitive).	-.149**
79. Read the transcript while listening to English (cognitive).	-.124*
81. Just pay attention to the meaning related to what … (cognitive).	-.120*
82. Often remember English grammatical rules based on … (cognitive).	.194**
83. Try to deduce the author's opinion and implied … (cognitive).	.123*
85. Often learn English grammar with reference to texts (cognitive).	.147**
91.Often translate what I learn in English into Chinese (cognitive).	-.166**
92. Try not to translate word-for-word when learning English (cognitive).	.127*
97. Make summaries of information that I hear or … (cognitive).	.116*
100. Make guesses based on contextual clues to … (compensation).	.126*
104. Use contextual clues to make guesses about …. (compensation).	.173**
105. Use background knowledge to make guesses …. (compensation).	.141*
106. Use background knowledge to make guesses …. (compensation).	.136*
110. Try to guess what the other person will say next … (compensation).	.135*
114. Give it up if not understanding what is heard and … (compensation).	-.114*
115. Often try to avoid using English (compensation).	-.194**
119. Use a word or phrase similar in meaning … (compensation).	.122*
120. Often try to link it with already known … (metacognitive).	.113*
121. Often try to link the topic with already known … (metacognitive).	.152**

155

124. Not look it up in a dictionary when coming … (metacognitive).	.130*
126. Definitely not use words learned long time ago … (metacognitive).	.129*
133. Try to use a variety of words when writing … (metacognitive).	.191**
134. Try to make as few grammatical mistakes … (metacognitive).	.226**
135. Try to make it coherent when writing in English (metacognitive).	.207**
140. Often focus on listening first and start to … (metacognitive).	.206**
141. Try to find out how to be a better learner of English (metacognitive).	.210**
157. Try to write notes and book reports in English (metacognitive).	.124*
162. Try to find as many ways as possible to use English (metacognitive).	.121*
163. Murmur the answer to myself when the English … (metacognitive).	.140*
165. Often speak English to myself (metacognitive).	.153**
173. Pay attention to the English used in various … (metacognitive).	.142*
183. Think about how to say things better after … (metacognitive).	.187**
190. Pay attention to the feedback given by the … (metacognitive).	.117*
191. Repeatedly read and revise it after completing … (metacognitive).	.163**
192. Check spelling and grammatical mistakes … (metacognitive).	.141*
194. Often self-test on English materials (metacognitive).	.137*
198. Self-encourage not to lose heart when not doing … (affective).	.132*
200. Often purposefully take chances to speak English … (affective).	.158**
202. Often purposefully make guesses when listening … (affective).	.138*
209. Ask the other person to slow down or repeat if not … (social).	.159**
210. Ask for clarification if not understanding … (social).	.156**

Notes: ** = p < .01;   * = p < .05;   P = performance

As noted in Table 6.14, four cognitive and two compensation strategies had a significant negative relationship with students' performance in English: strategy 78, "often read the transcript before listening to English" ($r = -.149$); 79, "read the transcript while listening to English" ($r = -.124$); 81, "just pay attention to the meaning related to what I am reading when looking up an English word in dictionary" ($r = -.120$); 91, "often translate what I learn in English into Chinese" ($r = -.166$); 114, "give it up if not understanding what is heard and just listen to the English that I can understand" ($r = -.114$); and 115, "often try to avoid using English" ($r = -.195$). The more frequently the BFU students used these strategies when learning English, the less proficient they were in English.

All the other strategies were positively related to the BFU students' performance in English. For example, strategy 49, "often review what I have learned in English" ($r = -.144$); 82, "often remember English grammatical rules based on understanding rather than rote memory" ($r = -.194$); 104, "use contextual clues to make guesses about what I have read in English" ($r = -.173$); 133, "try to use a variety of words when writing in

English" ($r = -.191$); 198, "self-encourage not to lose heart when not doing well in English exams" ($r = -.132$); and 210, "ask for clarification if not understanding something in English" ($r = -.156$). The more frequently the BFU respondents utilized these strategies in English learning, the more proficient they were in English. Moreover, among these strategies, the majority belonged to the metacognitive (19) category, followed by cognitive (14), compensation (8), memory (7), affective (3) and social (2) categories, which was probably due to the actual number of items included in each category.

As noted from Table 6.14, most of the metacognitive strategies were related to evaluating learning and seeking practice opportunities; most of the cognitive strategies were concerned with analyzing and reasoning. If a strategy was positively or actively used, it seemed to be positively correlated with students' test performance, otherwise, the relationship was negative.

6.4 English test-taking strategy use by the BFU sample

6.4.1 Broad profile of English test-taking strategy use by the BFU sample

Compared with their conscious knowledge of English learning strategies, the BFU participants seemed to know more about test-taking strategies and generally believed to be helpful, as evidenced by the analysis of their journal data. To deal with an English exam more effectively, they would memorize words and phrases, review notes, texts and mistakes, and do some simulated exam papers before the exam. During the exam, they would breathe deeply or close eyes or look out of window to stay calm, and tell themselves to 'believe yourself' to remain confident. When dealing with the test items, they would read first and then scan, do the easy first (from easy to difficult), arrange the time properly, and concentrate on the exam. After the exam, more than a third would review their performance in it to better their performance in future exams. All these were generally consistent with the survey results, as discussed below.

Based on BFU mean scores of English Test-taking Strategy Inventory (ETSI) items summarized in Appendix II, items in different use ranges were summarized and presented in Table 6.15 (please refer to section 4.3.3 for the analyzing key). Among the 91 ETSI items, 41 items were in the high use range, 47 in the medium use range and 3 in the low use range. The majority of the strategies were sometimes or usually/always used; only three were usually not used or even not used. It was the same with each of the six strategy categories. A review of the ETSI mean scores reported in Appendix II further indicates that mean scores for high use strategies rarely exceeded 4.00 and those for low use strategies never fell below 2.00. Alternatively, those high use strategies were just usually but not always used; while those low use strategies were just not usually used and none of them were never or almost never used, as were English learning strategies. In short, all the strategies were deployed by the BFU students to different extents during English tests and the majority were sometimes or more often used.

**Table 6.15: Number of Test-taking
Strategy Items in Different Use Ranges** (BFU)

Test-taking Strategy categories	High use	Medium use	Low use
Memory Strategy (TMS)	1	4	1
Cognitive Strategy (TCogS)	8	9	0
Compensation Strategy (TComS)	7	4	1
Metacognitive Strategy (TmetaS)	21	26	1
Affective Strategy (TAS)	2	2	0
Social Strategy (TSS)	2	2	0
English Test-Taking Strategy Inventory (ETSI)	41	47	3

According to Table 6.16, the mean of overall test-taking strategy use was 3.36 on the 5-point Likert scale. This implies "medium" strategy use (sometimes used) towards the upper end. It seems that the BFU participants employed quite frequent use of various strategies during English tests, close to high use but not to that extent, consistent with the analyses of mean scores of different English test-taking strategy items.

The mean scores for all the six test-taking strategy categories generally fell in the medium-use range. Among the six categories, the most frequently used were metacognitive and affective strategies with the same mean of 3.43, followed by compensation, cognitive and social strategies with a mean of 3.42, 3.35 and 3.22 respectively. The least frequently used were memory strategies with a mean of 2.89. That is, the BFU learners were able to deploy varying test-taking strategies to enhance their performance in English exams.

158

Table 6.16: Means and Standard Deviations
Indicating Test-taking Strategy Use (BFU) (N = 327)

Strategy category (most used to least used)	Frequency of strategy use	
	Mean/range	Standard deviation
Metacognitive	3.43 (medium use; upper end)	.42
Affective	3.43 (medium use; upper end)	.63
Compensation	3.42 (medium use; upper end)	.44
Cognitive	3.35 (medium use; upper end)	.50
Social	3.22 (medium use; upper end)	.67
Memory	2.89 (medium use; low end)	.68
ETSI	3.36 (medium use; upper end)	.40

6.4.2 The most and least used individual test-taking strategies by the BFU sample

As analyzed in section 6.5.1, most of the test-taking strategies were sometimes or usually used. Among these more often used strategies, twenty were identified to be the most frequently used by BFU undergraduate EFL learners during English tests, as demonstrated in Table 6.17.

Of these twenty most frequently used test-taking strategy items, all fell in the high-use range with means ranging from 3.81 to 4.35. To be better prepared for English tests, these BFU students would usually "attend 100% of my English classes" (mean = 4.35) and take good notes of the teacher' instructions about what would be on the test (mean = 3.96). When a test was coming, they would "try to get a good night's sleep" (mean = 3.87), "gather and organize all the needed supplies" (mean = 3.85), and "arrive at the test room on time" (mean = 4.14). During the test, they would look for "keywords" (mean = 3.94) and "clues" (mean = 3.88) while reading; listen to "keywords" (mean = 3.87), "questions carefully" (mean = 3.87) and "clues" (mean = 3.81) when doing listening comprehension"; and "read questions carefully" (mean = 3.94). When writing, they would try to make it "coherent and cohesive" (mean = 3.88) and make "as few mistakes as possible" (mean = 3.83). To better their performance, these learners would "eliminate certain answers when answering multiple-choice questions" (mean = 3.89); use background knowledge of the topic to help guess and deduce "while reading" (mean = 3.92) and "complete the cloze test" (mean = 3.86), and linguistic knowledge to help guess and deduce speakers' intention while listening (mean = 3.81) during the exam.

As noted in Table 6.17, the most frequently used strategies were of metacognitive category (13), followed by compensation (4), cognitive (2) and affective (1) categories. The high means show these BFU learners often attended classes, took notes and arrived at the test time on time to be prepared for an upcoming test. During the test, they would look for clues, make guesses, read instructions and questions carefully to perform better.

Table 6.17: The Twenty Most Frequently and Twenty Least Used Test-taking Strategies (BFU) (N = 327)

The twenty most frequently used strategies				
No.	Strategy	Mean	Category in which this strategy is classified	Comment
254	Attend 100% of my English classes.	4.35	Metacognitive	H
265	Always arrive at the test room on time.	4.14	Metacognitive	H
231	Take good notes as my English	3.96	Cognitive	H
282	Look for keywords while reading	3.94	Metacognitive	H
284	Read questions carefully	3.94	Metacognitive	H
248	Use background knowledge of	3.92	Compensation	H
236	Eliminate certain answers when	3.89	Cognitive	H
283	Look for clues while reading	3.88	Metacognitive	H
294	Try to make my writing coherent	3.88	Metacognitive	H
279	Listen to keywords when doing	3.87	Metacognitive	H
281	Listen to questions carefully	3.87	Metacognitive	H
302	Try to get a good night's sleep	3.87	Affective	H
247	Use background knowledge of	3.86	Compensation	H
264	Gather and organize all the supplies	3.85	Metacognitive	H
274	Try to better understand the	3.84	Metacognitive	H
285	Write legibly during tests.	3.83	Metacognitive	H
295	Try to make as few mistakes	3.83	Metacognitive	H
245	Make guesses based on different clues	3.82	Compensation	H
244	Use linguistic knowledge to help	3.81	Compensation	H
280	Listen to clues while doing listening	3.81	Metacognitive	H
The Twenty least frequently used strategies				
No.	Strategy	Mean	Category in which this strategy is classified	Comment
224	Often dump information on the back	2.22	Memory	L
271	I create study checklists before an	2.45	Metacognitive	L
250	Use Chinese when not knowing how	2.46	Compensation	L
269	Try to predict examination questions	2.53	Metacognitive	M
222	Create flashcards for words, phrases	2.68	Memory	M
256	Avoid speaking with other students	2.69	Metacognitive	M
270	Self-test in similar oral English	2.72	Metacognitive	M
232	Create summary notes and "maps"	2.74	Cognitive	M
221	Use high technology to help	2.75	Memory	M
242	Exchange with English teachers about	2.78	Compensation	M
243	Ask the instructor what to anticipate	2.81	Compensation	M

223	Memorize model texts/essays before ….	2.87	Memory	M
272	Self-test on the material before ….	2.88	Metacognitive	M
229	Practice writing by modeling good ….	2.91	Cognitive	M
226	Practice speaking English in different ….	2.92	Cognitive	M
228	Practice translating English into ….	2.96	Cognitive	M
263	Get familiar with the test room ….	2.97	Metacognitive	M
262	Finish studying the day before the ….	2.98	Metacognitive	M
260	Develop a timetable for exam ….	2.99	Metacognitive	M
305	Often self-reward if doing well in ….	2.99	Affective	M

Notes: H = high use;　　M = medium use;　　L = low use

Table 6.17 indicates that all of the twenty least frequently used strategies were distinctly in the medium-use range except the first three with means ranging from 2.22 to 2.99. For example, "dump information on the back of the English test paper" (mean = 2.22); "use Chinese when not knowing how to express myself in English during English tests" (mean = 2.46); "try to predict examination questions and then outline answers" (mean = 2.53); "create flashcards" (mean = 2.68); "exchange with English teachers about how and what to prepare before English tests" (mean = 2.78); "memorize model texts/essays before an English essay test" (mean = 2.87); and "finish studying the day before the English exam" (mean = 2.98).

Moreover, as seen from Table 6.17, the least often used strategies mainly belonged to metacognitive (8) category, followed by memory (4), cognitive (4), compensation (3) and affective (1) categories. To prepare and/or during an English test, these BFU learners, like their TU peers, would not use much such metacognitive strategies as creating study checklists, predicting, self testing, developing a preparation timetable, and scanning. They would not often depend on such memory strategies as dumping information, using high technology, memorization and review of homework and notes. Neither would they practice a lot or employ such compensation strategies as using the mother tongue and talking with their English teachers about exam preparation either.

Also, it is worth noting that although these strategies were the least frequently employed, the majority were in the medium-use range (sometimes used). This clearly implies these students were highly flexible in utilizing various strategies to help complete and/or better their performance in English tests. This might be part of the reasons why these learners often did better than most of their peers in other universities in the country.

161

6.4.3 BFU Gender differences in English test-taking strategy use

Table 6.18 shows that both male and female BFU students had a medium use of English test-taking strategies, as indicated by their ETSI mean scores (3.36 and 3.37 for males and females respectively). Their use of the six categories of test-taking strategies also fell in the medium or even high use range, as implied by their mean ranges (2.87~3.52 and 2.91~3.43 for males and females respectively). Moreover, BFU female students reported to be more frequent users of compensation and affective strategies but less frequent users of the other categories of test-taking strategies than their male counterparts. Nevertheless, no significant difference was found in any use of the categories of test-taking strategies, as revealed by the results of Independent-samples t-tests presented in Table 6.18.

Table 6.18: BFU Gender Differences in English Test-taking Strategy Use (N = 327)

		Mean	Standard Deviation	t-test results		
				t	p	t*
TMS	M (116)	2.87	.72	-.52	.601	1.96
	F (211)	2.91	.66			
TCogS	M (116)	3.32	.50	-1.03	.303	1.96
	F (211)	3.37	.45			
TCompS	M (116)	3.44	.50	.45	.652	1.96
	F (211)	3.41	.41			
TMetaS	M (116)	3.42	.47	-.36	.721	1.96
	F (211)	3.43	.39			
TAS	M (116)	3.52	.67	1.81	.071	1.96
	F (211)	3.39	.60			
TSS	M (116)	3.22	.72	.07	.947	1.96
	F (211)	3.22	.64			
ETSI	M (116)	3.36	.44	-.26	.796	1.96
	F (211)	3.37	.37			

Notes: M = male; F = female

t* → Critical t value at .05 level (Black, 1999).

6.4.4 Correlations between individual test-taking strategies and BFU students' performance in English

Correlation analyses revealed 27 test-taking strategy items were significantly correlated with the BFU students' performance in English with coefficients ranging from -.188 to .211. The results are reported in Table 6.19.

Table 6.19: Correlations between Individual English Test-taking Strategies and BFU Students' Performance in English (N = 327)

Items	P
220. Keep up my homework and review my notes regularly … (memory).	.124*
224. Often dump information on the back of the English … (memory).	-.188**
231. Take good notes as my English teacher tells … (cognitive).	.114*
234. Directly get to the point when writing answers … (cognitive).	.143*
235. Use both general and specific information … (cognitive).	.154**
236. Eliminate certain answers when answering … (cognitive).	.143*
237. Analyze the sentence structure before translating … (cognitive).	.120*
238. Break up run-on sentences into smaller parts to … (cognitive).	.175**
244. Use linguistic knowledge to help guess and … (compensation).	.146*
245. Make guesses based on different clues while reading (compensation).	.148**
246. Use linguistic knowledge to help complete … (compensation).	.187**
247. Use background knowledge of the topic to help … (compensation).	.151**
248. Use background knowledge of the topic to help … (compensation).	.211**
254. Attend 100% of my English classes (metacognitive).	.153**
256. Avoid speaking with other students who have not … (metacognitive).	.112*
266. Set a goal for myself before an English test (metacognitive).	-.141*
269. Try to predict examination questions and then … (metacognitive).	-.116*
271. Create study checklists before an English test (metacognitive).	-.171**
274. Try to better understand the sentence … (metacognitive).	.177**
281. Listen to questions carefully (metacognitive).	.119*
285. Write legibly during tests (metacognitive).	.128*
291. Paragraph my writing (metacognitive).	.143*
294. Try to make my writing coherent and cohesive (metacognitive).	.197**
295. Try to make as few mistakes as possible … (metacognitive).	.149**
302. Try to get a good night's sleep the night before … (affective).	.118*
303. Breathe deeply to calm down when I became nervous … (affective).	.112*
304. Approach the exam with confidence (affective).	.122**

Notes: ** = p < .01;   * = p < .05;   P = performance

According to Table 6.19, four strategies significantly negatively correlated with students' performance in English: strategy 224, "often dump information on the back of the English test paper as soon as I receive it"; 266, "set a goal for myself before an English test"; 269, "try to predict examination questions and then outline answers"; and 271, "create study checklists before an English test". The more frequently students used these strategies during English exams, the less they achieved the exams. It had been expected that setting goals, predicting exam questions and/or creating study checklists should help enhance students' achievements in English exams. Surprisingly, these strategies might actually exert a negative effect on students' performance in English. It might be because the more often students predicted exam questions and/or the higher goals they set for themselves, the more they expected of the exam, which resulted more anxiety. This anxiety might ultimately negatively affect their achievements in the exams.

The rest of the test-taking strategies were significantly positively related to students' performance in English. For example, strategy 234, "directly get to the point when writing answers to questions"; 246, "use linguistic knowledge to help complete the cloze test"; 254, "attend 100% of my English classes"; 281, "listen to questions carefully"; 291, "paragraph my writing"; and 304, "approach the exam with confidence". The more frequently the BFU learners employed these test-taking strategies during exams, the more proficient they were in English.

In addition, among these 27 test-taking strategy items, the majority belonged to metacognitive (11) category which were mainly concerned with paying attention and planning for a task, followed by cognitive (6), compensation (5), affective (3) and memory (2) categories.

6.5 Correlations among measured variables and BFU students' performance in English

To explore the relationships among the measured variables and the BFU participants' performance in English, correlation analyses were conducted. The results are reported in Table 6.20.

Table 6.20: Correlations among Measured Variables and BFU Students' Performance in English (N = 300-327)

	ELM	InSM	InM	ELInS	MS	CogS	CompS	MeasS	AS	SS	ELSI	TMS	TCogS	TCompS	TMeasS	TAS	TSS	ETSI	Performance
CAS	-.38**	-.13*	-.27**	-.30**	-.27**	-.33**	-.28**	-.40**	-.33**	-.32**	-.41**	-.07	-.28**	-.35**	-.30**	-.28**	-.21**	-.32**	-.20**
ELM	1	.08	.31**	.40**	.20**	.28**	.24**	.33**	.24**	.32**	.34**	.11	.30**	.17**	.23**	.19**	.11*	.25**	.22**
InSM		1	.36**	.76**	.19**	.23**	.24**	.22**	.20**	.17**	.26**	.12*	.22**	.20**	.25**	.20**	.15**	.25**	.05
InM			1	.86**	.34**	.43**	.29**	.47**	.39**	.36**	.49**	.16**	.32**	.27**	.33**	.29**	.19**	.34**	.17**
ELInS				1	.34**	.43**	.34**	.46**	.39**	.37**	.50**	.18**	.37**	.30**	.37**	.32**	.22**	.39**	.17**
MS					1	.65**	.39**	.59**	.52**	.44**	.73**	.28**	.47**	.36**	.45**	.38**	.35**	.49**	.17**
CogS						1	.43**	.71**	.61**	.53**	.86**	.30**	.52**	.39**	.54**	.41**	.32**	.56**	.12*
CompS							1	.53**	.39**	.35**	.63**	.22**	.41**	.50**	.48**	.29**	.29**	.50**	-.01
MeasS								1	.69**	.64**	.94**	.33**	.62**	.51**	.68**	.47**	.44**	.70**	.19**
AS									1	.54**	.76**	.35**	.50**	.45**	.51**	.46**	.34**	.56**	.07
SS										1	.69**	.25**	.46**	.40**	.45**	.36**	.30**	.49**	.10
ELSI											1	.36**	.65**	.55**	.69**	.50**	.44**	.71**	.18**
TMS												1	.51**	.38**	.48**	.29**	.35**	.60**	.004
TCogS													1	.65**	.79**	.53**	.47**	.88**	.15**
TCompS														1	.70**	.47**	.46**	.78**	.12*
TMeasS															1	.58**	.52**	.96**	.09
TAS																1	.36**	.63**	.11
TSS																	1	.59**	-.10
ETSI																		1	.10

Note: **. p < .01;   *. p < .05

165

As noted in Table 6.20, the majority of the measured variables were significantly correlated with one another and with the BFU students' performance in English.

Negative correlations were found between the Classroom Anxiety Scale (CAS) and English Learning Motivation Scale (ELMS) and its three subscales (ELM, InsM and IntM), English Learning Strategy Inventory (ELSI) and its six categories (MS, CogS, CompS, MetaS, AS and SS), English Test-taking Strategy Inventory (ETSI) and its six categories (TMS, TCogS, TCompS, TMetaS, TAS and TSS). All the correlations were statistically significant except that between the CAS and the TMS. That is, the more anxious a student was in English classrooms, the less motivated s/he was to learn English and the less frequently s/he used different strategies when learning English and taking English exams.

The ELMS and its three subscales significantly positively correlated with one another except the relationship between the ELM and the InsM which was positive but insignificant. The more instrumentally motivated student tended to be more integratively motivated to learn English. In addition, the ELMS and its subscales were all significantly positively correlated with the ELSI and the ETSI and their subcategories except the correlation between the ELM and the TMS which was insignificantly positive. The more (instrumentally/ integratively) motivated student tended to be the more frequent user of different categories of strategies when learning English and taking English exams.

Correlations among the ELSI, the ETSI and their subcategories were all significantly positive. For example, the more frequent user of memory strategies (MS) was generally also a more frequent user of cognitive, compensation, metacognitive, affective and social strategies when learning English. S/he also tended to utilize the six categories of test-taking strategies more frequently during English exams.

Finally, these measured variables generally positively correlated with the BFU students' performance in English. Among these variables, the CAS, CompS (compensation strategy), and TSS (test-taking social strategy) were negatively correlated with the students' performance in English (r = -.20, -.01 and -.10 respectively), with the first significantly while the other two insignificantly correlated. The InsM, AS, SS, TMS, TMetaS, TAS, TSS, and the ETSI were insignificantly positively related to students' performance in English. All the other measures significantly positively correlated with the students' performance in English. For example, the more integratively motivated a student was to learn English, the better s/he performed in English.

6.6 The structural model of the measured variables and performance of the BFU sample

The statistical analyses of the data discussed previously indicate that the data satisfied the statistical assumptions of SEM. In specifying a general model of the relationships between reported degree or use of the measured variables and the students' performance in English for the BFU group, we argued for a one-factor model of classroom anxiety (CAS), a three-factor model of motivation (ELMS), and a six-factor model of English learning and test-taking strategy use respectively, as detailed in Chapter 4.

Of the numerous models tested, the baseline model of the measured variables and performance for the BFU group, presented in Figure 6.1, seemed to fit the data well from both a statistical and substantive perspective. The model produced a CFI of .977, a TLI of .971, an IFI of .977, a RFI of .912, and a NFI of .931, indicating a fairly good representation of the sample data. All parameter estimates in the model were substantively plausible and statistically significant at the .001 level.

As shown in the structural model, classroom anxiety exerted a significant, negative effect (-3.44) on the students' performance in English; motivation (.82), English learning strategy use (.34) and English test-taking strategy use (.08) showed a significant, positive effect on the students' performance in English.

With regard to the effect of the measured variables on one another, motivation significantly negatively affected classroom anxiety (-.49) and English test-taking strategy use (-1.33); classroom anxiety yielded a significant, negative effect on English learning strategy use (-1.38) and English test-taking strategy use (-2.81). Finally, the model shows that English learning strategy use displayed a significant, positive effect on English test-taking strategy use (2.81).

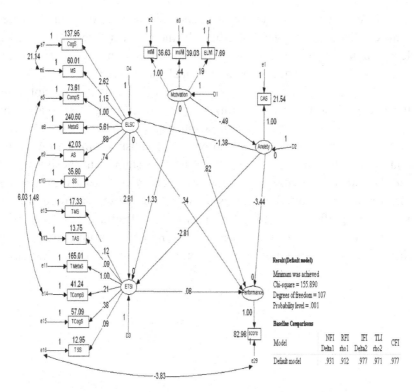

Figure 6.1: BFU Group Analysis—Measured Variables and Performance

6.7 Summary

As previously discussed, the BFU students were moderately anxious in English class due to various reasons such as low English proficiency, limited practice and low self-confidence. Having a high motivation to learn English, they were more motivated instrumentally than integratively motivated, with the most widely agreed motivations being finding a better job, going abroad and passing CET band 4.

Although knowing little about English learning strategies, the BFU learners had a medium use of the overall strategies. Among its six categories, the most frequently used were compensation strategies, followed by social, affective, metacognitive, cognitive, and memory strategies. Likewise, they had a medium us of the English test-taking strategies. Among its six categories, the most frequently used were metacognitive strategies, followed by affective strategies, compensation, cognitive, social, and memory strategies.

168

With regard to gender differences in these measured variables, female BFU students were significantly more integratively motivated to learn English than were their male peers, utilized compensation strategies significantly more frequently than their male peers in English learning.

In terms of the relationship between the measured variables and the students' performance in English, statistical analyses revealed that classroom anxiety exerted a significant, negative effect on the students' performance in English, while motivation, English learning strategy use and English test-taking strategy use showed a significant, positive effect on the latter. Moreover, motivation significantly negatively affected classroom anxiety and English test-taking strategy use; classroom anxiety yielded a significant, negative effect on English learning strategy use and English test-taking strategy use; and English learning strategy use displayed a significant, positive effect on English test-taking strategy use.

Chapter 7   Results of the CUP Sample

This chapter reports the results of the CUP (China University of Petroleum) sample. For each measured variable, descriptive analysis and analysis of ANOVA (Duncan's) were conducted. Subsequently, correlation coefficients were computed to determine the associations among the measured variables and performance in English. Finally, SEM was run to further explore these relationships.

7.1 English language classroom anxiety of the CUP sample

7.1.1 General picture of English language classroom anxiety of the CUP sample

7.1.1.1 Item analysis of the CAS of the CUP sample

The CUP students' responses (the first number means the real number and the second percentage) to the CAS (Classroom Anxiety Scale) items were reported in Table 7.1. All percentages refer to the number of students who (strongly) disagreed, neither disagreed nor agreed, or (strongly) agreed with the statements (percentages were rounded to the nearest whole number).

**Table 7.1: CAS Items with Numbers and
Percentages of CUP Students Selecting Each Alternative (N = 425)**

SD/D	N	A/SA

1. I don't usually get anxious when I have to respond to a question ....
    130/30.6   38/8.9   257/60.5
2. I am always afraid that other students would laugh at me if I speak ....
    301/70.8   44/10.4   80/18.8
3. I always feel that other students are more at ease than I am in ....
    215/50.6   93/21.9   117/27.5
4. I am never embarrassed to volunteer answers in English class.
    169/39.8   104/24.5   152/35.8
5. I am generally tense whenever participating in English class.
    333/78.4   49/11.5   43/10.1
6. I never understand why other students are so nervous in English class.

162/38.1   136/32.0   127/29.9
7. I usually feel relaxed and confident when active participation takes ....
    134/31.5   152/35.8   195/45.9
8. Whenever I have to answer a question, out loud, I get nervous and ....
    294/69.2   40/9.4   91/21.4

Notes: SD → Strongly disagree;   D → Disagree
N → Neither disagree nor agree; A → Agree; SA → Strongly agree

As noted in Table 7.1, around 70% of the CUP learners, like their TU and BFU peers, (strongly) disagreed statements expressing speech anxiety such as "whenever I have to answer a question, out loud, I get nervous and confused in English class" (item 8) (69.2%); "I am always afraid that other students would laugh at me if I speak up in English class" (item 2) (70.8%); "I am generally tense whenever participating in English class" (item 5) (78.4%). 50.6% of them vetoed item "I always feel that other students are more at ease than I am in English class". It seems that most CUP students did not feel anxious or even feel confident and relaxed in English class. However, still more than 30% of them rejected CAS items implicative of confidence when speaking in English class such as "I don't usually get anxious when I have to respond to a question in English class" (item 1) (30.6%); "I usually feel relaxed and confident when active participation takes place in English class" (item 7) (31.5%); "I never understand why other students are so nervous in English class" (item 6) (38.1%); and "I am never embarrassed to volunteer answers in English class" (item 4) (39.8%). It is clear that at least a third of the CUP participants were anxious to different degrees in English classrooms, as found with their TU and BFU counterparts.

This finding is generally in conformity with the result of the journal data. Of 83 CUP journal participants, 58 reported feeling (very/a little/sometimes) anxious in English classrooms, especially when speaking English publicly in class. The principal reasons were: low English proficiency, fear of making mistakes, lack of practice, personality, and so on, as detailed in Table 7.5.

7.1.1.2 General tendency of the CAS of the CUP sample

In order to know the general tendency of the CUP respondents' anxiety in English class, the total score, mean, standard deviation, median, mode, maximum and minimum of the CAS were computed (please refer to section 4.1.1.2 for detailed computing and interpreting scheme). Thus, the total score of the CAS revealed the CUP students' anxiety in English classrooms; the higher the score, the more anxious they felt. The results are reported in Table 7.2.

Table 7.2: Statistical Analyses of the CAS of CUP Students

	Mean	Standard Deviation	Median	Mode	Range
Male (312)	20.62	5.07	20.00	20.00	8.00-36.00
Female (113)	21.39	4.51	21.00	18.00	11.00-34.00
Total (425)	20.82	4.93	21.00	20.00	8.00-36.00

According to Table 7.2, the majority of the CUP students, like their TU and BFU peers, felt relaxed in English class, as supported by their CAS mean (20.82), median (21.00) and mode (20.00) which were all below the average 24.00. However, these scores also suggest at least a third of the students suffered from anxiety in English classrooms; some even felt extremely nervous, as indicated by the CAS score of 36.00.

Moreover, Table 7.2 shows female students with a mean of 21.39 reported to be more anxious than their male peers with a mean of 20.62 in English class. But the difference was statistically insignificant, as demonstrated by the Independent-samples t Test result: $t = -1.43$, $p = .153$.

7.1.2 Differences in English language classroom anxiety among CUP students at different proficiency levels

In order to know the differences in English language classroom anxiety among the CUP participants at two different proficiency levels, the total scores, means, standard deviations, medians, modes, maximums and minimums of the CAS were computed, as done in section 4.2.1.2. The results are presented in Table 7.3.

Table 7.3: Statistical Analyses of the CAS across Levels (CUP)

	Mean	Standard Deviation	Median	Mode	Range
Band 2 (289)	20.99	5.03	21.00	19.00	8.00-36.00
Band 3 (136)	20.46	4.72	21.00	20.00	8.00-34.00

Table 7.3 shows that the majority of each band group did not feel anxious in English class, as supported by their CAS means (20.99 and 20.46 for bands 2 and 3 respectively), medians (21.00 for both groups) and modes (19.00 and 20.00 for bands 2 and 3 respectively) which were all far below the average score of 24.00. Nevertheless, these scores also reveal at least a third of each band group experienced anxiety in English class; some

172

even reported to be extremely anxious and nervous, as suggested by the CAS scores (36.00 and 34.00 for bands 2 and 3 respectively).

As noted in Table 7.3, band 2 students had a higher mean (20.99) and maximum (36.00) but a lower mode (19.00) on the CAS than their band 3 peers though medians were the same for both groups. It appears band 2 students felt more anxious than their band 3 counterparts. Alternatively, students at the lower proficiency level suffered more anxiety in English class. Nevertheless, no significant difference in anxiety was found between band 2 and 3 groups, as proved by the Independent samples t-test results: $t = 1.03$, $p = .305$.

This finding again conforms to that of the journal data, as reported in Table 7.4.

Table 7.4: CUP Student Anxiety Reported in Journals

	Total No.	(Very) N N/%	A little N N/%	Sometimes N N/%	Not N N/%	Not mentioned N/%
Band 2	41	16/39%	8/25.8%	6/14.6%	8/25.8%	3/7.3%
Band 3	42	14/33.3%	7/16.7%	7/16.7%	12/28.6%	2/4.8%
Total	83	30/36.1%	15/18.1%	13/15.7%	20/24.1%	5/6%

Notes: N = nervous;   N/% = number/percentage

Table 7.4 shows that around 69% of the CUP journal participants reported feeling very, a little, or sometimes anxious in English class due to various reasons. A closer comparison of the two groups indicates that more band 2 students (79.4%) self-reported to be anxious than their band 3 (66.7%) peers. This further supports the statistical result that CUP band 2 students seemed to be more anxious in English classrooms.

7.1.3 Causes for and consequences of language classroom anxiety of the CUP sample

As discussed above, the majority of the TU students in three band groups reported feeling anxious in English class. Nevertheless, the reasons for anxiety might be different, as summarized in Table 7.5.

Table 7.5: Causes for Language Classroom Anxiety (CUP)
(Source: journals)

	Band 2 (Total N = 41) N/%	Band 3 (Total N = 42) N/%
Lack of /limited vocabulary	15/36.6%	6/14.3%
Personality	10/24.4%	6/14.3%
Low English proficiency	9/22%	5/11.9%

Lack of practice	9/22%	2/4.8%
Lack of preparation	6/14.6%	4/9.5%
Lack of confidence	6/14.6%	4/9.5%
Fear of making mistakes	5/12.2	2/4.8%
Poor oral English	3/7.3%	2/4.8%
Not knowing how to express oneself in English	4/9.8%	1/2.4%
English lessons being difficult	2/4.9%	1/2.4%
Other students' good English	2/4.9%	1/2.4%
Being unable to find appropriate words to express myself	3/7.3%	0
Being unable to catch classmates	0	3/7.1%
English being a foreign language	2/4.9%	0
Fear of being unable to understand the teacher	2/4.9%	0
Hating English	0	1/2.4%
The pressure given by the teacher	0	1/2.4%
English being difficult	1/2.4%	1/2.4%
Fear of being the center of attention	1/2.4%	0
Not understanding what the teacher is saying	1/2.4%	0
Lack of familiarity with classmates	1/2.4%	0

As shown in Table 7.5, the main factors leading to the CUP learners' anxiety in English classrooms lack of vocabulary (36.6% and 14.3% respectively), personality (mainly introversion and shyness based on their own description) (24.4% and 14.3% respectively), low English proficiency (22% and 11.9% respectively) and lack of practice (22% and 4.8% respectively). To these CUP students, lack of vocabulary was the most anxiety-provoking in English class. Like their TU peers, introverted and shy personality also drove some CUP learners anxious in English classrooms, especially when speaking the target language. Low English proficiency was another important contributor, as found in Liu's (2006a) study.

The next important reasons were lack of preparation (14.6% and 9.5% respectively) and lack of confidence (14.6% and 9.5%). Though probably not so good at English as their TU and BFU counterparts, these CUP correspondents were still fairly proficient in the language compared with most Chinese undergraduate non-English majors. They should have a (strong) belief in themselves. Nevertheless, due to the lack of preparation and confidence, some of them became anxious in English class. The other factors ranged from fear of being the focus of attentions, to English lessons being difficult, to English being difficult, etc., with varying weights assigned to them by different band students.

When confronted the question whether anxiety affected their performance in English, these CUP students, like their TU and BFU peers, gave varying comments, with bad effect being the most common comment, as demonstrated in Table 7.6. 58 of 83 journal participants maintained that anxiety negatively affected their performance in English, 4 believed that anxiety exerted a positive effect, 2 regarded anxiety as something both good and bad, 6 held that anxiety could produce no effect, and 13 didn't give any comment.

Table 7.6: Impact of Anxiety on CUP Students' Learning of English
(Source: journal)

	Bad	Good	Good and bad	No effect	No comment
Band 2 (41)	30/73.2%	3/7.3%	0	2/4.9%	6/14.6%
Band 3 (42)	28/66.7%	1/2.4%	2/4.8%	4/9.5%	7/16.7%
Total (83)	58/69.9%	4/4.8%	2/2.4%	6/7.2%	13/15.7%

Table 7.6 reveals that though a few students (3 band 2 and 1 band 3 respectively) asserted that anxiety was something good in that it could urge them to study harder, the majority of both band 2 (73.2%) and 3 (66.7%) students believed that the relationship between anxiety and performance was negative. The reasons were similar: anxiety made them prone to make mistakes, afraid of speaking English, and unable to listen to teachers carefully and/or improve English. Due to anxiety, they also tended to do things slowly, hate English, and lose confidence. It is clear as well that more band 2 students regarded anxiety as something bad than their band 3 peers.

Even so, few had intentionally taken some measures to cope with anxiety. They seemed to be helpless and just hoped that their anxiety would decrease as they had more and exposure to English. Nevertheless, they also offered a number of suggestions for language learners and teachers to help reduce/overcome anxiety, as listed in Table 7.7.

Table 7.7: CUP Students' Suggestions to Cope with
Anxiety for Language Learners and Teachers (Source: journal)

	Common to all	Create a relaxing and comfortable classroom environment.
Suggestions for EFL		Ask students in turn.
		Praise more.

175

teachers		Give students more chances to express themselves.
		Encourage students.
	Particular to band 2 students	Be friendly and helpful.
		Let students talk in pairs.
		Treat students equally.
		Choose interesting topics.
	Particular to band 3 students	Help students overcome some difficulties.
		Let students speak loud in the classroom.
		Have a talk with students.
		Make students feel free.
		Be good and humorous.
		Set proper assignments.
		Give more advice on how to study English.
		Give them some time to prepare for the answer.
		Ask certain students to answer questions.
Suggestions for EFL learners	Common to all	More practice.
		Be courageous.
		Be more self-confident.
		Remember more words.
	Particular to band 2 students	Don't be afraid of making mistakes.
		Improve English.
		Make a study plan.
	Particular to band 3 students	Enjoy English.
		Be more prepared.
		Communicate with other students.
		Study hard.
		Learn English songs.

Note: Ss → students.

According to Table 7.7, all the students suggested that they would become less nervous when using/speaking English in class if the teachers could create a relaxing classroom environment, encourage and praise them more, ask them in turn, and give them more chances for practicing the target language in class. Band 2 students held that they would feel (more) at ease if English teachers could be friendly and helpful, choose interesting topics, treat them equally and ask them to talk in pairs. Band 3 students hoped English teachers could help students overcome some difficulties, talk with students, give advice on how to learn English, and give them some thinking time before answering a question.

As far as the learners were concerned, all the participants commented that they should have more practice, be more confident, be courageous and remember more words. Band 2 students also suggested that language learners don't fear making mistakes, improve English and plan their study. Their band 3 peers advised other learners to enjoy English, be more prepared, communicate with other students, study hard and learn English songs.

7.2 English learning motivation of the CUP sample

7.2.1 General picture of English learning motivation of the CUP sample

7.2.1.1 Item analysis of the ELMS of the CUP sample

The CUP students' responses to ELMS (English Learning Motivation Scale) items (the first number means the real number and the second percentage) were reported in Table 7.8, in the same way as the presentation of their responses to CAS items.

Table 7.8: ELMS Items with Numbers and Percentages of CUP Students Selecting Each Alternative (N = 425)

SD/D	N	A/SA
9. Honestly, I don't know whether I am motivated to learn English.		
277/65.2	49/11.5	99/23.3
10. I have the impression that I am wasting my time in studying English.		
358/84.2	34/8.0	33/7.8
11. I study English in order to get a good job later on.		
113/26.6	55/12.9	257/60.5
12. I study English in order to earn more money later on.		
129/30.4	92/21.6	204/48.0
13. I study English for higher education later on.		
61/14.4	73/17.2	291/68.5
14. I study English in order to go abroad later on.		
96/22.6	103/24.2	226/53.1
15. I study English because I think it is important for my future work.		
62/14.6	59/13.9	304/71.5
16. I study English because I want to get high marks in English exams.		
145/34.1	63/14.8	217/51.1

17. I study English because it is required with credits at my university.
    185/43.5   62/14.6   178/41.9
18. I study English because I want to have different kinds of ....
    208/48.9   99/23.3   118/27.8
19. I study English because I have to pass English exams; otherwise, ...
    333/78.4   43/10.1   49/11.5
20. I study English because I am good at English listening, speaking, ...
    184/43.3   100/23.5   141/33.2
21. I study English because I want to improve my English abilities in ....
    72/16.9   63/14.8   290/68.2
22. I study English because I would feel guilty if I didn't know English.
    206/48.5   91/21.4   128/30.1
23. I study English because I would feel ashamed if I couldn't speak to ....
    167/39.3   93/21.9   165/38.8
24. ... I think it is important for my personal development.
    27/6.4   26/6.1   372/87.5
25. I study English because I choose to be the kind of person who can ....
    82/19.3   77/18.1   266/62.6
26. ... I choose to be the kind of person who can speak English.
    78/18.4   69/16.2   278/65.4
27. I study English for the satisfied feeling I get in finding out new things.
    108/25.4   132/31.1   185/43.5
28. I study English for the pleasure that I experience in knowing ....
    139/32.7   139/32.7   147/34.6
29. I study English because I enjoy the feeling of learning about ....
    166/39.1   117/27.5   142/33.4
30. I study English for the enjoyment I experience when I understand a ....
    185/43.5   124/29.2   116/27.3
31. ... satisfaction I feel when I am doing difficult exercises in English.
    235/55.3   107/25.2   83/19.6
32. I study English for the good feeling I get when I do better than ....
    115/27.1   99/23.3   211/49.6
33. I study English for the excitement that I get while speaking English.
    219/51.5   90/21.2   116/27.3
34. I study English for the excitement I feel when I hear someone ....
    220/51.8   99/23.3   106/24.9

Notes: SD → Strongly disagree;   D → Disagree

N → Neither disagree nor agree;   A → Agree;   SA → Strongly agree

According to Table 7.8, most CUP students reported to be motivated to learn English and considered it was worth learning the language, as supported by their rejection of ELMS items indicative of little English learning motivation: "Honestly, I don't know whether I am motivated to learn English (item 9)" (65.2%) and "I have the impression that I am wasting my time in studying English (item 10)" (84.2%).

Like their TU and CUP peers, these CUP students were also highly instrumentally motivated to learn English, as indicated by the frequencies and percentages of responses to items 9 to 21 shown in Table 7.4 and ELMS item mean scores reported in Appendix II. Some of the instrumental reasons highly agreed on by the students were: earning more money (item 12) (48.0%); getting high marks in English exams (item 16) (51.1%); going abroad (item 14) (53.1%); getting a good job (item 11) (60.5%); higher education (item 13) (68.5%); improving English abilities in four basic skills (item 21) (68.2%); future career (item 15) (71.5%); and personal development (item 24) (87.5%). As expected, they also denied learning English for certificates (item 18) (48.9%) and passing exams (item 19) (78.4%).

Table 7.8 shows many CUP non-English majors were also integratively motivated to learn the language. And the reasons with more credits were: the satisfaction of finding out new things (item 27) (43.5%); the good feeling of doing better than expected (item 32) (49.6%); choosing to speak more than one language (item 25) (62.6%) and English (item 26) (65.4%). At the same time, they denied being motivated to learn English for such reasons as feeling guilty (item 22) (48.5%); excitement of speaking English (item 33) (51.5%); excitement of hearing someone speaking English (item 34) (51.8%); and satisfaction of doing difficult exercises in English (item 31) (55.3%). Again, these integrative reasons were more utilitarian in nature.

This finding was also consistent with the results of the journal data. Of 83 CUP journal participants, 71 reported to be motivated to learn English in university because of a variety of reasons, as shown in Table 7.9.

Table 7.9: Reasons for CUP Students' Motivation to Learn English
(Source: Journal)

		Band 2 (41)	Band 3 (42)
Not mentioned		5/12.2%	4/9.5%
No motivation	Number	3/7.3%	0
	Reason	No interest in English	
Yes	Number	33/80.5%	38/90.5%
	Reason	To find a better job To go abroad To communicate with foreigners For further study To improve English English being useful English being important Being interested in English	To find a better/good job Interest in English English being useful English being important Desire to speak English fluently To learn more things from English books To pass examination To communicate with others better To study abroad To be happy in English class To improve English To do as teachers said To be better than friends

According to Table 7.9, what motivated both band 2 and 3 students to learn English was to find a good/better job, to go abroad, to pursue further study, and to improve English. Usefulness and importance of English and interest in the language were also the common motivations. The band 3 students were motivated also because they desired to speak English fluently, to learn more things from English books, to be better than friends, to pass exams, and to be happy in English classrooms. Generally speaking, these two band groups were motivated to learn English both instrumentally and integratively, apparently with more instrumental reasons.

7.2.1.2 General tendency of the ELMS of the CUP sample

In order to know the general tendency of the CUP learners' English learning motivation, the total score, mean, and standard deviation of the ELMS and its three subscales were computed, as done in section 4.2.1.3 (please refer to section 4.2.1.3 for detailed computing and interpreting scheme). The results are presented in Table 7.10.

Table 7.10: Statistical Analyses of the
ELMS and its Subscales of CUP Students

		Mean	Standard Deviation	Median	Mode	Range
ELMS	M (312)	82.31	10.57	82.00	80.00	50.00-122.00
	F (113)	84.95	10.57	85.00	81.00	60.00-124.00
	T (425)	83.01	10.62	83.00	80.00	50.00-124.00
ELM	M (312)	7.77	1.76	8.00	10.00	2.00-10.00
	F (113)	8.16	1.62	8.00	10.00	4.00-10.00
	T (425)	7.88	1.73	8.00	10.00	2.00-10.00
InsM	M (312)	38.71	5.59	38.00	38.00	23.00-55.00
	F (113)	39.67	5.47	40.00	44.00	24.00-56.00
	T (425)	38.97	5.57	39.00	38.00	23.00-56.00
IntM	M (312)	35.83	7.52	36.00	40.00	12.00-58.00
	F (113)	37.12	7.33	36.00	32.00	12.00-58.00
	T (425)	36.17	7.48	36.00	40.00	12.00-58.00

Notes: M = male; F = female;   T = total

As noted in Table 7.10, a mean of 83.01, a median of 83.00 and a mode of 80.00 on the ELMS, which all well exceeded the average score of 78.00, reveal the majority of the CUP students, like their TU and BFU peers, were highly motivated to learn English. This is further confirmed by their ELM mean (7.88), median (8.00) and mode (10.00) which were all far above the average 6.00.

Meanwhile, a mean of 38.97, a median of 39.00 and a mode of 38.00 on the InsM, all exceeding the average 36.00, imply most CUP students were (highly) instrumentally motivated to learn English. Likewise, their IntM mean (36.17), median (36.00) and mode (40.00) which were only narrowly above the average of 36.00 suggest these students were moderately integratively motivated to learn English. In addition, as indicated by their InsM and IntM means, these students reported to be more instrumentally than integratively motivated to learn the target language. And the difference was statistically significant, as proved by the paired-samples t test result: $t = 6.82$, $p = .000$.

Moreover, as shown in Table 7.10, female students scored higher than their male peers on the ELMS and its subscales. It seems that female CUP learners had a stronger motivation to learn English and were more motivated to learn the language both instrumentally and integratively. But significant difference was found only in the ELMS, as proved by the results of Independent-samples t Tests reported in Table 7.11. Therefore, female CUP students were only generally more motivated to learn the target language.

Table 7.11: Independent-samples t Test Results
for Gender Differences in the ELMS and its Subscales (CUP)

	ELM	InsM	IntM	ELMS
t	-2.04	-1.58	-1.57	-2.27
p	.042	.116	.118	.024
t*	1.96	1.96	1.96	2.326

Note: t* → Critical t values at .05 and .02 levels respectively (Black, 1999).

7.2.2 Differences in English learning motivation among CUP students at different proficiency levels

In order to know the differences in English learning motivation among the CUP students at different proficiency levels, the total scores, means, standard deviations, medians, modes, maximums and minimums of the ELMS and its subscales were computed, as done in section 4.2.1.3 (please refer to section 4.2.1.3 for detailed computing and interpreting scheme). The results are summarized in Table 7.12.

Table 7.12: Statistical Analyses of
the ELMS and its Subscales across Levels (CUP)

Measure	Level	Mean	Standard Deviation	Median	Mode	Minimum
ELMS	2 (289)	82.08	10.21	82.00	74.00	50.00-122.00
	3 (136)	84.99	11.22	85.00	93.00	56.00-124.00
ELM	2 (289)	7.75	1.72	8.00	8.00	2.00-10.00
	3 (136)	8.15	1.73	8.00	10.00	2.00-10.00
InsM	2 (289)	38.79	5.32	39.00	38.00	23.00-55.00
	3 (136)	39.35	6.06	40.00	40.00	23.00-56.00
IntM	2 (289)	35.55	7.47	35.00	34.00	12.00-58.00
	3 (136)	37.50	7.36	37.00	36.00	17.00-58.00

According to the mean scores, medians and modes of the two groups on the ELMS and its subscales presented in Table 7.12, it is clear that students at each proficiency level had a (strong) motivation to learn English for both instrumental and integrative reasons.

As seen from Table 7.12, band 3 students scored higher on all the scales than their band 2 counterparts. Not only did they report to have a stronger overall motivation to learn English, they also had a stronger instrumental and integrative motivation to learn the language. And significant differences emerged in the ELMS, the ELM and the IntM, as supported by the results of Independent t tests presented in Table 7.13. Namely, students at a higher proficiency level were generally more motivated to learn English; their integrative motivation was also stronger.

Table 7.13: Independent-samples t Test Results
for Proficiency Difference in the ELMS and its Subscales (CUP)

	ELM	InsM	IntM	ELMS
t	-2.23	-.96	-2.53	-2.65
p	.026	.337	.012	.008
t*	2.326	2.326	2.576	3.291

Note: t* → Critical t values at .02, .01 and .0001 levels respectively (Black, 1999).

7.3 English Learning strategy use by the CUP sample

7.3.1 CUP students' knowledge of English learning strategies

Of 83 CUP journal participants, 36 band 2 and 41 band 3 students reported using some strategies during the process of English learning, as Table 7.14 shows.

Table 7.14: CUP Students' Knowledge of English Learning Strategies

Band 2	Band 3
Memorize words and phrases	Memorize words
Recite	Preview
Review	Review
Practice	Recite texts
Read texts	Listen to English
Do exercises	Repeat
Take notes while listening to the teacher	Take notes
	Practice
Listen to tapes and radio programs	Read English books
Make a good plan	Do exercises
	Make good organization of time
	Make a plan
	Plan and revise

It seems that CUP band 2 and 3 students deployed similar strategies when learning English. They both were familiar with such memory strategies as memorizing, reciting and reviewing. They also made use of such cognitive strategies as practicing (e.g., doing exercises and/or repeating), using resources for receiving and sending messages (e.g., listen to English and read texts), and creating structure for input and output (e.g., taking notes). They both would plan for their study. As such, 29 band 2 and 30 band 3 correspondents maintained that these learning strategies were conducive to their learning of English. Because of these strategies, they felt confident, learned fast and effectively, saved time, achieved more and enhanced English proficiency.

7.3.2 Broad profile of English learning strategy use by the CUP sample

Based on CUP mean scores of English Learning Strategy Inventory (ELSI) items reported in Appendix II, items in different use ranges were summarized in Table 7.15 (please refer to section 4.3.3 for detailed analyzing key). Among the 184 ELSI items, 69 items fell in the high use range, 103 in the medium use range and 12 in the low use range. That is, more than 50% of the strategies were sometimes used; over a third of them were usually or always used; only a few were usually not used or even not used. The case was the same with each of the six strategy categories, as presented in Table 7.15. A review of the ELSI mean scores reported in Appendix II further shows that mean scores for high use strategies never exceeded 4.00 and those for low use strategies never fell below 2.00. Alternatively, those high use strategies were just usually but not always used, while those low use strategies were just usually not used and none of them were never or almost never used. It is thus clear that all the strategies were employed by the CUP students to different extents and the majority were sometimes or more often used.

Table 7.15: Number of English Learning
Strategy Items in Different Use Ranges (CUP)

English Learning Strategy categories	High use	Medium use	Low use
Memory Strategy (MS)	5	13	2
Cognitive Strategy (CogS)	10	34	0
Compensation Strategy (ComS)	13	7	1
Metacognitive Strategy (MetaS)	31	36	8
Affective Strategy (AS)	6	6	1
Social Strategy (SS)	4	7	0
English Learning Strategy Inventory (ELSI)	69	103	12

As reported in Table 7.16, the mean of overall strategy use was 3.25 on the 5-point Likert scale, which indicates "medium" strategy use (sometimes used) towards the upper end. It seems that the CUP participants, like their TU and BFU peers, were also used to using various strategies when learning English to different degrees, though not highly frequently.

Compensation strategies fell in the high use range, as implied by its mean (3.53) shown in Table 7.16; all the other five strategy categories fell in the medium-use range with means ranging from 3.09 to 3.28. Among the six categories, the most frequently used were compensation strategies with a mean of 3.53, followed by affective (mean = 3.28), social (mean = 3.26), and metacognitive (mean = 3.25) strategies, and then cognitive (3.15) and memory (mean = 3.09) strategies.

Table 7.16: Means and Standard Deviations
Indicating English Learning Strategy Use (CUP) (N = 425)

	Frequency of strategy use	
	Mean/range	Standard deviation
Compensation	3.53 (high use; low end)	.36
Affective	3.28 (medium use; upper end)	.45
Social	3.26 (medium use; upper end)	.49
Metacognitive	3.25 (medium use; upper end)	.39
Cognitive	3.15 (medium use; upper end)	.34
Memory	3.09 (medium use)	.43
ELSI	3.25 (medium use; upper end)	.32

7.3.3 The most and least used individual learning strategies by the CUP sample

As discussed above, the majority of the strategies were sometimes or usually used. Among these strategies, twenty were identified to be the most frequently used by CUP undergraduate EFL learners, as displayed in Table 7.17.

Among the twenty most often used English learning strategy items, all were in the high-use range with means ranging from 3.79 to 4.03. Most of these highly frequently used strategies fell into compensation (8) and metacognitive (8) categories; a few belonged to affective (2), memory (1) and cognitive (1) categories. Like those from the other two universities, the CUP participants would usually use contextual clues to "understand unfamiliar English words" (mean = 4.03) and "make guesses about English reading" (mean = 3.92) and background knowledge to make guesses when "reading in English" (mean = 3.87); make guesses "purposefully when listening to/reading English" (mean = 3.82) and "on

185

word formation to understand unfamiliar English words" (mean = 3.80). When being unable to recall or use the desired word(s)/phrase(s), they would use "words or phrases similar in meaning as substitutes" (mean = 3.97) and "simple English words, expressions and sentence structures as substitutes" (mean = 3.96). In addition, they tried to link "it with already known knowledge when reading or listening to English (mean = 3.80) and "the topic with already known knowledge when speaking/writing in English" (mean = 3.80). When writing in English, these CUP learners tried to "make it coherent" (mean = 3.90); "make as few grammatical mistakes as possible" (mean = 3.85); and "keep to the main idea" (mean = 3.84). When reading in English, they "adjust reading speed" according to the content (mean = 3.81) and "highlight certain phrases or sentences" (mean = 3.80) in order to promote comprehension. Meanwhile, they "self-encourage not to lose heart when not doing well in English exams" (mean = 3.96) and "try to find out how to be a better English learner" (mean = 3.79).

On the whole, as reported in Table 7.17, the CUP students made high use of such compensation strategies as making guesses based on linguistic and other clues and using synonyms. When employing metacognitive strategies, they mainly utilized such strategies as overviewing and linking with already known materials, paying attention, planning, and self-monitoring. Like that of the whole participant sample, only two affective strategies were highly frequently used by the TU learners. Apart from these, they hardly employed other types of strategies frequently.

Table 7.17: The Twenty Most Frequently and Twenty Least Used English Learning Strategies (CUP) (N = 425)

No.	Strategy	Mean	Category in which this strategy is classified	Comment
The twenty most frequently used English learning strategies				
100	Make guesses based on contextual	4.03	Compensation	H
119	Use words or phrases similar in	3.97	Compensation	H
117	Often use simple words, expressions	3.96	Compensation	H
198	Self-encourage not to lose heart	3.96	Affective	H
104	Use contextual clues to make	3.92	Compensation	H
108	Use visual aids to help better	3.91	Compensation	H
135	Try to make it coherent when	3.90	Metacognitive	H
48	Remember a new English word	3.89	Memory	H
127	Look up frequently occurring words	3.88	Metacognitive	H
105	Use background knowledge to	3.87	Compensation	H

134	Try to make as few grammatical	3.85	Metacognitive	H
202	Often purposefully make guesses	3.82	Affective	H
136	Keep to the main idea when writing	3.84	Metacognitive	H
189	Adjust reading speed according to	3.81	Metacognitive	H
98	Highlight certain phrases or	3.80	Cognitive	H
99	Make guesses based on word	3.80	Compensation	H
109	Try to predict the content according	3.80	Compensation	H
120	Often try to link it with already	3.80	Metacognitive	H
121	Often try to link the topic with	3.80	Metacognitive	H
141	Try to find out how to be a better	3.79	Metacognitive	H
The Twenty least frequently used English learning strategies				
No.	Strategy	Mean	Category in which this strategy is classified	Comment
168	Initiate to make friends with	2.24	Metacognitive	L
206	Write down my feelings in	2.24	Affective	L
169	Initiate to talk to teachers in English.	2.25	Metacognitive	L
78	Often read the transcript before	2.27	Cognitive	L
51	Physically act out new English words.	2.29	Memory	L
118	Make up new words when not	2.31	Metacognitive	L
167	Initiate to greet and converse	2.33	Metacognitive	L
52	Use flashcards to remember new	2.36	Memory	L
160	Try to write diaries and/or journals	2.37	Metacognitive	L
170	Often participate in various	2.40	Metacognitive	L
61	Often do really a lot of English	2.41	Cognitive	L
159	Write emails and/or letter in English	2.45	Metacognitive	L
171	Actively take part in various	2.47	Metacognitive	L
161	Have a notebook ready for writing	2.47	Metacognitive	L
59	Practice pronunciation according	2.50	Cognitive	M
217	Just care for what I need to say and	2.51	Social	M
53	Often memorize English words	2.52	Memory	M
176	Often search for various English	2.55	Metacognitive	M
205	Often use a checklist to note my	2.56	Affective	M
157	Try to write notes and book	2.57	Metacognitive	M

Notes: H = high use;   M = medium use;   L = low use

According to Table 7.17, 14 of the twenty least frequently used strategies were in the low-use range at the upper end with a mean range of 2.24 to 2.47; 6 fell in the medium-use range at the low end with means ranging from 2.50 to 2.57. For example, "write down my feelings in language learning diaries" (mean = 2.24); "initiate to talk to teachers in English" (mean = 2.25); "make up new words when not knowing the right ones in English" (mean = 2.31); "often participate in various English activities" (mean = 2.40); "actively take part in various English contests" (mean = 2.47); "practice pronunciation according to English phonological rules" (mean = 2.50); "often search for various English materials in libraries" (mean = 2.55); and "try to write notes and book reports in English" (mean = 2.57).

7.3.4 Differences in English learning strategy use between CUP male and female students and among those at different proficiency levels

As noted from Table 7.18, with mean ranges of 3.10 to 3.51 and of 3.08 to 3.61 for male and female students respectively, they both had a medium use of all the categories of strategies except the compensation category which fell in the high use range. Moreover, CUP female students reported to be more frequent users of compensation and social strategies and the ELSI when learning English, while the males used memory, cognitive, metacognitive and affective strategies more frequently. And the results of Independent-samples t-tests presented in Table 7.18 show that significant difference existed only in the use of compensation and social strategies. That is, females deployed compensation and social strategies significantly more frequently than their male peers in English learning.

Table 7.18: CUP Gender Differences in English Learning Strategy Use (N = 425)

		Mean	Standard Deviation	t-test results	
				t	p
MS	M (312)	3.10	.39	.26	.799
	F (113)	3.08	.52		
CogS	M (312)	3.16	.33	.56	.574
	F (113)	3.14	.36		
CompS	M (312)	3.51	.37	-2.78	.006
	F (113)	3.61	.33		
MetaS	M (312)	3.26	.38	.77	.443
	F (113)	3.23	.42		
AS	M (312)	3.28	.43	.16	.872
	F (113)	3.27	.51		
SS	M (312)	3.23	.48	-2.50	.013
	F (113)	3.36	.51		
ELSI	M (312)	3.25	.31	-.01	.994
	F (113)	3.25	.36		

Notes: M = male; F = female

To explore differences in English learning strategy use between the CUP students at two different proficiency levels, Independent-samples t-tests were conducted. The results are summed up in Table 7.19.

Table 7.19: Differences in English Learning Strategy Use between CUP Students across Levels (N = 425)

		Mean	Standard Deviation	t-test results	
				t	p
MS	2(289)	3.09	.45	-.47	.639
	3(136)	3.11	.39		
CogS	2(289)	3.14	.33	-1.41	.159
	3(136)	3.19	.35		
CompS	2(289)	3.53	.35	-.54	.588
	3(136)	3.55	.39		
MetaS	2(289)	3.23	.40	-2.11	.035
	3(136)	3.31	.37		
AS	2(289)	3.26	.46	-.77	.44
	3(136)	3.30	.44		
SS	2(289)	3.26	.49	-.21	.836
	3(136)	3.27	.49		
ELSI	2(289)	3.23	.33	-1.62	.107
	3(136)	3.28	.31		

Notes: t* → Critical t value at .02 level (Black, 1999).

According to Table 7.19, the CUP students at band 2 and 3 levels had a medium use of all the categories of strategies except the compensation category which were in the high use range. Band 3 students reported using all the strategies more frequently than their band 2 counterparts in learning English. But significant difference emerged only in the use of meatacognitive strategies, as revealed by the results of Independent-samples t-tests shown in Table 7.19. Alternatively, band 3 students utilized metacognitive strategies significantly more frequently than did their band 2 peers.

7.3.5 Correlations between individual English learning strategy use and CUP students' Performance in English

To address this question, correlation analyses were conducted, which revealed 45 English learning strategy items significantly correlated with

the CUP learners' performance in English with coefficients ranging from
-.155 to .209, as presented in Table 7.20.

**Table 7.20: Correlations between Individual English learning
Strategies and CUP Students' Performance in English** (N = 425)

Items	P
36. Remember English words according to pronunciation … (memory).	.133**
37. Remember a new word by its formation (memory).	.116*
38. Think of relationships between what I already know… (memory).	.156**
45. Remember a new English word by making a mental … (memory).	.108*
49. Often review what I have learned in English (memory).	.145**
50. Copy down new English words in a special notebook … (memory).	.119*
57. Reread an English text to enhance my understanding (cognitive).	.108*
63. Often practice reading English aloud (cognitive).	.114*
69. I read for pleasure in English (cognitive).	.100*
73. First skim an English passage then go back … (cognitive).	.108*
76. Make sure of its meaning and learn how to use it … (cognitive).	.108*
78. Often read the transcript before listening to English (cognitive).	-.155**
79. Read the transcript while listening to English (cognitive).	-.138**
82. Often remember English grammatical rules based on … (cognitive).	.103*
83. Try to deduce the author's opinion and implied … (cognitive).	.123*
98. Highlight certain phrases or sentences … (cognitive).	.105*
99. Make guesses based on word formation … (compensation).	.126*
101. Often use linguistic clues to make guesses if not … (compensation).	.123*
107. Make guesses about the speaker's intention … (compensation).	.108*
114. Give it up if not understanding what is … (compensation).	-.134**
115. Often try to avoid using English (compensation).	-.145**
119. Use a word or phrase similar in meaning … (compensation).	.107*
125. Pay attention to the beginning and ending of … (metacognitive).	.110*
127. Look up the words in dictionary that frequently … (metacognitive).	.148**
130. Pay attention when someone is speaking English (metacognitive).	.107*
132. Try to use a variety of sentence structures when … (metacognitive).	.170**
133. Try to use a variety of words when … (metacognitive).	.168**
134. Try to make as few grammatical mistakes as … (metacognitive).	.209**
135. Try to make it coherent when writing in English (metacognitive).	.100*
137. Pay attention to paragraphing when … (metacognitive).	.142**
138. Be attentive when my English teacher is … (metacognitive).	.112*
141. Try to find out how to be a better learner … (metacognitive).	.098*
142. Have my own English learning plan in addition … (metacognitive).	.165**
143. Plan my schedule in order to have enough time … (metacognitive).	.123*
144. Organize my ideas quite logically when writing … (metacognitive).	.192**
152. Select different learning strategies according to … (metacognitive).	.117*
163. Murmur the answer to myself when the … (metacognitive).	.123*

164.Try to voluntarily seek chances to answer ... (metacognitive).	.105*
166. Look for opportunities to read as much ... (metacognitive).	.135**
181. Notice my English mistakes and use that ... (metacognitive).	.098*
183. Think about how to say things better ... (metacognitive).	.103*
193. Usually read English articles repeatedly, ... (metacognitive).	.098*
200. Often purposefully take chances to speak English ... (affective).	.101*
202. Often purposefully make guesses when listening ... (affective).	.170**
212. Ask my English teachers to correct my writing (social).	.139**

Notes: ** = p < .01;   * = p < .05;   P = performance

As seen from Table 7.20, two cognitive and two compensation strategies had a significant negative relationship with the CUP students' performance in English: strategy 78, "often read the transcript before listening to English" (r = -.155); 79, "read the transcript while listening to English" (r = -.138); 114, "give it up if not understanding what is heard and just listen to the English that I can understand" (r = -.134); and 115, "often try to avoid using English" (r = -.145). The more frequently the CUP students used these strategies when learning English, the less proficient they were in English.

The rest of the strategies were significantly positively related to the CUP students' performance in English. For example, strategy 36, "remember English words according to pronunciation rules of letter clusters" (r = .133); 82, "often remember English grammatical rules based on understanding rather than rote memory" (r = .103); 119, "use a word or phrase similar in meaning as substitutes" (r = .107); 133, "try to use a variety of words when writing in English" (r = .168); 200, "often purposefully take chances to speak English even if I may not speak it well" (r = .101); and 212, "ask my English teachers to correct my writing" (r = .139). The more frequently the CUP learners employed these strategies in English learning, the more proficient they were in English.

Moreover, among these strategies, the majority belonged to the metacognitive (20) category, followed by cognitive (10), compensation (6), memory (6), affective (2) and social (1) categories. As Table 7.20 shows, the majority of the metacognitive strategies were concerned with paying attention, organizing and planning, seeking practice opportunities, and self monitoring and evaluating. The cognitive strategies are mainly related to repeating, practicing, using recourses for receiving and sending messages, reasoning deductively and highlighting. The compensation strategies mainly involved making guesses, avoiding using the target language totally or partially, and using synonyms. And the memory strategies were mainly of creating mental images and reviewing.

7.4 English test-taking strategy use by the CUP sample

Of 83 CUP journal participants, 20 band 2 and 24 band 3 students reported using some strategies when taking English exams, as listed in Table 7.21.

**Table 7.21: CUP Students' Knowledge
of English Test-taking Strategies** (Source: journal)

Band 2	Band 3
Read some English articles before the exams	Review notes, texts, words, grammar and all that have been learned
Review before exams	Memorize words
Memorize all the words	Recite texts
Do exercises	Have a good sleep before the exam
Listen to the tape	Do some simulated tests
Do a similar test to check myself	Do reading and listening comprehension
Do it from easy to difficult	Have a deep breath
Focus on the exam	Control the writing time
Review my performance during the test	Do the easy first, from easy to difficult
	Be concentrated
	Treat it carefully
	Guess the meaning of new words
	Try my best
	Review my performance during the test

Table 7.21 shows that the CUP students at both levels would prepare for a coming exam (carefully) by reviewing notes, memorizing words and phrases, doing exercises, and/or reading English articles. They also self-evaluated their proficiency in the language by doing some simulated tests before exams. During exams, they would solve the easy questions first and then difficult ones, and be concentrated. The band 3 participants would solve the questions with (great) care, guess the meanings of strange words, control the writing time, and try their best to perform well. Furthermore, both groups would review their performance in the exam(s), reflecting where they had done well and where they done poorly so that they could perform better in future exams. Consequently, these strategies helped them (18 band 2 & 3 participants respectively) remain relaxed and confident before and during the exams, according to their self-reports in the journals.

7.4.1 Broad profile of English test-taking strategy use by the CUP sample

Based on CUP mean scores of English Test-taking Strategy Inventory (ETSI) items presented in Appendix II, items in different use ranges were summarized and presented in Table 7.22 (please refer to section 4.3.3 for analyzing key). Among the 91 ETSI items, 44 items fell in the high use range, 44 in the medium use range and 3 in the low use range. It was the same with each of the six strategy categories. A review of the ETSI mean scores reported in Appendix II further reveals that mean scores for more high use strategies exceeded 4.00 and those for low use strategies never fell below 2.00. Namely, those high use strategies were often just usually and only a few were always used; while those low use strategies were just not usually used and none of them were never or almost never used. Therefore, all the strategies were deployed by the CUP participants to different extents during English exams and the majority were sometimes or more often used.

Table 7.22: Number of Test-taking Strategy Items in Different Use Ranges (CUP)

Test-taking Strategy categories	High use	Medium use	Low use
Memory Strategy (TMS)	1	4	1
Cognitive Strategy (TCogS)	8	9	0
Compensation Strategy (TComS)	7	4	1
Metacognitive Strategy (TMetaS)	24	23	1
Affective Strategy (TAS)	2	2	0
Social Strategy (TSS)	2	2	0
English Test-Taking Strategy Inventory (ETSI)	44	44	3

According to Table 7.23, the mean of overall test-taking strategy use was 3.43 on the 5-point Likert scale, which indicates "medium" strategy use (sometimes used) towards the upper end. This shows the CUP learners were frequent users of various test-taking strategies during English exams, as were their TU and BFU peers.

The mean scores for all the six test-taking strategy categories generally fell in the medium-use range. Among the six categories, the most frequently used were affective strategies with a mean of 3.53, followed by metacognitive (mean = 3.50), compensation (mean = 3.46), cognitive (mean = 3.41) and social (mean = 3.33) strategies. The least frequently used were memory strategies with a mean of 2.91.

Table 7.23: Means and Standard Deviations
Indicating Test-taking Strategy Use (CUP) (N = 425)

	Frequency of strategy use	
	Mean/range	Standard deviation
Affective	3.53 (medium use; upper end)	.60
Metacognitive	3.50 (medium use; upper end)	.38
Compensation	3.46 (medium use; upper end)	.43
Cognitive	3.41 (medium use; upper end)	.46
Social	3.33 (medium use; upper end)	.59
Memory	2.91 (medium use; low end)	.65
ETSI	3.43 (medium use; upper end)	.37

7.4.2 The most and least used individual test-taking strategies by the CUP sample

As previously analyzed, most of the test-taking strategies were sometimes or usually used. Among these more often used strategies, twenty were identified to be the most frequently used by CUP undergraduate non-English majors during English exams, as summarized in Table 7.24.

All of the twenty most often used test-taking strategy items fell in the high-use range with means ranging from 3.85 to 4.46. To be better prepared for English exams, the CUP students would usually "attend 100% of my English classes" (mean = 4.46) and "gather and organize all the needed supplies" (mean = 4.02). When a test was coming, they would "try to get a good night's sleep" (mean = 3.95) and "arrive at the test room on time" (mean = 4.26). During the exam, they would read (mean = 4.00) and listen to (mean = 3.91) questions carefully. When doing reading comprehension, they looked for "keywords" (mean = 4.09) and "clues" (mean = 4.06); made guesses based on different clues (mean = 3.95) and used background knowledge of the topic to help guess and deduce (mean = 3.92). When doing listening comprehension, these CUP respondents would listen to "keywords" (mean = 4.00), "clues" (mean = 3.92) and "directions carefully" (mean = 3.85). When writing, they would try to make it coherent and cohesive (mean = 3.98) and "make as few mistakes as possible" (mean = 3.93). To better their performance, these learners would "eliminate certain answers when answering multiple-choice questions" (mean = 4.00); use background knowledge of the topic (mean = 3.93) and linguistic knowledge (mean = 3.91) to help complete the cloze test; and "try to better understand the sentence according to its context when translating it into Chinese" (mean = 3.85).

Moreover, as seen from Table 7.24, most of the most frequently used strategies belonged to the metacognitive category (13), followed by compensation (5), cognitive (2) and affective (1) categories. The high means indicate these CUP learners preferred to attend every English class, arrive at the test room on time, look for clues, and make guesses based on various linguistic and background knowledge during English exams.

Table 7.24: The Twenty Most Frequently and Twenty Least Used Test-taking Strategies (CUP) (N = 425)

No.	Strategy	Mean	Category in which this strategy is classified	Comment
	The twenty most frequently used strategies			
254	Attend 100% of my English classes.	4.46	Metacognitive	H
265	Always arrive at the test room on time.	4.26	Metacognitive	H
282	Look for keywords while reading	4.09	Metacognitive	H
283	Look for clues while reading	4.06	Metacognitive	H
264	Gather and organize all the needed	4.02	Metacognitive	H
236	Eliminate certain answers when	4.00	Cognitive	H
279	Listen to keywords when	4.00	Metacognitive	H
284	Read questions carefully	4.00	Metacognitive	H
294	Try to make writing coherent	3.98	Metacognitive	H
302	Try to get a good night's sleep	3.95	Affective	H
245	Make guesses based on different	3.95	Compensation	H
247	Use background knowledge of the	3.93	Compensation	H
295	Try to make as few mistakes as	3.93	Metacognitive	H
280	Listen to clues while doing	3.92	Metacognitive	H
248	Use my background knowledge of	3.92	Compensation	H
246	Use linguistic knowledge to	3.91	Compensation	H
281	Listen to questions carefully	3.91	Metacognitive	H
244	Use linguistic knowledge to help	3.88	Compensation	H
238	Break up run-on sentences into	3.86	Cognitive	H
274	Try to better understand the	3.85	Metacognitive	H
278	Listen to directions carefully	3.85	Metacognitive	H
	The Twenty least frequently used strategies			
No.	Strategy	Mean	Category in which this strategy is classified	Comment
224	Often dump information on the	2.25	Memory	L
250	Use Chinese when not knowing	2.38	Compensation	L
271	Create study checklists	2.43	Metacognitive	L
221	Use high technology to help	2.50	Memory	M
307	Form a study group with classmates	2.58	Social	M
269	Try to predict examination	2.65	Metacognitive	M

232	Create summary notes and	2.67	Cognitive	M
222	Create flashcards for words, ...	2.70	Memory	M
270	Self-test in similar oral English	2.73	Metacognitive	M
256	Avoid speaking with other students	2.79	Metacognitive	M
242	Exchange with English teachers	2.81	Compensation	M
243	Ask the instructor what to anticipate	2.82	Compensation	M
272	Self-test on the material	2.84	Metacognitive	M
226	Practice speaking English in	2.94	Cognitive	M
263	Get familiar with the test room	2.99	Metacognitive	M
289	Plan and organize ideas	2.99	Metacognitive	M
251	Use body language to help	3.04	Compensation	M
260	Develop a timetable for	3.04	Metacognitive	M
233	Look for the central idea of	3.07	Cognitive	M
229	Practice writing by modeling	3.08	Cognitive	M

As reported in Table 7.24, all the twenty least frequently used strategies fell in the medium-use range except the first three with means ranging from 2.25 to 3.08. For example, "dump information on the back of the English test paper" (mean = 2.25); "use Chinese when not knowing how to express myself in English during English tests" (mean = 2.38); "create study checklists before an English test" (mean = 2.43); "use high technology to help review materials before English tests" (mean = 2.50); "create summary notes" (mean = 2.67) and flashcards" (mean = 2.70); "exchange with English teachers about how and what to prepare before English tests" (mean = 2.81); "get familiar with the test room before an English test" (mean = 2.94); "developed a timetable for exam preparation" (mean = 3.04); and "practice writing by modeling good essays before an English essay test" (mean = 3.08).

Table 7.24 also indicates that most of the least often used strategies were of the metacognitive (8) category, followed by compensation (4), cognitive (4), memory (3) and social (1) categories. To prepare and/or during an English test, these CUP learners, like their TU and BFU peers, would not use much such metacognitive strategies as creating study checklists, predicting, self testing, developing a preparation timetable, and scanning. They would not often depend on such memory strategies as dumping information, using high technology, memorization and review of homework and notes. They would not employ such compensation strategies as using the mother tongue and talking with their English teachers or instruction about exam preparation either.

7.4.3 Differences in test-taking strategy use between CUP male and female students and between those at different proficiency levels

According to able 7.25, CUP male (with a mean range of 2.89 to 3.50) and female (with a mean range of 2.98 to 3.61) students had either a medium or a high use of the six categories of English test-taking strategies. Their ETSI mean scores (3.42 and 3.46 for males and females respectively) also fell in the medium use range. Moreover, CUP female students scored higher than their male peers not only on the ETSI but also in the six strategy categories. But no significant difference was found in any test-taking strategy use, as revealed by the results of Independent-samples t tests shown in Table 7.25.

Table 7.25: CUP Gender Differences in English Test-taking Strategy Use (N = 425)

		Mean	Standard Deviation	t-test results	
				t	p
TMS	M (312)	2.89	.67	-1.30	.194
	F (113)	2.98	.60		
TCogS	M (312)	3.39	.46	-1.57	.116
	F (113)	3.47	.45		
TCompS	M (312)	3.46	.43	-.36	.719
	F (113)	3.47	.42		
TMetaS	M (312)	3.49	.39	-.37	-.712
	F (113)	3.51	.36		
TAS	M (312)	3.50	.61	-1.72	.086
	F (113)	3.61	.58		
TSS	M (312)	3.31	.58	-1.42	.158
	F (113)	3.40	.60		
ETSI	M (312)	3.42	.37	-.91	-.364
	F (113)	3.46	.35		

Notes: M = male; F = female

To investigate differences in English test-taking strategy use between the CUP respondents at two different proficiency levels, Independent-samples t-tests were conducted. The results are presented in Table 7.26.

Table 7.26: Differences in English Learning
Strategy Use between CUP Students across Levels (N = 425)

		Mean	Standard Deviation	t-test results	
				t	p
TMS	2(289)	2.93	.67	.60	.547
	3(136)	2.89	.62		
TCogS	2(289)	3.40	.47	-.71	.477
	3(136)	3.43	.44		
TCompS	2(289)	3.45	.43	-1.02	.310
	3(136)	3.49	.42		
TMetaS	2(289)	3.48	.40	-1.47	.143
	3(136)	3.54	.35		
TAS	2(289)	3.50	.60	-1.42	.156
	3(136)	3.59	.59		
TSS	2(289)	3.33	.62	-.16	.875
	3(136)	3.34	.51		
ETSI	2(289)	3.42	.38	-1.07	.285
	3(136)	3.46	.33		

Notes: t* → Critical t value at .05 level (Black, 1999).

As shown in Table 7.26, the CUP learners at band 2 (with means ranging from 2.93 to 3.50) and 3 (with means ranging from 2.89 to 3.59) levels had a medium or even high use of the six categories of test-taking strategies. Band 3 students reported to use memory strategies less frequently but all the other categories of strategies more frequently than their band 2 counterparts when taking English exams. But no significant difference was found, as revealed by the results of Independent-samples t-tests reported in Table 7.26.

7.4.4 Correlations between individual English test-taking strategies and CUP students' performance in English

To address this question, correlation analyses were conducted, the results of which were reported in Table 7.27. It shows 23 English test-taking strategy items significantly correlated with the CUP students' performance in English with coefficients ranging from -.130 to .208.

Of these 23 strategy items, only one compensation strategy (250) significantly negatively correlated with the CUP respondents' performance in English: "use Chinese when not knowing how to express myself in English" ($r = -.130$, p < .05). The more frequently the CUP students turned to their mother tongue—Chinese when not knowing how to express themselves in English, the less proficient they were in English.

The rest of the test-taking strategies were significantly positively related to the CUP learners' performance in English. For example, strategy 219, "review a lot before English exams" ($r = .153$); 233, "look for the central idea of each question" ($r = .129$); 253, "attend class when the instructor reviews the English exam" ($r = .176$); 279, "listen to keywords when doing listening comprehension" ($r = .171$); 288, "outline my answers to questions during an essay test" ($r = .105$); 304, "approach the exam with confidence" ($r = .208$); and 309, "support and help my partner during an oral English test" ($r = .118$). The more frequently the CUP learners employed these test-taking strategies during exams, the higher they achieved in English exams.

In addition, among these 23 test-taking strategy items, the majority belonged to the metacognitive (10) category, followed by cognitive (7), compensation (2), memory (2), affective (1) and social (1) categories. As presented in Table 7.26, most of the metacognitive strategies were related to paying attention, organizing and planning, and self-monitoring. The cognitive strategies were mainly concerned with analyzing, taking notes, highlighting, and getting the idea.

Table 7.27: Correlations between Individual English Test-taking Strategies and CUP Students' Performance in English (N = 425)

Items	P
219. Review a lot before English exams (memory).	.153**
220. Keep up my homework and review my notes … (memory).	.124*
230. Analyze past test papers to determine how to improve … (cognitive).	.134**
231. Take good notes as my English teacher tells what will … (cognitive).	.110*
233. Look for the central idea of each question (cognitive).	.129**
237. Analyze the sentence structure before translating … (cognitive).	.164**
238. Break up run-on sentences into smaller parts to … (cognitive).	.151**
239. Jot down information in the margin while listening … (cognitive).	.106*
241. Highlight some sentences or phrases while reading … (cognitive).	.114*
250. Use Chinese when not knowing how to express … (compensation).	-.130**
253. Attend class when the instructor reviews … (compensation).	.176**
254. Attend 100% of my English classes (metacognitive).	.161**
263. Get familiar with the test room before … (metacognitive).	.108*
274. Try to better understand the sentence according … (metacognitive).	.164**
279. Listen to keywords when doing listening … (metacognitive).	.171**

280. Listen to clues while doing listening comprehension (metacognitive).	.154**
285. Write legibly during tests (metacognitive).	.130**
288. Outline my answers to questions … (metacognitive).	.105*
294. Try to make my writing coherent and cohesive (metacognitive).	.116*
295. Try to make as few mistakes as possible … (metacognitive).	.100*
297. Double-check my answers when completing … (metacognitive).	.189**
304. Approach the exam with confidence (affective).	.208**
309. Support and help my partner during an oral English test (social).	.118*

Notes: ** = $p < .01$;   * = $p < .05$;   P = performance

7.5 Correlations among measured variables and CUP students' performance in English

To explore the relationships among the measured variables and the CUP respondents' performance in English, correlation analyses were conducted. The results are presented in Table 7.28.

Table 7.27: Correlations among Measured Variables and CUP Students' Proficiency in English (N = 438–451)

	ELM	hsSM	InsM	IntM	ELMS	MS	CogS	CompS	MetaS	AS	SS	ELSI	TMS	TCogS	TCompS	TMetaS	TAS	TSS	ETSI	Performance
CAS	-.32**	.07	-.20**	-.23**	-.33**	-.28**	-.21**	-.31**	-.17**	-.18**	-.33**	-.02	-.19**	-.20**	-.25**	-.25**	-.10*	-.17**	-.23**	-.15**
ELM	1	.04	.25**	.36**	.27**	.19**	.22**	.26**	.16**	.17**	.27**	.05	.24**	.18**	.18**	.25**	.17**	.16**	.24**	.24**
hsSM		1	.19**	.66**	.17**	.17**	.19**	.15**	.15**	.16**	.13**	.18**	.15**	.21**	.20**	.23**	.22**	.12*	.25**	.03
InsM			1	.84**	.41**	.41**	.27**	.40**	.37**	.31**	.18**	.45**	.14**	.22**	.23**	.27**	.29**	.25**	.29**	.14**
IntM				1	.30**	.38**	.41**	.40**	.37**	.32**	.43**	.46**	.19**	.30**	.23**	.35**	.35**	.26**	.37**	.15**
ELMS					1	.38**	.37**	.30**	.40**	.37**	.32**	.46**	.19**	.30**	.30**	.35**	.35**	.40**	.37**	.11*
MS						1	.66**	.37**	.61**	.47**	.43**	.74**	.34**	.47**	.35**	.46**	.35**	.42**	.50**	.05
CogS							1	.42**	.73**	.59**	.55**	.87**	.14**	.47**	.32**	.48**	.36**	.42**	.52**	.04
CompS								1	.43**	.37**	.34**	.56**	.14**	.41**	.40**	.40**	.29**	.32**	.44**	.13**
MetaS									1	.72**	.69**	.95**	.37**	.54**	.39**	.60**	.43**	.50**	.62**	.05
AS										1	.62**	.77**	.33**	.44**	.36**	.46**	.48**	.44**	.52**	.06
SS											1	.73**	.40**	.51**	.35**	.48**	.33**	.44**	.54**	.11*
ELSI												1	.39**	.59**	.44**	.62**	.46**	.53**	.66**	.05
TMS													1	.45**	.32**	.45**	.29**	.38**	.57**	.15**
TCogS														1	.55**	.77**	.47**	.51**	.86**	.10*
TCompS															1	.64**	.42**	.42**	.73**	.14**
TMetaS																1	.58**	.60**	.96**	.11*
TAS																	1	.40**	.63**	.04
TSS																		1	.66**	.14**
ETSI																			1	.14**

Note: **. p <.01;   *. p <.05

201

As seen from Table 7.28, the measured variables were generally highly correlated with one another and most of them significantly correlated with the CUP participants' performance in English.

The Classroom Anxiety Scale (CAS) was negatively correlated with English Learning Motivation Scale (ELMS) and its three subscales (ELM, InsM and IntM), English Learning Strategy Inventory (ELSI) and its six categories (MS, CogS, CompS, MetaS, AS and SS), English Test-taking Strategy Inventory (ETSI) and its six categories (TMS, TCogS, TCompS, TMetaS, TAS and TSS). All the correlations were statistically significant except those between the CAS and the InsM and TMS, as found with the TU sample. That is, the more anxious a CUP student was in English class, the less motivated s/he was to learn the language and the less frequently s/he resorted to various strategies when learning English and taking English exams.

The ELMS and its three subscales significantly positively correlated with one another except the ELM and the InsM whose relationship was positive but insignificant. The more instrumentally motivated student was, tended to be more integratively motivated. In addition, the ELMS and its subscales were all significantly positively correlated with the ELSI and the ETSI and their subcategories except the correlation between the ELM and the TMS which was insignificantly positive. The more (instrumentally/ integratively) motivated student was usually also the more frequent user of different categories of strategies when learning English and taking English exams.

The ELSI and the ETSI and their subcategories all significantly positively correlated with one another. For example, the more frequent user of metacognitive strategies (MetaS) tended to employ memory, compensation, cognitive, affective and social strategies more frequently in English learning. S/he often deployed the six categories of test-taking strategies more frequently during English exams as well.

Finally, these measured variables generally significantly correlated with the CUP learners' performance in English. Among these variables, the CAS was significantly negatively correlated with the CUP students' performance in English ($r = -.15$); the InsM, CompS, AS, SS, TMS, and TSS were insignificantly positively related to the CUP correspondents' performance in English; the rest significantly positively correlated with the students' performance in English. In other words, the more frequent user of English learning metacognitive strategies tended to achieve higher in English.

7.6 The structural model of the measured variables and performance of the CUP sample

The statistical analyses of the data discussed above demonstrate that the data satisfied the statistical assumptions of SEM. In specifying a general model of the relationships between reported degree or use of the measured variables and the students' performance in English for the whole sample, we argued for a one-factor model of classroom anxiety (CAS), a three-factor model of motivation (ELMS), and a six-factor model of English learning and test-taking strategy use respectively, as did with the whole sample.

Of the numerous models tested, the baseline model of the measured variables and performance for the whole sample, presented in Figure 7.1, seemed to fit the data well from both a statistical and substantive perspective. The model produced a CFI of .959, a TLI of .947, an IFI of .959, a RFI of .906, and a NFI of .926, indicating a fairly good representation of the sample data. All parameter estimates in the model were substantively plausible and statistically significant at the .000 level.

As noted in the structural model, classroom anxiety significantly negatively affected the students' performance in English (-.15.93), while motivation (6.37), English learning strategy use (1.86) and English test-taking strategy use (.24) exerted a significantly positive effect on the latter.

Regarding the effect of the measured variables on one another, motivation exerted a significant, negative effect on classroom anxiety (-.49) but a significantly positive effect on English test-taking strategy use (3.63); classroom anxiety displayed a significantly negative effect on English learning strategy use (-1.29) but a significant and positive effect on English test-taking strategy use (6.71). Finally, the model illustrates that English learning strategy use significantly positively affected English test-taking strategy use (3.00).

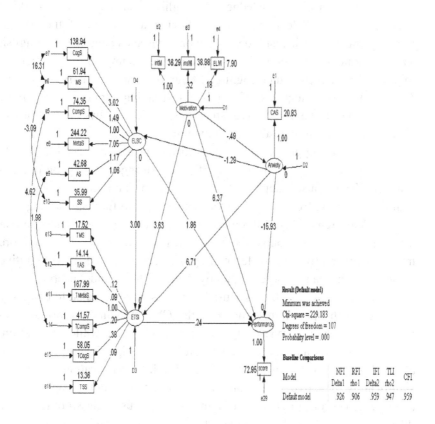

Figure 7.1: CUP Group Analysis—Measured Variables and Performance

7.7 Summary

As presented above, around a third of the CUP students were anxious to different degrees in English classrooms due to such reasons as lack of vocabulary, low English proficiency, lack of practice and lack of preparation. Meanwhile, most of them reported to be motivated and considered it worthwhile to learn English for such instrumental and integrative reasons as earning more money, getting high marks in English exams, going abroad, getting a good job, the satisfaction of finding out new things, and the good feeling of doing better than expected. Nevertheless, they were significantly more instrumentally than integratively motivated to learn the language.

204

With certain knowledge of English learning and test-taking strategies, the CUP learners reported having a medium of the overall learning and test-taking strategies. Among the six categories of English learning strategies, the most frequently used were compensation strategies, followed by affective, metacognitive, cognitive, and memory strategies. Among the six categories of English test-taking strategies, the most frequently used were affective strategies, followed by metacognitive, compensation, cognitive, social, and memory strategies.

Concerning gender differences in the measured variables, female CUP students reported to have a significantly stronger motivation to learn English. They also deployed compensation and social strategies significantly more frequently than their male peers in English learning.

With regard to differences in the measured variables among different proficiency groups, the band 3 learners were significantly more integratively motivated to learn English, and utilized metacognitive strategies significantly more frequently than did their band 2 peers.

Finally, most of the measured variables were revealed to be highly correlated with one another and with the CUP students' performance in English. Classroom anxiety significantly negatively, while motivation, English learning and test-taking strategy use significantly positively affected the students' performance in English. Motivation exerted a significantly negative effect on classroom anxiety but a significantly positive effect on English test-taking strategy use; classroom anxiety displayed a significantly negative effect on English learning strategy use but a significant and positive effect on English test-taking strategy use; and English learning strategy use significantly positively affected English test-taking strategy use.

Chapter 8   Discussion, Conclusions and Implications

This chapter mainly compares and discusses possible reasons for the similarities and differences in the findings of the three university samples presented in the previous chapters, draws conclusions, and provides implications and suggestions for future research in this area.

8.1 Discussion and conclusions

8.1.1 Foreign language anxiety

Considering foreign language anxiety, the three university samples' responses to the CAS (Classroom Anxiety Scale) items were basically similar: most of the participants from each university disagreed with statements indicative of speech anxiety, while around a third vetoed items implicative of confidence when speaking English in class. The case was the same with the statistical analyses of the CAS of the three university samples: about a third of each university sample experienced anxiety in English classrooms. This might be because almost 100% of the participants had had at least six years of exposure to English teaching and learning in schools, which enabled them to be used to English teaching and learning in class to varying degrees. However, English is after all a foreign language and seldom used in the participants' daily life. This, coupled with the fact that competition always exists and other factors such as low English proficiency, lack of vocabulary and introversion (Bailey, 1983; Liu, 2007b), unavoidably drove many of them anxious, especially when speaking the target language in class. All these conform to the findings of the whole participant sample presented in chapter 4, as found in Liu's (2006a, 2006b, 2007b) studies.

Despite these similarities, there exist certain differences. As presented in Tables 5.1, 6.1 and 7.1, the largest number of the BFU students (39.1%) (strongly) disagreed with the item "I don't usually get anxious when I have to respond to a question in English class" but the smallest number of them (48.9%) endorsed the item; whereas, the smallest number of the CUP learners (30.6%) (strongly) vetoed this item and the largest number of them (60.5%) agreed with it. The BFU students also (strongly) disagreed with the item "I always feel that other students are more at ease than I am in English class" the most (56.0%) while agreeing with it the least (21.4%); while the case was reversed with the TU sample (41.7% and 31.1% respectively). So did the BFU learners with the item "I am never embarrassed to volunteer answers in English class" (49.9% and 27.5% respectively), while their TU (39.5% and 35.7% respectively) and CUP (39.8% and 35.8% respectively) peers responded similarly to this item. However, statistical analyses reveal that the TU students reported to be the most anxious and the CUP learners the least anxious in English class though the difference was insignificant. This is surprising yet maybe reasonable in that the TU students, the best in English and other subjects, might compete with one another the hardest as well. That the CUP learners reported to be the least anxious might be due to the geographic location of the University and the high self-confidence in their abilities in English of the students.

Another difference is that the three samples endorsed the factors contributing to their anxiety in English class to varying degrees. As shown in Table 4.6, among the factors identified, generally many more BFU learners attributed their anxiety in English classrooms to the factors, especially to low English proficiency (51.6%), lack of vocabulary (32.2%), and lack of practice (41.9%), while fewer than 20% of the TU/CUP correspondents did so; many BFU participants also regarded failure to understand the teacher (29%), poor pronunciation (10%), poor listening (12.9%), and fear of being laughed at (16%) as main contributors of their anxiety in English class, whereas no more than 2.1% of the TU/CUP students believed so; 10.5% of the TU, 12.9% of the BFU, and 6% of the CUP participants considered poor oral English to be an important factor; 20% of the TU, 12.9% of the BFU, and 19.3% of the CUP learners thought of personality as a contributor; and 9.5% of the TU, 16% of the BFU, and 12% of the CUP respondents thought so of lack of confidence. Obviously, among the three university samples, proficiency in and exposure to English were of the much less concern to the TU and CUP, especially to the TU participants when identifying causes for their anxiety in English classrooms, while they were greatest worries for their BFU peers. This not only further confirms that the TU students were virtually at the highest proficiency level, as described in Chapter 3, who thus reported to suffer the least from the lack of confidence, but also suggests that a more communicative and student-oriented teaching style is conducive to reducing students' foreign language anxiety. Contrary to our expectation,

207

the BFU learners seemed to be at a lower proficiency level than their CUP counterparts, which might suggest that the present assumption of universities' ranks and the quality of their students was inappropriate, and that it would be detrimental if this assumption was incorporated into the teaching and learning of the target language in formal classrooms. Meanwhile, peer pressure seemed to be much more serious among the TU students, as implied by the fact that a lot more TU (14.7%) participants agreed that other students' wonderful performance was a great contributor to their anxiety in English class, while few of the other two samples thought so. It might be because top students were more self-conscious and held a greater self-esteem. As revealed in Liu's (2006a, 2006b) studies, these students usually tended to pursue perfection. A similar tendency is observed from those at different proficiency levels among the TU and CUP learners.

Generally, more of those at the lower proficiency level within a university also tended to consider foreign language anxiety to be a debilitator. Nevertheless, it is worth noting that more TU students at the highest proficiency level believed so, which might be also due to the fact that the smallest number of band 3 students was included in the sample.

Concerning the strategies to deal with foreign language anxiety, all the three samples hoped their EFL teachers to be helpful, friendly, and encouraging. However, comparatively, the TU learners preferred their EFL teachers to be a guide and facilitator, the CUP learners suggested EFL teachers being a helper and a friend, but their BFU peers hoped their EFL teachers to be a corrector and modify their speech accordingly. As for the learners, all the three samples suggested them being confident and brave, improving English and having more practice. Nevertheless, the TU participants' suggestions focused more on affect, while their BFU peers' were more concerned with motivation intensity when learning the language. A similar pattern is observed for those at different proficiency levels within a university sample.

8.1.2 English learning motivation

Similar to the CAS, the three university samples' responses to the ELMS items were generally conformant: consistent with the result of the whole participant sample, more than 60% of each university sample reported to have a strong English learning motivation, be both instrumentally and integratively motivated, and be more instrumentally than integratively motivated. This also conforms to the findings of motivation studies of Chinese EFL learners (Gao et al, 2004; Liu, 2007a).

Likewise, there also exist certain differences among the three university samples concerning English learning motivation. As presented in Tables 5.9, 6.6 and 7.8, the three university samples' responses to the ELMS items did not fluctuate much except items 11, 12, 16, 17, 18 and 32. The BFU and CUP students did not differ much from each other in terms of responses to these items. But a lot more TU learners (strongly) disagreed with while fewer endorsed these items—learning English for a good job, more money, high marks, requirement, certificates and the good feeling of doing better than expected. And the ANOVA results reveal that the TU students were significantly less motivated than their BFU and CUP peers, whereas no significant difference was found between the latter two. This might be attributed to the different policies and styles of English education adopted by the three universities, as described in chapter 3. With an aim of enhancing students' overall competence in English, a more student-oriented teaching style and a more autonomous learning style prevailed in Tsinghua University (TU). Without the pressure of passing CET band 4, the TU students might have a less strong motivation to learn English, yet they could also learn the language more for personal interests. By contrast, the BFU and CUP students had to pass CET band 4 in order to graduate on time. Thus, the teaching and learning of English in these two universities were more exam-oriented, which partially explained why these two samples were more motivated to learn the language. This also partly accounted for the fact that the BFU and CUP students were significantly more instrumentally than integratively motivated while the TU learners did not differ much in these two types of motivations.

A comparison of the specific motivations identified by the three samples revealed a similar pattern. It is worth noting that both the TU and CUP correspondents reported that the desire to do something for the Olympic Games 2008 motivated them to learn English, while no CUP participants reported so, which is interesting puzzling since the Beijing Organizing Committee for the Games has been recruiting volunteers all over the country.

Meanwhile, the TU or CUP students at the highest proficiency level were significantly more motivated to learn English than those least proficient in English; their integrative motivation was significantly stronger as well. But no significant difference existed in instrumental motivation between these two groups of learners. It is worth noting that no significant differences were found in the ELMS and its subscales between band 1 and 2 or between band 2 and 3 TU undergraduate non-English majors. This might be because band 1 and 2 or band 2 and 3 TU students actually did not differ much from each other in English proficiency.

8.1.3 English learning strategy use

When it comes to English learning strategy use, all the samples had a limited knowledge/awareness, with the TU participants being the most aware of the strategies they were using and their BFU learners being the least aware of the use, so did those at different proficiency levels within a university. And both the whole participant sample and each university sample had a medium use of the strategies. Among the three university samples, the BFU students had the smallest number of high-use strategy items and the largest number of strategy item in the medium-use range; whereas the other two samples had a similar distribution of the strategy items in different use ranges. But no significant difference was found in the overall English learning strategy use among the three university samples. As to the six categories of English learning strategy, compensation and memory strategies were the most and least frequently used respectively by all the samples. This is surprising in that it was often believed that Chinese students depended much on memory strategies in learning and that memory strategies were actually reported to be the most familiar to the participants from all universities. However, the present finding might imply that Chinese learners were changing their style of using different strategies, which justifies the continuous and further research in this area. The other four categories of strategies were utilized to varying degrees by the four samples, with the order for the whole participant sample and the TU students being the same. Concerning the use of these categories of strategies, significant differences were found in memory and metacognitive strategies among the three university samples.

Among the twenty most frequently used English learning strategies, most were shared by the three or two of the three university samples. The common features are: all fell in the high-use range; the majority of the most often used strategies fell into the compensation and metacognitive categories, with few belonging to the other strategy categories; each university sample would resort to both linguistic and background knowledge to make guesses to overcome obstacles in English learning, and center their learning by overviewing, linking and paying attention. But the following most frequently use strategies were peculiar to the TU learners: use background and linguistic knowledge to make guesses about English listening; use paralinguistic knowledge to make guesses about speakers' intentions; select English learning materials based on English proficiency; remember new English words by pronunciation; pay attention when someone is speaking English; try to use a variety of words when writing in English; and make a summary and restate the main idea in the concluding paragraph when writing in English. This, we think, can be mainly attributed to the aim and style of English teaching and learning in Tsinghua University. Since the four basic skills of English—reading, listening, speaking and writing were of the same importance for the TU EFL teachers and learners, strategies concerned with the learning of English listening, speaking and writing unavoidably caught the students' attention in the process of English learning. This also explains why these strategies were more or less neglected by the BFU and CUP learners in whose universities the teaching and learning of English was focused on reading and primarily aimed to pass CET band 4.

Of the twenty least often used English learning strategies, more common features could be found among the three university samples: most of the strategies fell in the medium-use range; the majority belonged to the metacognitive category, followed by cognitive, memory, affective and social categories. Each sample generally id not seek practice opportunities much in learning English; they did not practice much through repetition and/or formally practicing with sounds and writing systems; they would not use physical response or sensation much; and they would not resort to such affective strategies as using a checklist, writing a language learning diary often either, or talking about feelings to ease their anxiety, fear and/or doubt in English learning, as found in Liu's (2006a, 2006b, 2007b) studies.

Regarding differences in English learning strategy use, the TU students at the lowest (band 1) proficiency level used the overall strategies and all categories of strategies significantly less frequently than those better proficient in English (band 2 and 3 students); while no significant difference existed between band 2 and 3 students in any use of categories of strategies. The CUP band 2 students employed metacognitive strategies significantly less often than their band 3 peers; and no significant difference was found in the use of other categories of strategies between these two groups. This might be because band 2 and 3 students in both

211

universities did not differ much from each other in terms of English proficiency. However, it can still be said that students at the highest proficiency level tended to be the most frequent users of English learning strategies.

8.1.4 English test-taking strategy use

As the data analyses show, all the three university samples had more knowledge of English test-taking strategies, with the TU correspondents using the most various types of strategies during an English exam. It is almost the same with those at different proficiency levels within a university. Moreover, both the whole participant sample and each university sample had a medium use of English test-taking strategies and a similar distribution of strategy items in different use ranges. As to the six categories of English test-taking strategy, compensation, affective and metacognitive strategies were the most frequently utilized by the TU, BFU and CUP learners respectively; memory, social and cognitive strategies were the top three least often used by the three samples, with the order being the same. This is unexpected considering the nature of the three EFL learning situations described in chapter 3: the TU students emphasized spoken English the most; the BFU consisted of the largest number of female students who might turn to affective strategies the most often; the CUP students seemed to be the most comfortable at centering, arranging and planning and evaluating their learning. Concerning the use of these categories of strategies, significant differences existed in all strategy categories among the three university samples: the TU students were the least frequent user of memory strategies but the most frequent users of cognitive and compensation strategies; the BFU learners were the least frequent users of cognitive, compensation, metacognitive, affective, social and overall English test-taking strategies; and the CUP sample employed metacoginitive, affective, social and overall English-test-taking strategies the most often.

Among the twenty most frequently used test-taking strategies, the majority were shared by the three or two of the three university samples: all strategies fell in the high-use range; the majority fell into metacognitive and compensation categories; each university sample would turn to both linguistic and background knowledge and different clues to make guesses to overcome obstacles in English learning, and center their learning by overviewing, linking and paying attention. The case was similar with the twenty least often used test-taking strategies among the three university samples: the top two least often used strategies were the same—dump information and switch to the mother tongue, which was highly due to the fact that nothing except answers should be written on the answer sheet in formal exams; the majority were in the medium-use range and belonged to metacognitive, memory and compensation categories; before English exams, each sample generally did not employ such metacognitive strategies as planning the preparation carefully, predicting and self-testing, or such memory strategies as memorization and review; during the exams, they would not like such metacognitive strategies as scanning, or compensation strategies as switching to the mother tongue. These features reveal that each sample were aware of and might consciously use a variety of choices when strategies were needed before and/or during English exams on one hand, and that certain strategies were less frequently utilized due to various reasons such as the nature, importance and difficulty of exams, and experience of taking exams, which needs further exploration.

Concerning differences in English test-taking strategy use, the TU band 3 students employed memory strategies significantly less frequently than those less proficient in English (band 1 and 2 students); the TU students at the lowest (band 1) proficiency level used the overall strategies and other categories of strategies significantly less frequently than those better proficient in English (band 2 and 3 students. Though the CUP band 3 students employed memory strategies less frequently and other categories of strategies and the overall test-taking strategies more frequently than their band 2 peers, no significant difference was found. This might be because many more band 2 students participated in the study.

8.1.5 Gender differences in the measured variables

As to gender differences in the measured variables, probably due to the fact that different numbers of male and female participants were involved in the three university samples mixed findings were revealed.

Female students reported to be less anxious than male students of the whole participant sample, but the difference was insignificant. This tendency holds true for the TU and BFU male and female students: the TU females felt significantly less anxious than males while no significant difference was found between the BFU male and female learners in anxiety. Contrarily, the CUP female students reported to be more anxious than their male peers, but no significant difference was found. As to English learning motivation, female respondents scored significantly higher on the ELMS and its subscales than their male peers of the whole participant sample. Girl students of the three university samples tended to score higher on the ELMS and its subscales as well; however, significant difference was found only in the ELMS for the CUP sample, the BFU females were significantly more instrumentally motivated, and the TU girls had a significantly higher motivation and were significantly more integratively motivated as well. Concerning English learning strategies, the TU female learners scored higher on the ELSI and its subscales than their male peers, but significant difference was found only in the use of social strategies. Girl students of the whole participant sample and the other two university samples scored either higher or lower than boys on the ELSI and its subscales. And significant difference existed in the use of compensation and social strategies for the whole participant sample and the CUP students, and compensation strategies for the BFU sample. Regarding English test-taking strategies, female learners of the whole participant sample and the three universities tended to score higher on the ETSI and its subscales than their male peers, but no significant difference was found.

This difference that female students tended to be less anxious, more motivated, use more learning and test-taking strategies than their male counterparts is so interesting yet may be peculiar to the Chinese EL learning context. In China, the majority of EFL teachers in colleges and universities were female, which might have a certain positive impact on girl students in English learning. Nevertheless, whether it is true deserves further research.

8.1.6 Interaction of the measured variables and their impact on the students' performance in English

As presented in previous three chapters, for the whole participant sample and each university sample, all the measured variables generally significantly correlated with one another, with coefficients somehow fluctuating as the samples varied. The subscales of the ELMS, the ELSI and the ETSI were highly significantly related to one another and the overall measurement. These three scales and their subscales also generally significantly correlated with one another, but the coefficients seldom exceeded .40 except those between the ELSI and the ETSI. This suggests English learning and test-taking strategies might have a greater effect on each other while the interactive effect between motivation and English learning/test-taking strategies were significant but not prominent.

Meanwhile, the CAS was generally significantly negatively correlated with the ELMS, the ELSI, the ETSI and their subscales though the coefficients rarely exceeded .40.

Additionally, most of these measured variables significantly correlated with students' performance in English, though the coefficients hardly exceeded .30. Moreover, around 19% (TU) to 29.7% (BFU) English learning strategy items and about 24.2% (TU) to 29.7% (BFU) test-taking strategy items were significantly related to the students' performance in English, but the coefficients were not high.

The SEM results largely confirmed these findings: the measured variables significantly interrelatedly affected each other and the students' performance in English. However, some of the differences are worth attention. First, though foreign language anxiety yielded a negative effect the ETSI for both the whole participant sample and the BFU sample, it exerted a positive effect on the ETSI for the other two samples, producing an extraordinarily great effect on the ETSI (6.71) for the CUP sample. This is really unexpected in that correlation analyses reveal that the CAS negatively correlated with the ETSI for all the samples, with the coefficient being the lowest for the BFU sample. Similarly surprising is that foreign language anxiety displayed the greatest effect (-15.93) on the CUP students' performance in English which is a lot larger than that for the other three sample (-.80 to -3.44), although a lot more BFU journal participants believed it to be negative. Second, motivation's effect on foreign language anxiety (-1.57) was much greater for the TU sample than that for the other three samples (-.49 - -.85). Third, motivation's effect on the TU correspondents' performance in English (.18) was much lower than that for the other three samples (.50 – 6.37), while its effect was much larger for the CUP sample (6.37). Finally, the ETSI's effect on the CUP learners' performance in English (.24) was much greater than that for the other three samples (.06 - .08). All these might be closely related to the learning contexts described in chapter three. The CUP students might become more motivated learners simply because they were the least proficient in English and had to take CET band 4. And because they relatively had less exposure and access to English, they became more anxious when using the language, which negatively affected their performance. Contrarily, as the most advanced learners who were exempt from CET band 4, the TU participants were the least affected by motivation; so were they by anxiety since they comparatively had much more exposure and access to the target language. Nevertheless, all these need to be further investigated.

8.1.7 Conclusions

To summarize, concerning the study of anxiety, motivation, English learning and test-taking strategy use, and their effect on students' performance in English, the following conclusions can be drawn.

(1) The ELM, the InsM and the IntM were important components of the ELMS; so were MS, CogS, ComS, MetaS, AS and SS of the ELSI, and TMS, TcogS, TcomS, TmetaS, TAS and TSS of the ETSI.

(2) Around a third of the whole participant sample and each university sample experienced anxiety in English class.

(3) More than 60% of the whole participant sample and each university sample were (highly) motivated both instrumentally and integratively to learn English; they were generally more instrumentally than integratively motivated as well.

(4) Both the whole participant sample and each university sample had a medium use of English learning and test-taking strategies and a similar distribution of the strategy items in different use ranges.

(5) As to the six categories of English learning strategies, compensation and memory strategies were the most and least frequently used respectively by all the samples.

(6) As to the six categories of English test-taking strategies, compensation, affective and metacognitive strategies were the most frequently utilized by the TU, BFU and CUP learners respectively; memory, social and cognitive strategies were the top three least often used by the three samples, with the order being the same.

(7) Significant differences existed in English learning motivation, memory and metacognitive English learning strategies, and all six categories of English test-taking strategies between two or three university samples. Obviously, proficiency or the learning context played an important role in motivating the learners and in their use of English learning and test-taking strategies. Understandably, different methods teaching and learning were adopted in the three universities; and the focus of teaching and learning varied accordingly as well.

(8) Significant differences were found in general motivation, integrative motivation, English learning and test-taking strategies among students at different proficiency levels. This lends direct support to the validation of the band system executed in TU and CUP. More insightful

findings would have been revealed if the system had also been carried out in BFU.

(9) Concerning gender differences in foreign language anxiety and English learning motivation, mixed findings were found; no significant differences were found in English learning and test-taking strategy use. To cater for different needs of males and females, various teaching methods can be employed to motivate them accordingly, as discussed by Chavez (2001). It is also beneficial to encourage them to utilize various learning and test-taking strategies to improve their learning outcomes.

(10) Among the twenty most and least frequently used English learning/test-taking strategies, most were shared by the three or two of the three university samples.

(11) All the measured variables generally significantly correlated with one another and the students' performance in English, with coefficients somehow fluctuating as the samples varied

(12) The SEM results of the four samples were generally similar, however, due to various factors such as English proficiency, geographic location, teaching focus, teaching style and personality, some striking differences existed in the structural models of the measured variables and performance in English.

8.2 Implications

Though only around a third of the participants felt anxious in English, it is still an issue deserving attention and research to help these learners reduce or even overcome anxiety to enhance their learning of English. Therefore, primarily it is necessary to be aware of and acknowledge the existence of anxiety in EFL classrooms and its potential negative effect on students' performance in English. Then, it is desirable for EFL teachers to be empathetic to their students, especially those who appear the most anxious in class (Oxford, 1999), which will make them more comfortable when using English in class. In addition, to help students become less anxious in English lessons, it is advisable for EFL teachers to create a relaxing and supportive classroom-learning environment (Horwitz et al., 1986; Price, 1991; Yan, 2003). As Phillips claimed, "low-stress language learning environment is believed to facilitate acquisition of the foreign language by allowing students to concentrate more fully on communication rather than being distracted by self-deprecating worry and fear of evaluation, encouraging a relaxed atmosphere in the classroom may be a first step in alleviating anxiety related to oral testing (1992: 24)".

Moreover, though the participants reported not to use affective learning strategies such as writing dairies and taking body temperature much, writing reflective journals is actually both a low anxiety-producing learning strategy and an effective way of reducing anxiety levels (Horwitz et al., 1986; Onwuegbuzie, Bailey & Daley, 1999). By doing this, EFL learners can be better conscious of the issue of anxiety and thus actively seek strategies to cope with the issue to promote their learning of the target language.

As the analyses of the data revealed, the correspondents from all universities were motivated to learn English for various reasons, most of which were instrumental. It may be helpful to share these motivations among the students to encourage them to learn the target language for a certain purpose. In this way, the motivated students may continue to remain motivated in spite of any difficulty and those without any motivation may thus become motivated because of peer pressure. Nevertheless, more importantly, it will be highly useful to increase EFL learners' English learning motivation in that it is so closely related to their performance in the target language.

Since the participants of all universities reported having limited knowledge of both English learning and test strategies, EFL teachers "are encouraged to start by raising students' awareness of the strategies they have already been using" (Lan & Oxford, 2003: 375). Being aware of the strategies, EFL learners may consciously employ certain strategies beneficial to their English learning or adjust some strategies that are not so helpful. To help students better understand the strategies and strategy use, it is also desirable for EFL teachers to explain the strategies via various means including the use of native language (Lan & Oxford, 2003). Only with a clear understanding of the strategies and strategy use can EFL students utilize the strategies accordingly when confronting different tasks in varying situations.

8.3 Limitations and suggestions for future research
As described in previous chapter(s), the present research adopted a triangulated method in collecting data, and the survey contained substantial information. Nevertheless, the design of reflective journals was not so informative and powerful. If a more complicated triangulation of

methodology (e.g., more reflective journals were required and more related topics were involved in the journals, interviews were conducted, etc.), more inside views of the issues (anxiety, motivation and strategy use) from the learners could have been obtained to complement the survey results.

Though this research recruited a large number of participants from different EFL learning situations in Beijing, the whole sample apparently had many more males; so did the TU and CUP samples. And the ration of male and females participants varied from university to university. The findings might be different if there were even numbers of male and female participants and/or an even proportion of men and women learners among different samples. Thus, research on gender differences in English learning and test-taking strategy use, anxiety and motivation needs to be continuously conducted in various learning and testing situations.

Still, the self-developed survey items, primarily the English learning Strategy Use Inventory and the Test-taking Strategy Use Inventory, in this study may need to be continuously researched in various situations to further confirm its reliability and validity. This need is also evidenced by the low coefficients revealed by the factor analyses of the two inventories and the correlation analysis of strategy use and the students' performance in English.

It is worth noting that some strategies, especially affective and social strategies, though not found to be significantly related to students' proficiency in English, might be specifically significantly correlated with students' proficiency in oral English, which was not measured as a separate part in the present study. Thus, it is worthwhile to be further researched in this area.

About the authors

Dr. Meihua Liu is associate professor of English at the Department of Foreign Languages, Tsinghua University, China. Her research interests mainly include second/foreign language teaching and learning, classroom research, and second language writing. She is reader for such journals as *the Journal of Asia TEFL, Indonesian Journal of English Language Teaching,* and *China EFL journal.* She has published widely in journals such as *Modern Language Journal, TESL Canada Journal, TESL Reporter, System, ITL: International Journal of Applied Linguistics, Asian Journal of English Language Teaching, Indonesian Journal of English Language Teaching, the Journal of Asia TEFL, Asian EFL Journal, Foreign Language Teaching (外语教学)，and Education and Career (教育与职业).* Her book called *Reticence and Anxiety in Oral English Lessons* came out by Peter Lang in 2009. Presently, she lives in Beijing, China.

Dr. Wenxia Zhang is professor of English at the Department of Foreign Languages, Tsinghua University, China. Her major research interests cover EFL teaching and learning, language testing, and EFL writing. She is on the board of *Assessing Writing* and has written for such journals as *Indonesian Journal of English Language Teaching, the Journal of Asia TEFL, Foreign Language World* (外语界), *Foreign Language Education* (外语教学), *China University Teaching* (中国大学教学), *Educational Technology for Foreign Language Teaching* (外语电化教学), *Teaching English in China, the Journal of Tsinghua University* (清华大学学报). Her book entitled *the Rhetorical Patterns Found in Chinese EFL Student Writers' Examination Essays in English and the Influence of These Patterns on Rater Response* was published by Tsinghua University Press in 2004. Presently, she lives in Beijing, China.

Bibliography

Abraham, R. G., and Vann, R. J. (1987). Strategies of two language learners: a case study. In A. Werden and J. Rubin (Eds.), *Learner strategies in language learning* (85-102). London: Prentice Hall International.

Aida, Y. (1994). Examination of Horwitz, Horwitz, and Cope's construct of foreign language anxiety: the case of students of Japanese. *The Modern Language Journal* 78: 155-168.

Allwright, D. (1983). Classroom-centered research on language teaching and learning: A brief historical overview. *TESOL Quarterly, 17, 191-204.*

Anderson, N. J. (1991). Individual differences in strategy use in second language reading and testing. *The Modern Language Journal, 75 (4), 460-472.*

Akbari, R., and Hosseini, K. (2008). Multiple intelligences and language learning strategies: Investigating possible relations. System (upcoming).

Bacon, S. M. (1992a). The relationship between gender, comprehension, processing strategies, and cognitive and affective response in foreign language listening. *Modern Language Journal, 76(2), 160-178.*

Bailey, K. M. (1983). Competitiveness and anxiety in adult second language learning: looking at and through the dairy studies. In H. W. Seliger and M. H. Long (Eds.), *Classroom Oriented Research in Second Language Acquisition* (pp. 67-103). Rowley, Mass.: Newbury House Publishers, Inc.

Bailey, P., Daley, C. E., and Onwuegbuzie, A. J. (1999). Foreign language anxiety and learning style. *Foreign Language Annals.* 32/1, 63-76.

Belmechri, F., and Hummel, K. (1998). Orientations and motivation in the acquisition of English as a second language among high school students in Quebec city. *Language Learning*, 2, 219-244.

Bialystok, E. (1981). The role of conscious strategies in second language proficiency. *Modern Language Journal, 65, 24-35.*

Bialystok, E. (1983). Some factors in the selection and implementation of communication strategies. In C. Faerch and G. Kasper (eds.), Strategies in interlanguage communication (pp. 103-126). London: Longman.

Black, J. H. (1993). Learning and reception strategy use and the cloze procedure. *The Canadian Modern Language Review, 49(3), 418-445.*

Black, T. R. (1999). *Doing quantitative research in the social sciences.* London: Sage Publications.

Block, E. (1986). The comprehension strategies of second language readers. *TESOL Quarterly, 20, 463-394.*

Bremner, S. (1999). Language learning strategies and language proficiency: investigating the relationship in Hong Kong. *The Canadian Modern Language Review, 55(4), 496-514.*

Brown, H. D. (1973). Affective variables in second language acquisition. *Language Learning. 23, 231-244.*

Bruen, J. (2001). Strategies for success: profiling the effective learner of German. *Foreign Language Annals, 34(3), 216-225.*

Chamot, A. U. (1987). The learning strategies of ESL students. In A. Wenden and J. Rubin (Eds.), *Learner strategies in language learning* (pp. 71-85). Hemel Hempstead: Prentice-Hall.

Chamot, A. U., and El-Dinary, P. B. (1999). Children's learning strategies in language immersion classrooms. *The Modern Language Journal, 83, 319-338.*

Chamot, A. U., and Küpper, L. (1989). Learning strategies in foreign language instruction. *Foreign Language Annals, 22, 13-24.*

Chamot, A. M., Küpper, L., and Impink-Hernandez, M. (1988). *A study of learning strategies in foreign language instruction: findings of the longitudinal study.* McLean, VA: Interstate Research Associates.

Chavez, M. (2001). *Gender in the language classroom.* Boston: McGraw Hill.

Chen, H., 2002. *College students' English learning anxiety and their coping styles.* China: Southwest Normal University, unpublished M. A. dissertation.

Cheng, Y., Horwitz, E. K., and Schallert, D. L. (1999). Language anxiety: differentiating writing and speaking components. *Language Learning. 49/3, 417-446.*

Clément, R., Dörnyei, Z.n, Noels, K. A. (1994). Motivation, self-confidence, and group cohesion in the foreign language. *Language Learning, 3, 417-448.*

Cohen, A. D. (1998a). Strategies and processes in test taking and SLA. In L. F. Bachman and A. D. Cohen (Eds.), *Interfaces between second language acquisition and language testing research* (pp. 90-111). Cambridge: Cambridge University Press.

Cohen, A. D. (1998b). *Strategies in learning and using second language.* London and New York: Longman.

Cohen, A. D., 2000. *Strategies in language and using a second language.* Beijing: Foreign Language Teaching and Research Press

College English Curriculum. 1999. Beijing: Higher Education Press.

Cortazzi, M., and Jin, L. (1996). Cultures of learning: language classrooms in China. In H. Coleman (ed.) *Society and the language classroom.* Cambridge: Cambridge University Press, 169-206.

Crookes, R., and Schmidt, R. (1989). Motivation: reopening the research agenda. *University of Hawaii Working Papers in ESL, 8, 217-256.*

Daly, J. A., Vangelisti, A. L., and Weber, D. J. (1995). Speech anxiety affects how people prepare speeches: a protocol analysis of the preparation processes of speakers. *Communication Monographs.* 62, 383–397.

Donley, P. (1998). Ten ways to cope with foreign language anxiety. In A. Mollica (Ed.) *Teaching and learning language: selected reading from Mosaic* (pp. 109-110). Welland, ON.: Soleil Publishing Inc.

Dörnyei, Zoltán. (1990). Conceptualizing motivation in foreign language learning. *Language Learning, 40, 45-78.*

Dörnyei, Z. (1994). Motivation and motivating in the foreign language classroom. *Modern Language Journal, 78, 273-284.*

Dörnyei, Z. (2001). *Teaching and researching motivation.* Longman: Pearson Education Limited.

Ehrman, M. E., and Oxford, R. L. (1989). Effects of sex differences, career choice, and psychological type on adult language learning strategies. *Modern Language Journal, 73, 1-13.*

Ehrman, M. E., and Oxford, R. L. (1995). Cognition plus: correlates of language learning success. *The Modern Language Journal. 79/1,* 67-89.

Ellis, R. (1985). *Understanding second language acquisition.* Oxford: Oxford University Press.

Ellis, R. (1999). *The study of second language acquisition.* Shanghai: Shanghai Foreign Language Education Press.

Ellis, R., and Sinclair, B. (1989). *Learning to learn English: a course in learner training* (teacher's book). Cambridge: Cambridge University Press.

Ely, C. M. (1986). An analysis of discomfort, risk-taking, sociability, and motivation in the L2 classroom. *Language Learning*. 36, 1-25.

Gao Y., Zhao, Y., Cheng, Y., and Zhou, Y. (2004). Motivation types of Chinese university students. *Asian Journal of English Language Teaching, 14, 45-64.*

Gardner, R. C. (1983). Learning another language: A true social psychological experiment. *Journal of Language and Social Psychology, 2, 219-239.*

Gardner, R. C. (1985). *Social psychology and second language learning.* Edward Arnold.

Gardner, R. C., and Lambert, W. E. (1972). *Attitudes and motivation in second language learning.* Rowley, MA: Newbury House.

Gardner, R. C., and MacIntyre, P. D. (1991). An instrumental motivation in language study. *Studies in Second Language Acquisition. 13, 57-72.*

Gardner, R. C., and MacIntyre, P. D. (1992). Integrative motivation, induced anxiety, and language learning in a controlled environment. *Studies in Second Language Acquisition.* 14/2, 197-214.

Gardner, R. C., and MacIntyre, P. D. (1993). A student's contribution to second language learning: Part II, affective factors. *Language Learning, 26, 1-11.*

Gardner, R. C., Day, J. B., and MacIntyre, P. D. (1992). Integrative motivation, induced anxiety, and language learning in a controlled environment. *Studies in Second Language Acquisition, 14, 197-214.*

Gardner, R. C., Lalonde, R. N., and Moorcroft, R. (1985). The role of attitudes and motivation in second language learning: Correlational and experimental considerations. *Language Learning, 35, 207-227.*

Gardner, R. C., Lalonde, R. N., Moorcroft, R., and Evers, F. T. (1987). Second language attrition: The role of motivation and use. *Journal of Language and Social Psychology, 6, 29-47.*

Gardner, R. C., Lalonde, R. N., and Pierson, R. (1983). The socio-educational model of second language acquisition: An investigation using LISREL causal modeling. *Journal of Language and Social Psychology, 2, 1-15.*

Gardner, R. C., and MacIntyre, P. D. (1992). Integrative motivation, induced anxiety, and language learning in a controlled environment. *Studies in Second Language Acquisition, 14(2), 197-214.*

Gardner, R. C., Moorcroft, R., and Metford, J. (1989). Second language learning in an immersion program: Factors influencing acquisition and retention. *Journal of Language and Social Psychology, 8, 287-305.*

Grainger, P. R. (1997). Language-learning strategies for learners of Japanese: investigating ethnicity. *Foreign Language Annals, 30(3), 378-385.*

Grainger, P. (2003). Second language learning strategies and Japanese: does orthography make a difference? System, 33, 327-339.

Green, J. M., and Oxford, R. (1995). A closer look at learning strategies, L2 proficiency, and gender. *TESOL Quarterly, 29(2), 261-297.*

Griffiths, C. (2003). Patterns of language learning strategy use. *System, 31, 467-383.*

Halbach, A. (2000). Finding out about students' learning strategies by looking at their diaries: A case study. *System, 28, 85-96.*

Hao, M., Liu, M., Hao, R. P. (2004). An Empirical Study on Anxiety and Motivation in English as a Foreign Language. *Asian Journal of English Language Teaching, 14, 89-104.*

Hilleson, M. (1996). "I want to talk with them, but I don't want them to hear": An introspective study of second langue anxiety in an English-medium school. In K. M. Bailey and D. Nunan (eds) *Voices from the language classroom.* Cambridge: Cambridge University Press, 248-282.

Hong-Nam, K., and Alexandra, G. L. (2006). Language learning strategy use of ESL students in an intensive English learning context. *System, 34, 399-415.*

Horwitz, E. K. (1995). Student affective reactions and the teaching and learning of foreign languages. *Journal of Educational Research.* 23/7, 569-652.

Horwitz, E. K. (2001). Language anxiety and achievement. *Annual Review of Applied Linguistics, 21, 112-126.*

Horwitz, E. K., Horwitz, M., and Cope, J. (1986). Foreign language classroom anxiety. *The Modern Language Journal.* 1, 125–132.

Horwitz, E. K., and Young, D. J. (1991). *Language anxiety: from theory and research to classroom implications.* NJ: Prentice Hall.

Hsiao, T-Y., and Oxford, R. L. (2002). Comparing theories of language learning strategies: a confirmatory factor analysis. Modern Language Journal, 86, 368-383.

Hu, J. (2002). Dörnyei's three-leveled learning motivation model and oral English teaching. *Shangdong Foreign Language Teaching, 1, 8-12.*

Huang, H., and Wen, W. (2005). An empirical study of English learners' motivation in a Chinese setting. *Foreign Language Teaching Abroad, (3), 30-38.*

Huang, X.-H., and Van Naerssen, M. (1985). Learning strategies for oral communication. *Applied Linguistics, 6, 287-307.*

Jackson, J. (2002). Reticence in second language case discussions: anxiety and aspirations. *System, 30(1), 65-84.*

Kitano, K., 2001. Anxiety in the college Japanese language classroom. *The Modern Language Journal, 85, 549-566.*

Ko, Yih-wen W. (2002). *Perceptual style preferences and their relationship to English achievement and learning strategies of junior high EFL learners in Taiwan.* Master's thesis, National Gaushung University of Education.

Krashen, S. (1982). *Principles and practice in second language acquisition.* Oxford: Pergamon.

Krippendorff, K. (1980). *Content analysis: an introduction to its methodology.* Beverly Hills: Sage Publications

Ku, P-Y. N. (1995). *Strategies associated with proficiency and predictors of strategy choice: a study of language learning strategies of EFL students at three educational levels in Taiwan.* Unpublished doctoral dissertation, Indiana University, Bloomington.

Lan, R., and Oxford, R. L. (2003). Language learning strategy profiles of elementary school students in Taiwan. *IRAL, 41, 339-379.*

Li, L. (2005). *An investigation of the learning strategy use of college English learners.* Unpublished M.A. dissertation. Beijing: Tsinghua University.

Liao, Yen-Fen. (2002). *A study of Taiwanese junior high school students' EFL learning motivation and learning strategies.* Master's thesis, National Gaushung University of Education.

Liu, M. (2006a). Anxiety in EFL classrooms: causes and consequences. *TESL Reporter, 39(1), 13-32.*

Liu, M. (2006b). Anxiety in Chinese EFL students at different proficiency levels. *System, 34(3).*

Liu, M. (2007a). Chinese students' motivation to learn English at the tertiary level. *Asian EFL Journal, 9(1), 126-146.*

Liu, M. (2007b). Anxiety in oral English classrooms: a case study in China. Indonesian Journal of English Language Teaching, 3(1), 119-137.

Liu, M. (2009). *Reticence and anxiety in oral English lessons*. Berne: Peter Lang.

Liu, M. and Jackson, J. (2008). An Exploration of Chinese EFL Learners' Unwillingness to Communicate and Foreign Language Anxiety. *The Modern Language Journal, 92(1), 71-86.*

MacIntyre, P. D. (1994). Toward a social psychological model of strategy use. *Foreign Language Annals, 27, 185-195.*

Lozanov, G. (1978). *Suggestology and outlines of suggestopedy*. New York: Gordon & Breach.

MacIntyre, P. D., Baker, S. C., Clément, R., and Conrod, S. (2001). Willingness to communicate, social support, and language-learning orientations of immersion students. *Studies in Second Language Acquisition, 28, 369-388.*

MacIntyre, P. D., Clément, R., Dörnyei, Z., and Noels, K. A. (1998). Conceptualizing willingness to communicate in a L2: a situational model of L2 confidence and affiliation. *The Modern Language Journal, 82(4), 545-562.*

MacIntyre, P. D., and Gardner, R. C. (1989). Anxiety and second-language learning: Toward a theoretical clarification. *Language Learning.* 39, 251–275.

MacIntyre, P. D., and Gardner, R. C. (1991a). Methods and results in the study of anxiety and language learning: A review of the literature. *Language Learning.* 41, 85-117.

MacIntyre, P. D., and Gardner, R. C. (1991b). Investigating language class anxiety using the focused essay technique. *The Modern Language Journal.* 75, 296-304.

MacIntyre, P. D., and Gardner, R. C. (1994a). The effects of induced anxiety on three stages of cognitive processing in computerized vocabulary learning. *Studies in Second Language Acquisition.* 16, 1-17.

MacIntyre, P. D., and Gardner, R. C. (1994b). The subtle effects of language anxiety on cognitive processing in the second language. *Language Learning, 44, 283-305.*

MacIntyre, P. D., Noels, K. A., and Clément, R. (1997). Biases in self-ratings of second language proficiency: the role of language anxiety. *Language Learning, 47(2), 265-287.*

MacIntyre, P. D., and Thivierge, K. A. (1995). The effects of audience pleasantness, audience familiarity, and speaking contexts on public speaking anxiety and willingness to speak. *Communication Quarterly, 43(4), 456-466.*

Magogwe, J. M., and Oliver, R. (2007). The relationship between language learning strategies, proficiency, age and self-efficacy beliefs: a study of language learners in Botswana. *System, 35, 338-352.*

Mangubhai, F. (1991). The processing behaviors of adult second language learners and their relationship to second language proficiency. *Applied Linguistics, 12, 268-298.*

Matsumoto, K. (1994). Introspection, verbal reports and second language learning strategy research. *The Canadian Modern Language Review, 50(2), 363-386.*

McDonough, S. H. (1999). Learner strategies: state of the art. *Language Teaching, 32, 1-18.*

McLaughlin, B. (1987). *Theories of second-language learning.* London: Edward Arnold.

Naiman, N., F., M., Stern, H. H., and Todesco, A. (1978). The good language learner. *Research in Education, No. 7.* Ontario Institute for Studies in Education.

Nam, C., and Oxford, R. L. (1998). Portrait of a future teacher: case study of learning styles, strategies, and language disabilities. *System, 26, 51-63.*

Neuendorf, K. A. (2002). *The content analysis: guidebook.* Thousand Oaks, Calif.: Sage Publications.

Noels, K. A., Clément, R., and Pelletier, A. G. (2001). Intrinsic, extrinsic, and integrative orientations of French Canadian learners of English. *The Canadian Language Review, 57, 424-442.*

Nunan, D. (1992). *Research methods in language learning.* Cambridge: Cambridge University Press.

O'Malley, J. M., and Chamot, A. U. (1990). Learning strategies in language acquisition. Cambridge: Cambridge University Press.

O'Malley, J. M., Chamot, A. U., Stewner-Manzanares, K., L., and Russo, R. P. (1985a). Learning strategies used by beginning and intermediate ESL students. *Language learning, 35(1), 21-46.*

O'Malley, J. M., Russo, R. P., Chamot, A.U., Stewner-Manzanares, G., and Kupper, L. (1985b). Learning strategy applications with students of English as a second language. *TESOL Quarterly, 19 (3), 557-584.*

Onwuegbuzie, A. J., Bailey, P., and Daley, C. E. (1999). Factors associated with foreign language anxiety. *Applied Psycholinguistics, 20(2), 217-239.*

Onwuegbuzie, A. J., Bailey, P., and Daley, C. E. (2000). Cognitive, affective, personality, and demographic predictors of foreign-language achievement. *Journal of Educational Research, 94/1, 3-15.*

Oxford, R. L. (1989). Use of language learning strategies: a synthesis of studies with implications for strategy training. *System, 17, 235-247.*

Oxford, R. L. (1990). *Language learning strategies: what every teacher should know.* New York: Newbury House/Harper & Row.

Oxford, R. (1993). Research update on L2 listening. *System, 21, 205-211.*

Oxford, R. L. (1999). "Style wars" as a source of anxiety in language classrooms. In D. J. Young (ed.) *Affect in foreign language and second language learning: a practical guide to creating a low-anxiety classroom atmosphere.* Boston: McGraw-Hill, 216-237.

Oxford, R. L., and Burry-Stock, J. (1995). Assessing the use of language learning strategies worldwide with the ESL/EFL version with the strategy inventory of language learning (SILL). *System, 23, 1-23.*

Oxford, R. L., Cho, Y., Leung, S., and Kim, H-J. (2004). Effect of the presence and difficulty of task on strategy use: an exploratory study. *IRAL, 42, 1-47.*

Oxford, R. L., and Cohen, A. D. (1992). Language learning strategies: crucial issues in concept and definition. *Applied Language Learning, 3, 1-35.*

Oxford, R. L., and Cohen, A. D. (2004). *Teaching and researching language learning strategies.* London: Addison Wesley Longman.

Oxford, R. L., and Ehrman, M. E. (1995). Adults' language learning strategies in an intensive foreign language program in the United States. *System, 23(3), 359-386.*

Oxford, R. L., and Nyikos, M. (1989). Variables affecting choice of language learning strategies by university students. *Modern Language Journal, 73, 291-300.*

Oxford, R. L., and Shearin, J. (1994). Broadening the theoretical framework of language learning motivation. *Modern Language Journal, 78, 12-28*.

Peck, S. (1996). Language learning diaries as mirrors of students' cultural sensitivity. In K. M. Bailey, and D. Nunan (Eds.), *Voices from the language classroom* (pp. 236-247). Cambridge: Cambridge University Press.

Peng, I-Ning. (2001). *EFL motivation and strategy use among Taiwanese senior high school learners*. Master's thesis, National Normal University.

Phakiti, A. (2003). A closer look at gender and strategy use in L2 reading. *Language Learning, 53(4), 649-702*.

Phillips, E. M. (1992). The effects of language anxiety on students' oral test performance and attitudes. *The Modern Language Journal, 76, 14-26*.

Politzer, R. L., and McGroarty, M. (1985). An exploratory study of learning behaviors and their relationship to gains in linguistic and communicative competence. *TESOL Quarterly, 19, 103-123*.

Price, M. L. (1991). The subjective experience of foreign language anxiety: interviews with highly anxious students. In E. K. Horwitz, and D. J. Young (Eds.), *Language anxiety: from theory and research to classroom implications* (pp. 101-108). Englewood Cliffs, New Jersey: Prentice Hall, Inc.

Purpura, J. E. (1997). An analysis of the relationships between test takers' cognitive and metacognitive strategy use and second language test performance. *Language Learning, 47, 289-325*.

Purpura, J. E. (1998). Investigating the effects of strategy use and second language test performance with high- and low-ability test takers: a structural equation modeling approach. *Language Testing, 15(3), 333-379*.

Qin, X., and Wen, Q. (2002). The internal structure of learning motivation among undergraduate students. *Foreign Language Teaching and Research, 34 (1), 51-58*.

Reid, J. M. (1987). The learning style preferences of ESL students. *TESOL Quarterly, 21(1), 87-111*.

Richards, J. C. (2001). *Curriculum development in language teaching*. Cambridge: Cambridge University Press.

Rubin, J. (1975). What the 'good language learner' can teach us. *TESOL Quarterly, 9, 41-51.*

Rubin, J. (1981). Study of cognitive processes in second language learning. *Applied Linguistics, 2, 117-131.*

Rubin, J. (1987). Learner strategies: theoretical assumptions, research, history, and typology. In A. Wenden and J. Rubin (Eds.), *Learner strategies in language learning* (pp. 15-30). Englewood cliff, N. Y.: Prentice-Hall.

Saito, Y., Horwitz, E. K. and Garza, T. J. (1999). Foreign language reading anxiety. *The Modern Language Journal* 83: 202-218.

Saito, Y. and Samimy, K. K. (1996). Foreign language anxiety and language performance: a study of learner anxiety in beginning, intermediate, and advanced-level college students of Japan. *Foreign Language Annals* 29: 239-251.

Sellers, V. D. (2000). Anxiety and reading comprehension in Spanish as a foreign language. *Foreign Language Annals, 33/5, 512-521.*

Skehan, P. (1989). *Individual differences in second language learning.* London: Edward Arnold.

Spolsky, Bernard. (2000). Anniversary article language motivation revisited. *Applied Linguistics, 21, 157-169.*

Stern, H. H. (1975). What can we learn from the good language learner? *Canadian Modern Language Review, 31, 304-318.*

Takeuchi, O. (2003). What can we learn from good foreign language learners? A qualitative study in the Japanese foreign language context. *System, 31, 385-392.*

Tran, T.V. (1988). Sex differences in English language acculturation and learning strategies among Vietnamese adults aged 40 and over in the United States. *Sex Roles, 19, 747-758.*

Tremblay, Paul F., and Gardner, Robert C. (1995). Expanding the motivation construct in language learning. *The Modern Language Journal, 79, 505-518.*

Tsui, A. B. M. (1996). Reticence and anxiety in second language learning. In K. M. Bailey and D. Nunan (Eds.) *Voices from the language classroom.* Cambridge: Cambridge University Press, 145-167.

Vandergrift, L. (1996). Listening strategies of core French high school students. *Canadian Modern Language Review, 52(2), 200-223.*

Vandergrift, L. (1997). The comprehension strategies of second language (French) listeners. *Foreign Language Annals, 30, 387-409.*

Vandergrift, L. (2003). Orchestrating strategy use: toward a model of the skilled second language listener. Language Learning, 53(3), 463-496.

Vandergrift, L. (2005). Relationships among motivation orientations, metacognitive awareness and proficiency in L2 listening. *Applied Linguistics, 26(1), 70-89.*

Vann, R., and Abraham, R. (1990). Strategies of unsuccessful language learners. *TESOL Quarterly, 24, 177-199.*

Wakamoto, N. (2000). Language learning strategy and personality variables: focusing on extroversion and introversion. *IRAL, 38, 71-81.*

Wallace, M. J. (1998). *Action research for language teachers.* Cambridge: Cambridge University Press.

Wang, C. (2003). Report of the FLCAS in college students. *Journal of Psychology Science, 26(2), 281-284.*

Wang, Q., and Ding, X. (2001). Language anxiety among rural middle school students in west China. *Journal of Northwest Normal University, 38(5), 68-73.*

Wang, W-Y. (2002). *Effects of gender and proficiency on listening comprehension strategy use by Taiwanese EFL senior high school students: a case from Changhua, Taiwan.* Master's thesis, National Changhua University of Education.

Weinstein, C. E., and Mayer, R. E. (1986). *The teaching of learning strategies.* New York: MacMillan.

Wen, Q. (1993). *Advanced level English learning in China: the relationship of modifiable learner variables to L2 learning outcomes.* Hong Kong University: Unpublished Doctoral Thesis.

Wen, Q. (1996). *English learning strategies.* Shanghai: Shanghai Publisher.

Wen, Q. (2001). Developmental patterns in motivation, beliefs and strategies of English learners in China. *Foreign Language Teaching and Research, 33 (2), 105-110.*

Wenden, A. L. (1985). Learner strategies. *TESOL Newsletter, 19, 1-7.*

Wenden, A. L. (1986). What do second-language learners know about their language learning? A second look at retrospective accounts. *Applied Linguistics, 7, 186-201.*

Wenden, A. L. (1987). Incorporating learner training in the classroom. In A. Wenden and J. Rubin (Eds.), *Learner strategies in language learning* (pp. 159-168). Hemel Hempstead: Prentice-Hall.

Wesche, M. (1987). Second language performance testing: the Ontario Test of ESL as an example. *Language Testing, 4, 28-47.*

Wharton, G. (2000). Language learning strategy use of bilingual foreign language learners in Singapore. *Language Learning, 50 (2), 203-243.*

Williams, K. (1991). Anxiety and formal second/foreign language learning. *RELC Journal. 22/2, 19-28.*

Wong-Fillmore, L. (1976). *The second time around: cognitive and social strategies in second language acquisition.* Unpublished Ph. D dissertation, Stanford University.

Wong-Fillmore, L. (1979). Individual differences in second language acquisition. In C. J. Fillmore, W-S. Y. Wang and D. Kempler (Eds.), *Individual differences in language ability and language behavior.* New York: Academic Press.

Wu, R-H. (2000). Exploring language learning strategies. *Min-Chung Japanese Education Report, 3, 109-126.*

Yan, X., and Wang, P. (2001). The impact of language anxiety on students' Mandarin learning in Hong Kong. *Language Teaching and Research. 6, 1-7.*

Yan, Y. (2003). Language anxiety and the teaching of spoken English. *Journal of Liaoning Technical University, 5(4), 73-74.*

Yang, Nae-Dong. (1996). Effective awareness-raising in language learning strategy instruction. In R. L. Oxford (Ed.), *Language learning strategies around the world: Cross-cultural perspectives* (pp. 205-210). Manoa: University of Hawaii Press.

Yang, H., and Weir, C. (1998). *Validation study of the national college English test.* Shanghai: Shanghai Foreign Language Education Press.

Yang, N-D. (1999). The relationship between EFL learners' beliefs and learning strategy use. *System, 27, 515-535.*

Young, D. J. (1991a). Creating a low-anxiety classroom environment: what does language anxiety research suggest? *The Modern Language Journal. 75/4, 426-439.*

Young, D. J. (1991b). The relationship between anxiety and foreign language oral proficiency ratings. In E. K. Horwitz and D. J. Young (eds) *Language anxiety: from theory and research to classroom implications* (pp. 57-63). New Jersey: Prentice Hall.

Young, D. J. (ed.). (1999). *Affect in foreign language and second language learning: a practical guide to creating a low-anxiety classroom atmosphere* (pp. 13-23). McGraw-Hill College.

Young, D. J., and Oxford, R. (1997). A gender-related analysis of strategies used to process written input in the native language and a foreign language. *Applied Language Learning, 8, 43-73.*

Zhang, W., and Liu, M. (2008). Investigating cognitive and metacognitive strategy use during an English proficiency test. *Indonesian Journal of English Language Teaching* (upcoming).

Zou, S. (1998). *Test validity of TEM.* Shanghai: Shanghai Foreign Language Education Press.

Zou, S. (2002). The relationship between item strategy use and reading test scores. *Foreign Language and Foreign Language Teaching, 5, 19-22.*

Zhou, J. F. (1998). How to motivate students to learn. *The Journal of the College of PLA Foreign Languages, 5, 84-88.*

Appendix I: Focus for reflective journals
Journal 1: English-learning experience

You are required to write for at least 150 words on the topic according to the guides given below. Besides, you can write about other aspects related to your language learning experience. If you can't find appropriate English words or phrases to express yourself, you can use Chinese. Please write honestly.

- **Motivation and anxiety in Chinese university English classrooms: causes and consequences**

a. Were you motivated to learn English in the secondary school? Why or why not? If yes, what was it? Are you motivated to learn English at the University? Why or why not? If yes, what is it (e.g., going abroad, for a better job, etc.)?

b. Generally speaking, are you nervous/anxious in university English classrooms? Why or why not (English proficiency, personality, etc.)? When do you feel the most nervous/anxious in class (e.g., listening, speaking, reading, or writing)? Why?

c. Do you think most of other (Chinese) students are nervous/anxious in university English classrooms as well? What do you think causes them to be nervous/anxious in university English classrooms (e.g., inadequate grammatical knowledge, lack of vocabulary, lack of practice, personality, lack of preparation, difficulty of the task, etc.)? Please give an example.

d. Do you think nervousness/anxiety affects your English proficiency? Why or why not? If yes, in what ways and to what extent? Please explain with examples.

e. If anxiety has a bad/negative effect on English proficiency, what do you think can be done by the students to overcome anxiety and become more confident? What have you done to be more confident? What can English teachers do to encourage students to be more confident in English classrooms?

......

- **大学英语学习动机及课堂焦虑：原因及影响**

a. 中学时你有学习英语的动力吗？为什么（没有）？如果有，是什么？现在在大学有学英语的动力吗？为什么（没有）？如果有，请问是什么样的动力（如出国、将来找工作等）？

b. 总的来说，你在大学英语课堂上感觉紧张焦虑吗？为什么（不）（如英语水平、性格等）？你在课堂上什么时候感觉最紧张焦虑（如听、说、读、写）？爲什麼？

  c. 你认为大部分中国学生在大学英语课堂上也紧张焦虑吗？为什么（如语法知识缺乏、词汇缺乏、操练不够、准备不足、性格等）（不）？

d. 你认为焦虑影响你的英语水平吗？为什么（不）？如果有影响，请问是如何影响的？达到什么程度？请举例说明。

e. 如果课堂焦虑对学生的英语水平有负面影响，你认为学生应该如何克服焦虑从而变得更积极？你在這方面是如何做的？你认为英语老师应该采取什么措施，以鼓励学生在课堂上变得更积极？…

235

Journal 2: English-learning experience

You are required to write for at least 150 words on the topic according to the guides given below. Besides, you can write about other aspects related to your language learning experience. If you can't find appropriate English words or phrases to express yourself, you can use Chinese. Please write honestly.

- **Learning and test-taking strategies**

 a. What do you know about learning strategies? What are they? Where did you learn about them? What strategies do you often use when learning English (e.g., memorize words, recite texts, planning and organizing, etc.)?

 b. Do you use the same strategies when learning English reading, speaking, listening and writing? If not, what is the difference? What strategies do you often use when learning these different aspects of English? Are they effective? Why? In what part of learning do you use strategies the most? Why?

 c. Do you think learning strategies can help enhance your proficiency in English reading, speaking, listening and writing? Why?

 d. Do you feel nervous before and during English tests? Why or why not? If you feel nervous before and during English tests, what do you usually do to make you less nervous?

 e. How do you usually prepare for your English tests? What strategies do you use to pass or get high marks in English tests (e.g., memorize facts, review notes and texts, etc.)? Are they effective? Why or why not? What strategies do usually use during English tests? Are they different when taking a written and an oral English test? Do you review your performance after finishing an English test? If not, what do you usually do (e.g., totally forget the test, reflect on what you've done well or bad, etc.)?

 ......

- **学习和考试策略**

a. 你对学习策略有什么了解？是从哪儿得知这些信息的？学习英语时你通常采用什么样的学习策略（如背单词、背课文、计划、组织等）？

b. 你在学习英语阅读、口语、听力及写作时采用同样的学习策略吗？如果不是，请问其区别是什么？那么在学习这些不同英语技能时，你分别采取什么样的策略？这些策略有用吗？为什么（不）？在学习何种技能时你采用的策略最多？为什么？

c. 你认为学习策略有助于你提高自己的英语阅读、口语、听力及写作水平吗？为什么（不）？

d. 你在英语考试前、期间感到紧张吗？为什么（不）？如果你觉得紧张，你是如何使自己不那么紧张的？

 e. 你通常是如何准备英语考试的？你采用什么样的策略以使自己通过英语考试或在考试中取得高分（如熟记事实、复习笔记课本等）？这些策略有用吗？为什么（不）？考试期间会采用什么策略吗？考英语笔试及口试时采用的策略有什么不一样？英语考试结束后你会总结自己在考试中的表现吗？如果不会，英语考试结束后你通常会做什么（如完全忘掉考试、回顾一下哪里做得好哪里做得不好等）？

...

Appendix II: Survey on English Learning

Direction: This survey aims to help better understand your language learning experiences. Please answer the following items by circling the letter of the alternative which appears most applicable to you. We would urge you to be as accurate as possible since the success of this investigation depends upon it.

Name: _____ Sex: _____ Department: _____ Age _____ Band _____
Level _____ Email: _____

	Total	TU	BFU	CUP
1. I don't usually get anxious when I have to respond to a question in English class.	2.72	2.73	2.88	2.59
2. I am always afraid that other students would laugh at me if I speak up in English class.	2.22	2.27	2.13	2.23
3. I always feel that other students are more at ease than I am in English class.	2.70	2.83	2.54	2.69
4. I am never embarrassed to volunteer answers in English class.	3.08	3.01	3.27	3.01
5. I am generally tense whenever participating in English class.	2.06	2.17	1.99	2.01
6. I never understand why other students are so nervous in English class.	3.19	3.26	3.24	3.07
7. I usually feel relaxed and confident when active participation takes place in English class.	2.86	2.81	3.00	2.80
8. Whenever I have to answer a question, out loud, I get nervous and confused in English class.	2.46	2.49	2.46	2.42
9. Honestly, I don't know whether I am motivated to learn English.	3.66	3.64	3.69	3.67
10. I have the impression that I am wasting my time in studying English.	4.15	4.21	3.98	4.20
11. I study English in order to get a good job later on.	3.15	2.78	3.31	3.42
12. I study English in order to earn more money later on.	2.97	2.62	3.15	3.21
13. I study English for higher education later on.	3.65	3.65	3.65	3.66
14. I study English in order to go abroad later on.	3.45	3.46	3.54	3.37
15. I study English because I think it is important for my future work.	3.70	3.70	3.71	3.70
16. I study English because I want to get high marks in English exams.	2.95	2.64	3.12	3.16
17. I study English because it is required with credits at my university.	2.84	2.54	3.11	2.95
18. I study English because I want to have different kinds of certificates showing my competence in the language (e.g., BEC certificate and PETS certificate, etc.).	2.58	2.30	2.76	2.73
19. I study English because I have to pass English exams; otherwise, I would not learn it.	2.05	2.00	2.09	2.07
20. I study English because I am good at English listening, speaking, reading and/or writing and thus interested in it.	2.91	2.95	2.84	2.91
21. I study English because I want to improve my English abilities in listening, speaking, reading and/or writing.	3.66	3.74	3.59	3.64
22. I study English because I think it is important for my personal development.	4.08	4.05	4.06	4.14
23. I study English because I would feel guilty if I didn't know English.	2.65	2.60	2.60	2.74
24. I study English because I would feel ashamed if I couldn't speak to my English-speaking friends in English.	2.88	2.84	2.83	2.97
25. I study English because I choose to be the kind of person who can speak more than one language.	3.60	3.59	3.69	3.55
26. I study English because I choose to be the kind of person who can speak English.	3.62	3.65	3.63	3.59
27. I study English for the satisfied feeling I get in finding out new things.	3.32	3.37	3.33	3.25
28. I study English for the pleasure that I experience in knowing more about English literature.	3.10	3.12	3.13	3.04
29. I study English because I enjoy the feeling of learning about English-speaking people and their way of life.	3.05	3.15	3.07	2.93
30. I study English for the enjoyment I experience when I understand a difficult idea in English.	2.79	2.71	2.88	2.82
31. I study English for the satisfaction I feel when I am doing difficult exercises in English.	2.54	2.39	2.69	2.59
32. I study English for the good feeling I get when I do better than I thought in English class.	3.12	2.94	3.18	3.28
33. I study English for the excitement that I get while speaking English.	2.78	2.80	2.81	2.75
34. I study English for the excitement I feel when I hear someone speaking a foreign language.	2.65	2.63	2.65	2.68
35. I remember English words by grouping them together according to their semantic relations such as super-ordinates and synonyms.	2.91	2.92	2.80	2.98
36. I remember English words according to pronunciation rules of letter clusters.	3.70	3.65	3.65	3.78

37. I remember a new word by its formation.	3.50	3.56	3.42	3.49
38. I think of relationships between what I already know and new things I learn in English.	3.54	3.62	3.42	3.54
39. When learning a new word, I associate it with those I already know.	3.51	3.57	3.42	3.50
40. I remember new English words by associating them with others.	2.99	3.07	2.94	2.93
41. I use new English words in a sentence so I can remember them.	2.91	3.00	2.81	2.89
42. I use the English words I know in different ways.	3.02	3.10	2.90	3.04
43. I connect the sound of a new English word and an image or picture of the word to help me remember the word.	3.30	3.27	3.33	3.30
44. I remember new English words or phrases by remembering their location on the page, on the board, or on a street sign.	2.89	2.82	2.99	2.88
45. I remember a new English word by making a mental picture of a situation in which the word might be used.	3.29	3.33	3.20	3.31
46. I remember new English words by establishing semantic relations.	3.47	3.49	3.37	3.53
47. I use rhymes to remember new English words (e.g., rice and ice; no vs. know).	2.71	2.68	2.62	2.80
48. I remember a new English word by its pronunciation.	3.79	3.73	3.73	3.89
49. I often review what I have learned in English.	2.99	2.94	2.90	3.09
50. I copy down new English words in a special notebook so that I can review them regularly.	2.80	2.83	2.76	2.80
51. I physically act out new English words.	2.25	2.24	2.20	2.29
52. I use flashcards to remember new English words.	2.41	2.50	2.36	2.36
53. I often memorize English words according to a vocabulary book or a dictionary.	2.61	2.66	2.66	2.52
54. I often recite English essays.	2.66	2.54	2.53	2.90
55. I often listen to/watch an English episode repeatedly until I understand every word.	2.77	2.83	2.69	2.76
56. I say or write new English words several times.	3.50	3.36	3.65	3.55
57. I reread an English text to enhance my understanding.	3.31	3.32	3.31	3.29
58. I practice the sounds of English.	3.29	3.26	3.28	3.32
59. I practice pronunciation according to English phonological rules such as strong and weak syllables and liaison.	2.56	2.59	2.62	2.50
60. I try to imitate the pronunciation of English native speakers.	3.14	3.23	3.13	3.04
61. I often do really a lot of English listening exercises.	2.51	2.56	2.56	2.41
62. I try to talk like native English speakers.	2.98	3.06	2.93	2.92
63. I often practice reading English aloud.	2.91	2.89	2.84	2.98
64. When learning English, I often find out and deduce grammatical rules myself.	2.87	2.92	2.87	2.81
65. I often try to use the prefabricated expressions I have learned when writing/talking in English.	3.43	3.51	3.37	3.40
66. I try to find patterns in English.	3.20	3.25	3.13	3.20
67. I often try to put together the English words and expressions I have learned.	3.12	3.13	3.11	3.13
68. I watch English language TV shows or English movies.	3.39	3.49	3.38	3.31
69. I read for pleasure in English.	3.25	3.37	3.17	3.19
70. I'm much concerned with whether I understand every sentence I hear in English.	3.08	3.00	3.10	3.16
71. I keep on listening to English if I come across an unfamiliar word.	3.68	3.66	3.66	3.70
72. As long as I can understand what I am reading in English, I won't pay attention to grammar.	3.62	3.57	3.61	3.68
73. I first skim an English passage (read over the passage quickly) then go back and read carefully.	3.41	3.35	3.34	3.52
74. When reading, I skip unimportant information.	3.56	3.59	3.48	3.60
75. I often try to enlarge my vocabulary by reading English as much as I can.	2.99	3.11	2.90	2.94
76. When looking up an English word in a dictionary, I not only make sure of its meaning but learn how to use it.	3.26	3.35	3.11	3.28
77. I read English without looking up every new word.	3.76	3.77	3.73	3.76
78. I often read the transcript before listening to English.	2.22	2.14	2.26	2.27
79. While listening to English, I read the transcript.	2.53	2.45	2.56	2.59
80. When learning English, I often turn to an English-Chinese or Chinese-English dictionary.	3.44	3.53	3.47	3.31
81. When looking up an English word in dictionary, I just pay attention to the meaning related to what I am reading.	3.04	2.95	3.04	3.15

238

82. I often remember English grammatical rules based on understanding rather than rote memory. 3.56 3.57 3.56 3.56

83. When reading English, I try to deduce the author's opinion and implied intention. 3.50 3.59 3.45 3.45

84. When reading English, I analyze the structure of the text. 2.77 2.84 2.83 2.65

85. I often learn English grammar with reference to texts. 3.25 3.29 3.13 3.30

86. When reading English, I often try to analyze the sentence structures. 2.95 2.98 2.88 2.96

87. I find the meaning of an English word by dividing it into parts that I understand. 3.18 3.15 3.20 3.20

88. I often analyze the structure of complicated sentences when learning English. 2.98 3.15 2.86 2.90

89. I often pay attention to the difference between Chinese and English when learning English. 3.13 3.22 2.30 3.12

90. I look for words in my own language that are similar to new words in English. 3.51 3.39 3.57 3.59

91. I often translate what I learn in English into Chinese. 3.07 2.88 3.13 3.23

92. I try not to translate word-for-word when learning English. 3.52 3.49 3.45 3.62

93. I practice writing by modeling good English essays to improve my writing ability. 3.04 2.97 3.03 3.12

94. I often transfer my knowledge about learning Chinese to English-learning. 2.87 2.84 2.81 2.96

95. I take notes while reading English. 2.94 2.97 3.05 2.94

96. I take notes while listening to English. 2.76 2.71 2.83 2.78

97. I make summaries of information that I hear or read in English. 2.72 2.69 2.76 2.72

98. I highlight certain phrases or sentences while reading English. 3.72 3.63 3.73 3.80

99. To understand unfamiliar English words, I make guesses based on word formation. 3.77 3.77 3.72 3.80

100. To understand unfamiliar English words, I make guesses based on contextual clues. 3.98 3.97 3.91 4.03

101. I often use linguistic clues such as context to make guesses if I can't
understand what I have heard in English. 3.66 3.73 3.64 3.60

102. If I hear an unfamiliar English word, I often try to remember its pronunciation,
based on which I make guesses about its spelling and meaning. 3.27 3.28 3.33 3.20

103. I try to guess what the other person will say next in English
according to what s/he has said before. 3.45 3.51 3.39 3.44

104. I use contextual clues to make guesses about what I have read in English. 3.87 3.86 3.80 3.92

105. I use background knowledge to make guesses about what I have read in English. 3.81 3.82 3.72 3.87

106. I use background knowledge to make guesses about what I have heard in English. 3.74 3.75 3.70 3.76

107. I make guesses about the speaker's intention according to his/her tone, intonation and pauses. 3.71 3.75 3.70 3.68

108. When watching English movies, I use such visual aids as subtitles, pictures,
and performers' facial expression to help me better understand the movies. 3.92 3.92 3.91 3.91

109. I try to predict the content according to the title when reading English. 3.73 3.68 3.70 3.80

110. I try to guess what the other person will say next in English according to
his/her tone, intonation, gestures and facial expressions, etc. 3.54 3.61 3.50 3.51

111. I often switch to Chinese when I don't know how to express myself in English. 3.32 3.28 3.32 3.36

112. I often ask for other people's help when I have difficulties in learning/using English. 3.33 3.36 3.28 3.34

113. When I can't think of a word during a conversation in English, I use body
language such as gestures. 3.50 3.58 3.48 3.44

114. I will give it up if I can't understand what I have heard. I just listen to the English
that I can understand. 2.72 2.70 2.66 2.80

115. I often try to avoid using English (such as speaking or writing in English). 2.68 2.65 2.63 2.74

116. I often choose the topics which I feel comfortable with when using English. 3.69 3.65 3.63 3.77

117. I often turn to use simple words, expressions and sentence structures when I can't
use more difficult or desired ones when using English in speech and/or writing. 3.88 3.83 3.86 3.96

118. I make up new words if I do not know the right ones in English. 2.32 2.27 2.40 2.31

119. If I can't think of an English word, I use a word or phrase that means the same thing. 3.89 3.82 3.90 3.97

120. When reading or listening to English, I often try to link it with what I have known. 3.79 3.78 3.77 3.80

121. When speaking/writing in English, I often try to link the topic with what I have known. 3.75 3.72 3.74 3.80

122. I pay attention to the conjunctions when reading. 3.46 3.46 3.42 3.50

123. When reading English, I try to find out topic sentences in the text. 3.51 3.48 3.57 3.50

124. I won't look it up in a dictionary when I come across a strange word in English reading. 3.60 3.62 3.47 3.67

125. I pay attention to the beginning and ending of an English text. 3.66 3.65 3.62 3.69

126. When writing in English, I definitely don't use words learned long time ago if I
can use those recently learned. 3.06 3.00 2.94 3.21

127. I look up the words in dictionary that frequently occur in English reading.	3.87	3.90	3.80	3.88
128. I look up in dictionary only the words that can affect my understanding of a sentence or even the whole text when reading English.	3.67	3.59	3.69	3.73
129. I look up in dictionary only those words that look familiar to me.	3.68	3.72	3.65	3.65
130. I pay attention when someone is speaking English.	3.70	3.73	3.64	3.72
131. I pay attention to new grammatical points and try to understand them when reading English outside class.	3.00	3.01	3.01	2.97
132. I try to use a variety of sentence structures when writing in English.	3.52	3.62	3.38	3.53
133. I try to use a variety of words when writing in English.	3.61	3.73	3.48	3.56
134. I try to make as few grammatical mistakes as possible when writing in English.	3.81	3.82	3.76	3.85
135. I try to make it coherent when writing in English.	3.86	3.85	3.82	3.90
136. I keep to the main idea when writing in English.	3.79	3.76	3.77	3.84
137. I pay attention to paragraphing when writing in English.	3.65	3.71	3.63	3.61
138. I am attentive when my English teacher is explaining how to write in English such as its requirement, format and methods.	3.61	3.56	3.64	3.65
139. When communicating in English, I focus my attention on expression of meanings rather than on grammaticality.	3.50	3.52	3.40	3.56
140. I often focus on listening first and start to speak English later.	3.51	3.49	3.46	3.56
141. I try to find out how to be a better learner of English.	3.75	3.77	3.69	3.79
142. In addition to the assignments, I have my own English-learning plan.	3.22	3.26	3.18	3.21
143. I plan my schedule so I will have enough time to study English.	3.17	3.15	3.14	3.20
144. When writing in English, I organize my ideas quite logically.	3.59	3.60	3.55	3.59
145. I often put forward a new question which sets readers thinking at the end of a piece of English writing.	2.96	3.06	2.86	2.94
146. I have clear goals for improving my English skills.	3.17	3.17	3.20	3.13
147. I often set short-term and long-term goals when learning English.	3.09	3.14	3.07	3.04
148. I often identify the purpose of an English-learning task first (e.g., getting the main idea and finding details, etc.).	3.10	3.06	3.15	3.10
149. When writing in English, I often make a paragraph evolve around an idea.	3.38	3.52	3.32	3.29
150. When writing in English, I often state the main idea in the first paragraph.	3.53	3.62	3.49	3.47
151. When writing in English, I often make a summary and restate the main idea in the concluding paragraph(s).	3.70	3.73	3.63	3.72
152. I select different learning strategies according to different tasks.	3.50	3.47	3.50	3.53
153. I often outline before starting to write in English.	2.97	3.09	2.98	2.84
154. Before writing in English, I often try to list the ideas related to the topic.	3.42	3.44	3.41	3.40
155. I select English learning materials based on my English proficiency.	3.67	3.74	3.57	3.68
156. I often think out a title according to the requirement before starting to write in English.	3.37	3.33	3.36	3.43
157. I try to write notes and book reports in English.	2.65	2.78	2.58	2.57
158. I keep on listening to the English even if I don't understand it.	3.37	3.42	3.35	3.34
159. I write emails and/or letter in English to my friends.	2.56	2.72	2.50	2.45
160. I try to write diaries and/or journals in English.	2.29	2.51	1.88	2.37
161. I have a notebook ready for writing down any good idea or sentence in English.	2.51	2.49	2.57	2.47
162. I try to find as many ways as I can to use my English.	2.98	3.01	2.91	3.00
163. I murmur the answer to myself when the English teacher asks other student(s) to answer questions in class.	3.15	3.10	3.09	3.25
164. I try to voluntarily seek chances to answer questions in English lessons.	2.66	2.68	2.53	2.76
165. I often speak English to myself.	2.93	3.12	2.73	2.89
166. I look for opportunities to read as much as possible in English.	2.93	3.02	2.81	2.94
167. I initiate to greet and converse with foreigners in English.	2.47	2.63	2.42	2.33
168. I initiate to make friends with international students and form one-to-to language learning groups with them.	2.33	2.40	2.33	2.24
169. I initiate to talk to teachers in English.	2.36	2.50	2.33	2.25
170. I often participate in various English activities such as English corners lectures and talks.	2.46	2.52	2.45	2.40
171. I actively take part in various English contests like speech contests.	2.45	2.48	2.38	2.47

240

172. I pay attention to the introduction in English when visiting a tourist site. 3.18 3.31 2.99 3.17
173. I pay attention to the English used in various international events and conferences. 3.34 3.45 3.16 3.36
174. I pay attention to the English used in streets (such as road signs and street nameplates). 3.49 3.50 3.41 3.56
175. I read English instructions of a product. 3.07 3.11 3.00 3.09
176. I often search for various English materials in libraries. 2.57 2.65 2.50 2.55
177. I often download audio materials from the Internet and listen to them with MP3. 3.03 3.11 2.97 2.99
178. I often surf various English websites for different kinds of information. 2.70 2.87 2.54 2.64
179. When communicating in English, I don't pursue grammaticality so much. 3.56 3.62 3.50 3.54
180. I repeatedly revise my English writing. 2.96 2.93 2.91 3.03
181. I notice my English mistakes and use that information to help me do better. 3.57 3.59 3.47 3.64
182. When writing in English, I note down the cases that I don't know how to express
    myself in English for later improvement. 2.95 2.84 2.95 3.08
183. After finishing a conversation in English, I think about how I could say things better. 3.51 3.43 3.49 3.62
184. I pay attention to learning from mistakes and often read my teacher(s)' feedback carefully. 3.47 3.49 3.37 3.52
185. I make adjustment once I find some strategies are of little effect when learning English. 3.53 3.51 3.56 3.54
186. I check my progress in English learning so that I can find out my weaknesses for improvement. 3.43 3.41 3.43 3.44
187. I assess my English-learning strategies in order to find out problems and solutions. 3.38 3.35 3.35 3.45
188. I study my personality to find out what is conducive to my English learning and
    what is not so that I can take corresponding measures to make better use of my
    advantages and try to get rid of my weaknesses. 3.39 3.29 3.44 3.46
189. I adjust my reading speed according to what I am reading. 3.69 3.61 3.65 3.81
190. After completing my writing in English, I pay attention to the feedback given
    by my teacher or other students and revise thereafter carefully. 3.34 3.38 3.39 3.27
191. After completing my writing in English, I repeatedly read and revise it. 2.99 3.09 2.98 2.88
192. After completing my writing in English, I check spelling and grammatical
    mistakes times and again .3.17 3.19 3.23 3.10
193. I usually read English articles repeatedly, listening to and evaluating
    my own pronunciation and intonation. 3.24 3.23 3.22 3.27
194. I often test myself on English materials. 2.78 2.76 2.85 2.76
195. I try to relax whenever I feel afraid of using English. 3.49 3.45 3.45 3.56
196. I breathe deeply whenever I feel anxious in using English. 3.22 3.19 3.24 3.24
197. I often try to laugh when learning English with others. 2.73 2.73 2.76 2.72
198. I encourage myself not to lose heart when I don't do well in English exams. 3.87 3.79 3.86 3.96
199. I encourage myself to use English even when I am afraid of making a mistake. 3.60 3.60 3.57 3.63
200. I often purposefully take chances to speak English even if I may not speak it well. 3.28 3.31 3.18 3.31
201. I often purposefully use certain English words or phrases even though I am
    not sure whether I'm using them appropriately. 3.51 3.51 3.46 3.55
202. I often purposefully make guesses when listening to/reading English. 3.74 3.73 3.65 3.82
203. I give myself a reward or treat when I do well in English. 3.25 3.17 3.31 3.28
204. I notice if I am tense or nervous when I am studying or using English. 3.63 3.58 3.61 3.69
205. I often use a checklist to note my attitudes toward and feeling for English learning. 2.57 2.61 2.52 2.56
206. I write down my feelings in language learning diaries. 2.25 2.18 2.34 2.24
207. I talk to someone else about how I feel when I am learning English. 2.96 2.88 3.01 3.02
208. I ask for help from English speakers when having difficulties in learning English. 3.03 3.04 3.02 3.02
209. If I do not understand something in English, I ask the other person to slow down or say it again. 3.70 3.65 3.72 3.75
210. If I do not understand something in English in class or during a talk, I ask for clarification. 3.48 3.43 3.54 3.48
211. I ask English speakers to correct me when I talk. 3.19 3.01 3.24 3.34
212. I ask my English teachers to correct my writing. 3.58 3.56 3.59 3.58
213. I practice English with other students outside class. 2.78 2.91 2.73 2.68
214. I talk to my peers about how to learn English. 3.10 3.13 3.05 3.12
215. I talk to more proficient learners about how to learn English. 3.29 3.26 3.30 3.32
216. I try to learn about the culture of English speakers. 3.60 3.65 3.60 3.55
217. During face-to-face English conversations, I just care for what I need to say
    and how to say it, while not listening to the other speaker carefully. 2.45 2.38 2.46 2.51

241

218. During English conversations, I use various ways to make active responses to the speaker.   3.56   3.60   3.50   3.57

Other English learning strategies: _____

_____

_____

219. I review a lot before English exams.	3.52	3.39	3.58	3.61
220. To prepare for English exams, I keep up my homework and review my notes regularly.	3.21	3.12	3.26	3.26
221. I use high technology to help me review materials (e.g., MP3) before English tests.	2.56	2.48	2.75	2.50
222. I create flashcards for words, phrases and sentence structures, etc. that I need to memorize before an English exam.	2.70	2.71	2.68	2.70
223. I memorize model texts/essays before an English essay test.	2.97	2.85	2.87	3.16
224. I often dump information on the back of the English test paper as soon as I receive it.	2.25	2.28	2.22	2.25
225. I practice a lot before English tests.	3.14	3.19	3.01	3.18
226. I practice speaking English in different situations before an oral test.	3.04	3.23	2.92	2.94
227. I practice writing answers to sample questions before an essay test.	3.15	3.18	3.01	3.23
228. I practice translating English into Chinese before an English test.	3.02	2.96	2.96	3.14
229. I practice writing by modeling good essays before an English essay test.	3.06	3.14	2.91	3.08
230. I analyze past test papers to determine how I can improve my test result before an important English test.	3.56	3.51	3.57	3.60
231. I take good notes as my English teacher tells what will be on the test.	3.81	3.75	3.96	3.77
232. I create summary notes and "maps" before an English test.	2.71	2.72	2.74	2.67
233. I look for the central idea of each question.	3.13	3.24	3.06	3.07
234. I directly get to the point when writing answers to questions during the test.	3.63	3.65	3.52	3.71
235. I use both general and specific information when answering an essay question.	3.49	3.60	3.37	3.48
236. I eliminate certain answers when answering multiple-choice questions.	3.94	3.93	3.89	4.00
237. I analyze the sentence structure before translating it into Chinese.	3.69	3.76	3.61	3.67
238. I break up run-on sentences into smaller parts to understand them better during an English test. 3.83	3.84	3.77	3.86	
239. I jot down information in the margin while listening during English tests.	3.63	3.69	3.63	3.56
240. In English essay exams, I jot down important ideas that come to mind as an outline in the margin.	3.29	3.37	3.27	3.22
241. I highlight some sentences or phrases while reading during English tests.	3.78	3.78	3.78	3.79
242. I exchange with English teachers about how and what to prepare before English tests.	2.88	3.01	2.78	2.81
243. I ask the instructor what to anticipate on the English test if he/she does not volunteer the information.	2.90	3.05	2.81	2.82
244. I use my linguistic knowledge to help guess and deduce what the speaker says while doing listening comprehension during English tests.	3.85	3.86	3.81	3.88
245. I make guesses based on different clues while reading during an English test.	3.90	3.92	3.82	3.95
246. I use my linguistic knowledge to help me complete the cloze test.	3.88	3.91	3.79	3.91
247. I use my background knowledge of the topic to help me complete the cloze test.	3.89	3.86	3.86	3.93
248. I use my background knowledge of the topic to help guess and deduce while reading during English tests.	3.92	3.92	3.92	3.92
249. I use my background knowledge of the topic to help guess and deduce what the speaker says while doing listening comprehension during English tests.	3.76	3.79	3.74	3.74
250. I use Chinese when I don't know how to express myself in English during English tests.	2.42	2.42	2.46	2.38
251. I use body language such as gestures to help express my ideas during an oral English test.	3.10	3.20	3.03	3.04
252. I try to translate the main idea into Chinese when I didn't know a word or phrase.	3.62	3.56	3.63	3.67
253. I attend class when the instructor reviews the English exam.	3.44	3.46	3.42	3.44
254. I attend 100% of my English classes.	4.36	4.28	4.35	4.46
255. In reviewing notes and text, I look for main topics and key ideas.	3.72	3.68	3.67	3.81
256. Before English tests, I avoid speaking with other students who have not prepared to avoid distraction from my preparation.	2.73	2.71	2.69	2.79
257. I pay particular attention to any study guides that the instructor hands out in class before the English exam, or even at the beginning of the course!	3.46	3.32	3.47	3.60

258. I pay particular attention—just prior to the English exam—to points the
instructor brings up during class lectures. 3.49 3.34 3.56 3.60

259. I pay particular attention to clues that indicate an instructor might test for a particular idea. 3.60 3.37 3.71 3.76

260. I develop a timetable for exam preparation and stick to it. 2.98 2.92 2.99 3.04

261. I estimate the time I'll need to review materials. 3.49 3.42 3.47 3.59

262. I finish my studying the day before the English exam. 3.09 3.14 2.98 3.13

263. I get familiar with the test room before an English test. 2.99 3.01 2.97 2.99

264. I gather and organize all the supplies I need before an English test. 3.85 3.70 3.85 4.02

265. I always arrive at the test room on time. 4.16 4.09 4.14 4.26

266. I set a goal for myself (such as how many scores I want to achieve) before an English test. 3.07 3.04 3.06 3.10

267. I read old exam papers before English tests. 3.40 3.56 3.27 3.34

268. I know exactly the format and content of an English test before it is taken. 3.46 3.47 3.43 3.48

269. I try to predict examination questions and then outline my answers. 2.65 2.73 2.53 2.65

270. I test myself in similar oral English testing situations before an oral English test. 2.81 2.94 2.72 2.73

271. I create study checklists before an English test. 2.48 2.56 2.45 2.43

272. I test myself on the material before an English test. 2.94 3.09 2.88 2.84

273. During an oral English test, I use whatever information given to
help me generate and organize ideas. 3.58 3.62 3.54 3.57

274. I try to better understand the sentence according to its context when translating it into Chinese. 3.85 3.87 3.84 3.85

275. I make a good use of my past experiences to finish an oral English test. 3.45 3.45 3.43 3.46

276. I listen to instructions carefully during oral English tests. 3.70 3.68 3.65 3.75

277. I read test directions carefully during an English test. 3.80 3.80 3.79 3.82

278. I listen to directions carefully when doing listening comprehension during an English test. 3.80 3.80 3.73 3.85

279. I listen to keywords when doing listening comprehension during English tests. 3.94 3.93 3.87 4.00

280. I listen to clues while doing listening comprehension during English tests. 3.88 3.90 3.81 3.92

281. I listen to questions carefully during an English test. 3.85 3.78 3.87 3.91

282. I look for keywords while reading during an English test. 3.97 3.88 3.94 4.09

283. I look for clues while reading during English tests. 3.95 3.91 3.88 4.06

284. I read questions carefully during an English test. 3.94 3.87 3.94 4.00

285. I write legibly during tests. 3.78 3.70 3.83 3.81

286. I answer easy questions first during an English test. 3.36 3.26 3.35 3.47

287. I scan the test first and then develop a plan for completing the test. 3.09 3.07 3.09 3.12

288. I outline my answers to questions during an essay test. 3.22 3.35 3.17 3.11

289. I plan and organize my ideas before answering an essay question. 3.08 3.20 3.06 2.99

290. I select a title for each question during an essay test to help me organize my ideas. 3.26 3.33 3.19 3.23

291. I paragraph my writing during English tests. 3.58 3.64 3.58 3.50

292. I write a topic sentence for each paragraph when writing during English tests. 3.24 3.40 3.14 3.14

293. I make a good use of the preparation time during an oral English test. 3.55 3.51 3.49 3.65

294. I try to make my writing coherent and cohesive during English tests. 3.91 3.86 3.88 3.98

295. I try to make as few mistakes as possible when writing during English tests. 3.89 3.90 3.83 3.93

296. I try to make my translation more like Chinese during an English exam. 3.41 3.57 3.24 3.37

297. I double-check my answers when I complete an English test. 3.48 3.60 3.37 3.45

298. After an English test, I list what did not work for improvement. 3.17 3.15 3.13 3.23

299. I forget about it immediately after an English test. 3.17 3.21 3.06 3.20

300. I summarize my performance after an English test. 3.33 3.35 3.28 3.35

301. After an English test, I list what worked and hold onto those strategies. 3.40 3.35 3.40 3.45

302. The night before an English exam I try to get a good night's sleep. 3.93 3.94 3.87 3.95

303. I breathe deeply to calm down when I became nervous before and/or during the test. 3.61 3.59 3.57 3.68

304. I approach the exam with confidence. 3.34 3.33 3.29 3.40

305. If I do well in an English test, I often reward myself such as having
a nice meal or buying a gift for myself. 3.07 3.10 2.99 3.09

306. I exchange with fellow students about how and what to prepare before English tests. 3.21 3.21 3.12 3.29

307. I form a study group with other students in my class to discuss and quiz each
other on important materials before an English test. 2.61 2.67 2.56 2.58

308. I listen to my partner carefully during an oral English test.   3.67   3.66   3.60   3.73
309. I support and help my partner during an oral English test.   3.68   3.67   3.60   3.74

Other English test-taking strategies: _____
_____
_____